THE SPIRIT OF
CLOVELLY PARK

Also by Frances-Marie Coke

The Balm of Dusk Lilies

Intersections

THE SPIRIT OF CLOVELLY PARK

Learning and Teaching at Kingston College

Frances-Marie Coke

THE SPIRIT OF CLOVELLY PARK
LEARNING AND TEACHING AT
KINGSTON COLLEGE

iUniverse books may be ordered through booksellers or by contacting:

iUniverse
1663 Liberty Drive
Bloomington, IN 47403
www.iuniverse.com
1-800-Authors (1-800-288-4677)

Cover photo by Ronnie Chin

ISBN: 978-1-5320-9080-6 (sc)
ISBN: 978-1-5320-9079-0 (e)

Library of Congress Control Number: 2019920129

Print information available on the last page.

iUniverse rev. date: 01/03/2020

Contents

Author's Note

This story reflects the author's recollection of events. Some names, locations, and identifying characteristics have been changed to protect the privacy of those depicted. Dialogue has been re-created from memory.

Foreword

One day, they cleared a space and made a park
There in the city slums;
and suddenly came stark glory
like lighting in the dark ... [1]

—Dennis Craig

Frances-Marie Coke has given us a personal and a professional memoir which shares her memory of events and the emotions generated by those events as she navigated her teaching career at Kingston College (KC). The book has significant historical value: it not

[1] Dennis Craig, "Flowers", in Nahdjla Carasco Bailey, A Time for Poetry: A Workshop Approach for CXC (Cheltenham, UK: Nelson Caribbean, 1988).

only captures the KC environment in the 1960s and 1970s, but also provides the context within which the education system in Jamaica, including schools like KC, functioned and survived during this time of considerable social, political. and economic change.

The opening chapter paints a graphic picture of the author as "the reluctant teacher", the physical reality of the school setting with its boisterous boys, her near panic, and the possibility of her retreat. Throughout, the reader shares glimpses of her life through vignettes of her own school experiences and significant events in her adult life, providing an intimate glimpse into who she is, why she sees things in a certain way, and what motivated her to make certain decisions about her life and career.

The writer's first meeting with the headmaster of KC, Mr Douglas Forrest, takes place in an unusual setting and establishes what became an indelible reminder to her of what KC was established to be—a rose blooming in the arid earth of inadequate schooling opportunities for poor Jamaican boys.

Observations of classroom interaction provide insights which should resonate with teachers everywhere. The writer identifies students who represent "types" inhabiting every classroom. She uses flashbacks to her own schooldays to analyse the differing ways in which boys and girls approach the authority of the teacher, the work of the class, and the behaviour they display. What makes the recounting of the writer's KC experience real is that it is not all plain sailing and instant success. Her frustration at the various challenges and the strategies she employed provide guidelines for teachers who are facing difficult classroom situations, but who realise in the final analysis that what will work depends on the personalities and the needs of the students facing them in their classrooms.

Most interesting is the discussion of the physical, mental, and psychological drain of preparation, delivery, and interaction involved in meeting the needs of a classroom of boys, the extent to which this can almost take over one's life, and the constant balancing of one's personal emotional state with these demands.

When the author leaves KC and takes on "The Job I Always Wanted", she realises the extent of the attachment she had established with KC. Also, she recognises that in this private-sector world "there were no mud-splattered rose petals"!

Her return—"Back to the Classroom"—is now her choice: a reflection of her value system and her need to make a difference. The chapter "Every Rose Garden Has Its Thorns" provides a contextual analysis which is very powerful. It succinctly yet graphically captures the social complexity of the 1970s and how it laid bare the troubling issues of skin colour and social class.

A central focus of the teaching and learning experience which the author describes is the television programme *Schools' Challenge Quiz* (SCQ). She and KC both needed SCQ. The novel, innovative way in which she approached this new challenge engaged the true KC "Fortis" spirit, previously demonstrated mainly in the sporting arena but now transported from sport to the academics and demonstrating excellence in both!

Her "Back to the Mona Campus" experience marked a transition both personally and professionally. The writer's elaboration and inclusion of her feelings help readers understand the introspection, thought process, and final decision-making in the next phase of her KC attachment.

The analysis of the teenage awakening and student revolution teachers faced in the 1970s accurately depicts the interplay of factors operating in the school and the wider society, instigated and fostered by the Black Power Movement and nurtured by the music of the time—Tosh and Marley's lyrics and the rhythm of reggae. The bold statement of the author's feelings about the revolution taking place at KC reflected, as she acknowledges, the feelings of several of her colleagues.

> I identified with the new-found self-awareness of the young men around me. I empathised with their passion about the new beliefs and alliances drawing them away from tradition. But I also saw that some boys were slipping towards the edge of a precipice that nobody understood.

"The Worst and Best of Times" is a case study of how a stimulus like SCQ can be used as a catalyst for achieving educational objectives which extend far beyond a classroom setting or extracurricular club. The description of effectively dealing with teaching and learning in a nontraditional fashion, victory and loss, and the involvement and development of the boys as team members as well as shining examples of school spirit will stir readers and inspire teachers.

KC's role as a safe place or refuge in the economic, social, and political upheaval of the 1970s is vividly recounted in the chapter "A Bigger Picture". The tragedy of the fire and the disruption it brought to this safe place, coupled with the disequilibrium of the environment external to the school, policy changes, and other factors, made the "safe haven" less effective as such in the lives of the students.

The personal response of the author to this disruption, as well as to other unsettling factors in her life, leads us to the chapter "The Blue Room". Here she shares with readers not just the day-to-day experience of being alone in a country overseas, but also the recognition of the value of separation from the familiar in self-discovery and her own emotional growth and development, despite doubts and concerns.

The description of returning to a changed physical environment at KC, assuming a new role, and facing new challenges gives the reader a valuable historical snapshot of the Jamaica of the 1970s and the apprehensions experienced by most Jamaicans, who were witnessing and living through rapid and discomfiting change. It also communicates the sense of dissonance which the writer experienced: the recognition that KC and Jamaica had changed, but that she had also. Her narrative describes her need to recapture the thrill and excitement she felt before "The Blue Room", but also recognition that the changes in herself and the school made this nearly impossible.

"I Felt a Parting" reveals the evolving feelings of disillusionment and betrayal she experienced and exposes her need for new and different challenges to energise her—challenges similar to SCQ maybe, but in a different setting and with different players. Sadly, separation from KC was justified.

Throughout the narrative, the author paints vivid word portraits of special teachers and acknowledges their significant roles in her journey as learner and teacher. She captures very well the atmosphere of the staffroom and the varied personalities and activities which created that unique environment. Mrs Riley, Peter Maxwell, Missa Johnno, Helen Douglas, and of course Mr Forrest loom large in the tapestry she creates.

"Epilogue 2014", so many years later, brings the readers back full circle to the writer as teacher—in the new tech-driven world, but still a learner and a teacher. Then comes the SCQ recap—a reiteration and analysis of the true educational value and impact of SCQ in the cognitive and affective growth of the young men who participated. She rounds off the narrative by allowing messages from former students to reinforce the centrality of SCQ and its catalytic role in the education of the grown men who became the writers of this string of emails. They give meaning to her statement that, from the very beginning:

> The boys sitting before me were promises the world was waiting for. I could be their poison, causing them to

droop and wither, robbing the world of what they could become. Or, I could be their nurturer, feeding their hunger for knowledge and growth.

That the writer fulfilled her initial (and consistent) objective of being their nurturer is clear.

The author is to be commended on her memory of these chapters of her life, the emotions evoked by the significant events, and the nuances of meaning which surround the period and create a depth and texture that permeate the entire manuscript. The writer holds the reader captive throughout.

This book should appeal to a very wide audience: the KC "Fortis" community, parents, and aspiring, current, and former teachers in all schools. The chapter on *Schools' Challenge Quiz* in particular should be required reading, analysis, and discussion for teacher trainees. Frances-Marie Coke must be congratulated on providing a fascinating self-reveal, a valuable resource on experiences rarely documented, and a significant stimulus for thought and analysis among those who are interested in or involved in the education of young people.

Elsa Leo-Rhynie, OJ, CD, PhD
Professor Emerita
The University of the West Indies

August 2019

Acknowledgements

This memoir would not have been possible without the hundreds of students of Kingston College who walked with me on the journey to becoming a teacher. Nor could I have written it without the numerous *Schools' Challenge Quiz* enthusiasts (team members, reserves, question writers, cheerleaders, teachers, buzzer builders, timekeepers, recorders, and assistant coaches) who contributed to building our foundation and making KC a force to be reckoned with throughout the life of the competition. I am grateful for all the alumni who were moved to share their feelings in numerous email messages on the occasion of KC's 2014 victory and ever since. It was their words that planted the idea that became the book. It was their anecdotes and their detailed records of matches that allowed me to write the chapters describing our exploits each year. To the teachers, coaches, students, and numerous "old boys" (the name for all past students of KC, no matter how old) who have kept the tradition going all these years, I salute your spirit and appreciate your respect for what you inherited from the earlier campaigners.

I am grateful to my friends and colleagues from KC, some no longer with us, who made it possible for me to learn and grow in the environment of support and collegiality that contributed to the environment in Hardie House and the spirit of Clovelly Park.

I commend the then Jamaica Broadcasting Corporation (JBC) and its successor Television Jamaica Ltd. (TVJ) for its role in bringing the *Schools' Challenge Quiz* competition to the region over all these years. Congratulations on the celebration of the fiftieth year!

To my sisters who were there from the start, always supporting and encouraging, thank you. Thanks also to my daughter, Kimberley, who shares her initials with KC and who inherited the spirit. And to Isabel, thank you for always asking "Did you work on your project today, Grammie?"

To Miss Barnett: You know who you are and what you did. I am forever grateful.

To my friends who read the manuscript and gave me both the encouragement and the constructive criticism necessary to bring it to its final state, I will always appreciate your feedback.

To Professor Emerita Elsa Leo-Rhynie, thank you for being who you are, and for the foreword.

Me? A Teacher?

It was 11:25 a.m. and still no one could find him. The heat bore down and my blouse stuck to my skin. I alternated between perching on the edge of the chair and pacing the floor helplessly while a couple of uneasy ladies came and went, embarrassed and flustered that they still couldn't find the headmaster for my interview. Being stuck there between grey walls hugging a narrow passageway made me claustrophobic and anxious; my slender frame felt as if it had no substance. I longed for the oats I'd left on my kitchen sink before rushing to catch the bus earlier that morning. I struggled with why the waiting area felt so familiar—could it be so frightening just because I didn't want to be there?

The answer dawned on me as I felt all five feet seven inches of myself shrinking into someone half my height, cowering in a similar setting where I'd sweated and wrung my hands so many times, so many years before. *Of course it feels like I've been here before! It's exactly like that other corridor outside that forbidding door at my high school!*

I had been in my third-form year at Alpha Academy. and one teacher or another had made a habit of sending me to the office for being in some kind of trouble. Now, all these years later, I could hardly distinguish between the cold sweat from memories of waiting for trouble outside Sister's door and the cold sweat of waiting for this headmaster.

Trouble was exactly what I felt coming on that blistering August morning of 1970. The feeling had hovered over me from the moment I'd stepped onto the Number 22 bus at Cross Roads. It had only worsened as the bus trundled along South Camp Road, taking me closer and closer to the destination I never wanted to reach. Walking along North Street and through the rusty iron gate dislodged from one of its hinges, I'd felt no conviction, only a large dose of trepidation about what lay ahead.

The long wait for the missing headmaster had given me all the time to worry about how crazy my curly brown hair must look after the breeze through the bus window had gusted through it like a storm. I glanced down on my dressy, size 10 patent-leather shoes, borrowed from their box for this occasion that was nowhere as happy as the few other times I had gently removed them from their light wrapping paper.

Now their shine was covered with dust that had settled over them as I walked all the way from the gate. I stood up every few minutes, shaking out the numbness in my legs and running my hands over my wrinkled black skirt, trying to restore its ironed look.

But those worries were nothing like the concerns that were rattling in my brain. My best efforts to dress the part and assume a quiet voice and sober facial expressions were steadily failing. I felt out of place, and I guessed I looked the same in the eyes of the two earnest women who were fluttering around me. *What am I doing here? How did I get myself into this*?

My exciting venture into television news had come to an abrupt but unavoidable end after just a year, leaving me shaken and without any moorings. Broke and lacking job prospects, I'd had no choice but to follow the halfhearted advice of my university's career placement officer to "go and see if the headmaster down there will consider you for his English teacher's job". My meeting with that chilly woman had unnerved me from the start. And my response was an immature, ill-considered outburst that started tentatively and suddenly picked up speed.

"I'm sorry. I really don't want to seem ungrateful, but I just can't be a teacher. I wouldn't know where to begin. I hated school for a long time, and I got in a whole lot of trouble. I didn't do all that well, so—"

"Stop right there, Miss Phillips. Let me see if I understand you." She rose deliberately from her desk and walked around in circles as if trying to protect herself from an imminent conniption. By the time she spoke again, her sarcasm dripped like ice cubes carried in bare hands. "I suppose you think there are hundreds of employers lining up out there, waiting to hire English graduates like you?" Her withering look, along with the recollection of my depleted savings account and the months of rent ahead, was what finally shoved me onto the bus that brought me to 2A North Street.

My eyes stung every time the mild breeze whipped up a whirlwind of dust from the expanse of drought-stricken earth that swallowed up the occasional patches of grass. They glazed over more and more as I sat, hungry and perplexed, in that "reception" area that was no more than a dreary passage with a small, littered desk and two metal classroom chairs with rust peeping out from their joints. I squirmed and sweated, wondering what I was doing waiting for a missing headmaster in a place that was anything but inviting—the last place to which I'd wanted an invitation. *Me waiting to be interviewed for a teaching job—how in the world can this be real?*

I could just see the faces of my grandmother; of Sister Bernadette, the first Jamaican woman to be appointed Alpha's principal; and of the many other teachers at my old school. Every one of them would question mightily what I thought I was doing. "Frances Phillips teaching?" they would ask in absolute shock. "Frances Phillips, who was the bane of our existence during her turbulent years between third and fifth form? Frances, who spent hour after hour kneeling in the school office as punishment for hurling her shoes into the Sweetie-Come-Brush-Me mango tree, and more often for 'staring impertinently' at sundry math teachers frustrated at her refusal to try with algebra?"

The secretary returned, bewildered and embarrassed, "I am so very sorry, Miss Phillips. Something must have come up. Can you wait a little longer?" The small voice was a surprise coming from the five-feet, nine-inch tall, extremely "church choir" type of woman who couldn't bring herself to look me in the face.

Thinking this was an act of God to rescue me from my decision to attend an interview for which I was completely ill-equipped, I answered in a rush, "It's okay. I understand, (Of course I didn't.) I have a little time … but wait; you know what? I think I will just go. I can call and make another … I can just come back—"

"Come this way, miss. I will take you to Mr Forrest." The older of the two women had come up so quietly that her voice startled the secretary and me. In her pale, pristine blouse with its tiny pearl buttons, pintucks, and frilly collar that almost brushed against her chin, she could have stepped right off page 183 of a George Eliot novel and landed by mistake in Jamaica. She guided me under the cobwebbed staircase, through corridors whose splintered wood floors longed for a broom. I was no more encouraged as I gazed at broken sash windows, aged paint peeling from dingy walls, orange juice boxes tightly rolled into crude miniature footballs, and little piles of garbage huddling in the corners. The lumps of curdled milk leaking from a blue-and-white Cremo box almost made me head straight for the bus stop. I checked off another reason to regret that this gentle lady had found the missing man. And as we journeyed to wherever she was taking me, I encountered more than enough reasons for that regret.

The determination to walk away was rising in my throat when the sound hit me: thundering footsteps from what sounded like two hundred boys in a small space just above my head. *Where are the deathly quiet classrooms I remember at Alpha, where the least outburst of noise would result in a "Sit down and be quiet!" command from whichever teacher was in charge*? Instead, these footsteps sounded like the beginning of a stampede. *How can the school allow them to make all that noise? They don't have teachers in charge?*

I got the answer to my unspoken question in an instant. A horde of bodies came barging down the stairs, rattling the old wooden walls like an earthquake and me right along with them. I pressed myself against the flimsy partition as a mass of white shirts and khaki pants stormed through the crammed corridor, ties flying and hands gesticulating as their owners shouted out their lunch orders.

"Two patty and one orange juice!"

"One bun an' a box a milk, *Rasta*!"

"Don' forget the cheese, Star—yellow cheese, not the pale, bilious one!"

"You better come get it yuself if you goin' fuss 'bout cheese colour!"

I was still shaking from the stampede when my George Eliot character and I walked out of the building and made our way to the side. She pointed ahead to a narrow space between two buildings that were as bedraggled as the one we'd just left.

"Nearly there," she said. "He's right around the corner there." She quickly stepped past me and made her way around the building, calling out to someone I couldn't see. "Sir, this is the young lady who is here to see you; I brought her along as you said."

Douglas Wrexham Eric Forrest unspooled slowly from his collection of body angles crouching over the square of damp earth. Stretched to what looked like my father's full height, he towered over both of us, his eyes twinkling from his sunburnt face like the lights atop a country lighthouse. I craned my neck and mentally decided he was about six feet three inches tall. My eyes fell to his feet, planted next to the reason he'd been missing from his office—a shock of red, yellow and orange! Yes, roses, in a glorious space surrounded by parched earth, dried-out grass, rocks, and rubble. Three or four boys were weeding and digging, tiptoeing around a leaky old water hose that snaked its way around the building and suddenly disappeared.

"Oh … Is this Miss Phillips? Thanks for bringing her around. Welcome, welcome, Miss Phillips! I'm sorry I didn't wait for you in the office, but I know you will understand now you see what I'm up to."

Luckily, he didn't give me a moment to get a word in; what could I have said?

"Come, boys. Tell this young lady what we are doing around here!" His fingers were muddy, one shoelace was undone, and a once-white handkerchief hung from his back pocket, its mud-stained edge sticking out, finishing off the image of a man who cared nothing about appearances. Excitement enlivened his voice, and I was stunned at the difference between what I saw in him and the demeanour I considered the birthmark of every headmaster or headmistress I had ever met or heard about before that moment.

Mr Forrest looked like an ordinary man—someone anyone could approach and speak to without shaking all over. His eyes were warm and comforting, the smile beneath his manicured moustache an invitation to tell him how frightened I was. Still, he was a headmaster, and I was there to be interviewed. I was overcome with worry that the scorching heat of the sun, now directly above us, must have added two more crescents of anxious armpit sweat to my sticky blouse.

Ten minutes later, after I'd listened to his lecture about the character and formation of each bloom, I reached down to grasp a long-stemmed orange rosebud thrust shyly at me by the smallest boy, now perched on one knee.

"Okay, back to class now, boys. Come with me, please, Miss Phillips," the headmaster said, gathering his rose clippers and wiping the sweat from his brow.

"Yes, sir," the little boys chirped as they scampered away, echoing one another's "Bye, Miss Young Lady."

Another Giant of North Street

My feet felt weighed down as I followed Mr Forrest back along the same path I'd wanted to run away from a few minutes earlier. This time there was less noise, and my thoughts about the sounds and sights were displaced by the confusion still rattling in my head about a rose between my fingers, a muddy headmaster in his garden, and the forces that had brought me for the first time to this place.

By the early 1970s, many Jamaicans thought North Street had only one glorious spot left—the Roman Catholic cathedral. But the boys of St George's College thought their glorious campus was the real giant. Now

I was walking across the fields of Clovelly Park—home of Kingston College (KC).

The boys of KC had gone quite unnoticed by most of the girls I knew while at Alpha Academy; after all, we were virtually promised to our Catholic brothers at St George's. The Sisters of Mercy fiercely managed our participation in the school events we shared with them to ensure we would fulfil that promise. Not once in all my seven years at Alpha did we visit KC or participate in any activities with them.

When we attended events at the cathedral or at the Winchester Park home of St George's, we *never* walked on North Street to get there. No, the ladies of Alpha Academy walked in orderly pairs, clad in blue tunics with white crocheted belts and white round-collared blouses. The warnings about looking tidy led to streams of hair sweat leaking from the despised navy-blue felt berets that kept the blistering heat simmering on our heads and brought instant destruction to the most elaborate hairstyle.

Stepping briskly half a mile down South Camp Road, we teetered between behaving like the brats we were and heeding the admonitions to act the part of "decent Catholic young ladies". It was a constant struggle to conceal the confusion and the misery, the awkward anticipation and the feverish anxiety that beset every girl about to land in the presence of her male counterparts. Whether visiting the cathedral or St George's, none of this could be visible to the sisters who constantly admonished, "Best behaviour, ladies; Alpha is on display."

Always, we turned right from South Camp Road and headed for Emerald Road, giggling with excitement, our faces averted from the harsh looks of Sister Rosa and Sister Pat, the screw-faced captains invariably in charge of our daring and nerve-wracking expeditions into the presence of boys. When we headed for the cathedral to celebrate special Masses and cast our longing eyes at our Georgian brothers while chanting our squeaky alleluias, we followed the same path, always entering from the side gate on Emerald Road—never looking across the street to KC.

When we were old enough to cheer for our Georgian brothers as they chased sporting accolades, it was the same thing, minus the nuns. In the dingy girls' bathrooms, we unravelled clothes from paper bags stuffed into bursting schoolbags, and quickly made our way, transformed into football fans, through Alpha's gate. It was for Sabina Park that we headed—straight into the sweat and excitement of the St George's College stand, where hearts were lifted and crushed over the fortunes of each year's heart-stopping heroes hustling to bring home the coveted trophy. It didn't matter that we knew precious little about football; the game was the last thing on the Alpha girls' agendas.

We rarely glanced over into the stands the KC boys occupied. In fact, no one heard the name of that school except when we caught snippets of chatter among girls who came from Vineyard Town, and whose eyes turned into glass as they walked to the Number 11 bus stop to gaze at gawky boys from that other side of North Street.

Now, I was not gazing from a distance. Mr Forrest and I stood on the threshold of the helter-skelter room I assumed was his office. He signalled me to sit across from a desk covered with loose paper, scissors, registers, reports, and a book with a piano on the cover. He wiped his hands vigorously and turned to a small shelf behind him. Beyond where I could see, he fiddled with something or another while I sat uncomfortably balanced on a straight-backed wooden chair and waited, bones rattling in my empty stomach and my chest, eventually lodging themselves in the middle of my parched throat. *Lord, let this be over with soon. Don't let him have a place for me.*

But the interview was not on Mr Forrest's mind— not yet. He shuffled paper, fiddled with pencils and pens, cleaned the glasses he fished from an open desk drawer, perched them on his nose, and looked over the heavy black frame into my face.

My unease moved down into my feet. As if disconnected from my brain, they tapped my shoes incessantly on the wooden floor. Mr Forrest glanced down at my flimsy one-page CV and remained silent. I thought, *He must be asking himself, "Did I interrupt caring for my roses for this?"*

"So, Miss Phillips … one of Sister Bernadette's girls from up the road at Alpha, eh?"

What would he say if he really knew of my stormy relationship with my own headmistress? What if he knew how many teachers up the road at Alpha considered me a troublemaker?

"Miss Phillips?" He was leaning over the desk towards me now.

"Sorry, sir, I didn't quite get that."

"I asked what made you leave the excitement of the TV newsroom?"

"Oh. Yes, sir. Well, the truth is I actually left the newsroom before I left the station. They moved me to the programmes department to promote upcoming shows and—"

He got up abruptly and walked slowly from behind his desk. My words had come out in the voice of a scared child. I looked to my black patent-leather pumps, heels and toes stained with the damp dust from my trek around the patch of roses.

"You know, Miss Phillips, the first job after leaving university is not always the best one, or the one we will stick with," he said, his tone so calm and reassuring that it reminded me of my father. "And our boys here at KC are not what you might have heard about, you know," he added, as if he knew at least one of the things that worried me. "Bishop Gibson had a good reason for starting this school, and although we have challenges, we are doing something here that changes lives."

My father came to KC, I longed to say. *His two brothers came too, and they sang in the choir.* I'd never thought any of that important enough to mention to anyone outside of my family. But I didn't want to sound too familiar. How could I be sure the *real* headmaster wouldn't jump out of nowhere at me, or that his gentleness wouldn't disappear in a haze of quickly restored authority?

He was fiddling again with the thing I couldn't see. His words broke the silence in a gentle murmur. "Do you hear that, Miss Phillips? Shh … Just listen for one minute." My eyes returned to his face. His eyes were sparkling like the eyes of an infant with a secret.

It started almost inaudibly—just a single repetitive drumbeat, coming from what I now realised was the gramophone he'd been fiddling with. A plaintive sound from an instrument I didn't recognise crept up to the beat of the insistent drum. It brushed the air like a baby's shuddering breath. Slowly and stunningly it rose, filling the room and doing something to my head that I struggled to name as he moved his hands like a conductor and lifted the album cover to show me.

"Ravel's *Bolero*", he said, as if that explained everything.

What's really going on? I wondered, feeling the moments tick by. The music diminished into silence as I wrestled with what to think or say. Satisfied that Ravel had done whatever he intended, Mr Forrest launched into a spirited recitation of the reasons why KC boys needed music, of what the school meant to Jamaica and to him, of what it would mean if more "bright young women" joined the staff to help him make "our boys gentler". *No, no, no; please don't ask me to be one of those women!*

After the minutes had stretched out before me like hours, he wrote something on a yellow notepad, stuck the torn-off page in an envelope with my CV, and scribbled a name on it. "You'll find her upstairs," he said, directing me across the schoolyard, pointing to the chapel and then to the building across a dusty walkway.

A Meeting over Lunch?

I stepped through a wide-open wooden door and down one giant step into a huge room filled with light and air from its well-spaced floor-to-ceiling windows. Columns and long tables divided the space into smaller sections. Every surface was littered with books and papers, thermos flasks and orange juice boxes, a *Daily Gleaner* centrespread, handbags, lunch bags, and stacks of exercise books. Unlike the area where I'd waited for Mr Forrest, the staffroom felt completely unfamiliar. As girls, we had hardly ever been allowed to cross the threshold into our teachers' domain. If you were unlucky enough to be sent there for any reason, you stood at the door and raised your forefinger, hoping for someone to look up and give permission to enter.

I hugged the side of the building, passed quickly through the sobering drabness before being spotted, and made my way up a truncated flight of steps that groaned with my every movement. My unsteady feet planted on the landing, I stood unnoticed, wondering which way to go. To my right, sunbeams lit up mahogany tables and chairs, across from numerous windows that extended almost the entire length of the high wall. Comforted by the emptiness, I tiptoed across the wooden floor and through the door, and leaned on one of two huge columns on either side of the intricate metal railings that propped up what looked like twenty-two concrete steps down into the yard. A clutch of small boys huddled at the foot of the steps, gesticulating wildly.

"Come on, Tony, or we goin' late for class and Missa Johnno soon start patrol." The boy scrunched up a greasy brown bag, brushed the last patty crumbs from his khaki shirt, and hauled Tony by the waist of his pants across the smatterings of grass toward another cluster of classrooms.

Back inside, there was still not a sign of anyone to ask for the name on the envelope—just rushes of cooling air, billowing yellow curtains, and the rustle of papers on dark wooden tables. As I turned to go back downstairs, I noticed out of the corner of my eye another door, half-open. I sneaked up toward this smaller room and peeked in. A narrow, rickety bookshelf lined one wall; a tired-looking couch pressed up against the other. In the middle of the room, five women huddled around a table, chatting and eating, their hands punctuating their animated conversation.

The trappings of the English teacher's profession lay strewn across the table and on the shelves: the *Oxford English Dictionary*, Nesfield's *English Grammar*, sundry English composition textbooks, novels, poetry collections, red-and-white cardboard boxes with various lengths of used and unused white chalk, wooden-backed blackboard erasers whitened with chalk dust, red pens, class registers, and stacks of familiar students' exercise books, all bearing the face of Queen Elizabeth on the front covers. I rapped on the door and stood back.

"Yes? What is it?" someone called out.

"Ahm … good morning … ladies; I'm sorry to disturb you. I'm looking for (glancing at the name Mr Forrest had scribbled on the envelope) … Mrs Riley?" My words sounded like the uncertain whisper of a child surrounded by the threatening eyes of unfamiliar adults.

The woman closest to the door leaned over and shoved one side open. Eight impassive eyes glanced in my direction, and the hush stretched out between us.

"Who wants to see her?" The tone was sharp and unforgiving of the interruption, but the face was emotionless. *God, don't let her be Mrs Riley; she looks really fierce.*

"Mr Forrest sent me," I said, hoping to lend a modicum of legitimacy to my obviously unwelcome visit. "I mean … Mr Forrest asked me to come and see if Mrs Riley might be able to speak with me."

"And you are?" This one was a slightly less hostile voice that came with the mere suggestion of a smile hovering around her lips, but still nothing near welcoming.

"Sorry; I … my name … I should have said … I am Frances … Frances Phillips." I remembered the envelope Mr Forrest had thrust into my hands, now damp with my sweat. I reached out gingerly and gave it to the hand belonging to the less hostile voice. She passed it to the younger woman on her left, whose eyes reminded me of the Half-Chinese girls at Alpha. *Let it be her*, I prayed. *At least she looks youngish.*

Too late! She passed it to Mrs Who Wants to See Her. I knew it was time to find an excuse and beat a hasty retreat. All heads turned as Mrs Who Wants to See Her turned into Mrs Riley, unfolding the note slowly and passing her eyes over it deliberately, moving from top to bottom and back.

"That Mr Forrest, you see? He knows it's lunchtime and still …" She addressed no one in particular. Though she said nothing more, her annoyance was palpable. Of course I knew her message was meant for me. The short, plump one with the almost friendly voice looked up and paused, a spoonful of rice and peas held at a standstill in the space between her blue plastic container and her mouth. She nudged Mrs Riley with her shoulder as if to suggest she would take the conversation from there.

"Just give us a minute, Miss Phillips," the one with the suspended rice and peas said. "Go around that corner and you'll see a small room. A chair should be there, so you can sit."

I wasn't sure any more which of them would be taking charge of my presence, so I made sure to include all of them in my answer. "I'm really sorry, ladies. I didn't know it was lunchtime. What if I just come back another time that is convenient?" My words still sounded jumbled like a toddler's, but I felt growing relief that this job was already slipping from my grasp.

At the same time, the gentle, encouraging words of Mr Forrest echoed, like his music, in another corner of my head, bringing back images of his roses and his mud-stained handkerchief—and the strains of *Bolero*. Between these two contradictions, one thought hammered behind my forehead: *I really have no choice. I have thirty-two dollars in my savings account, and that miserable landlord will soon be slipping notes under the door, badgering me for his rent.*

In a voice that reminded me of my history teacher at Alpha, the sternest one spoke, "Miss Phillips, I don't know what kind of work you do, my dear, but teachers don't have much time. Before lunch, we teach; after a measly lunch break, we go back to the classroom and we teach; in between classes, we mark the students' work and plan lessons. As Mrs Reid said, there's a room around there. Take a seat, and I will come as soon as I can." Mrs Riley promptly returned to her sandwich, still languishing on its square of wax paper, her teeth clearly outlined across the hard-dough bread.

So this is the real world of the English teacher here at KC; it's not Mr Forrest's rose garden or his music. I eased myself around the corner, hoping I wouldn't encounter one of the dreaded lizards I knew could emerge at any minute between the cobwebs hanging from the treacherous ceiling panels. As I searched for any sign of movement, the table came into view. I fell into the chair next to it, eager to get off my unreliable feet.

In the distance, I could see the interior of the chapel. Through the smallest of six stained-glass windows, the midday sun cast a slanted ray of light across the altar. "That's the St Augustine Chapel way over there," Mr Forrest had said before despatching me to the formidable lady I was now waiting for. *Over there in the dim quiet of that chapel is where I want to be right now.*

"So … Miss Phillips, what brings you to our part of the world?" Mrs Riley had slipped into the other chair without a sound.

"Sorry, Miss … Mrs Riley. I didn't hear you come in." I was surprised to hear the new tone in her voice and to see the possibility of a smile lurking on her face.

She quickly introduced herself as Muriel and moved right along. "Well, are you going to tell me?"

"Mrs Riley, the truth is—"

"Spare me, Miss Phillips. I know you've never taught. But for some reason, our Mr Forrest thinks you can replace one of our best teachers, who is off on study leave doing her master's in education".

Of course, perfect—me replacing someone doing a master's in education! Oh God, why did I step on that bus at Cross Roads this morning?

Mrs Riley obviously had no time or inclination to wait for my musings to end. She had finished scanning, probably for the third time, the thin information Mr Forrest had sent her. "Okay, I see that you studied literature at UWI[2]. Maybe we can start there. Maybe you can tell me why."

"It was my best subject at school. I loved … love reading; I love books; I read all the time. My English teacher at Alpha was the one who— I just loved all those poems and novels that we read in—" I stopped, realising my answer was juvenile and fractured. I fully expected Mrs Riley to be annoyed about me wasting her time.

"Well, I suppose if you can get excited like that when you talk about reading, maybe you can do something—I don't know what—to get our boys to read. They would do math and science all day long if they could. And of course they love everything to do with sports, so no time to read literature. Don't get me wrong: many of our boys are very bright boys and we get good results; but some people want to believe the boys only care

---

[2] The University of the West Indies is a regional institution serving mainly the Caribbean countries, sometimes known as the West Indies. It was founded as the University College of the West Indies, a college of London University. as part of British education policy for its colonies. Commonly known as UWI by the 1970s, it had campuses in Jamaica (at Mona), Trinidad and Barbados.

about sports. That is exactly why we have to keep up our results in other areas, especially English."

The last sentence landed like a blow. *What chance do I, a green UWI graduate, have of contributing to that?*

The formidable veteran hammered me with a few more questions and caustic comments between my tongue-tied answers. She gave one or two explanations about the KC approach to teaching English, peppering them with sharp warnings about how challenging the task of teaching was. Her closing statement was as mystifying as the explanations she had given.

"You know what, Miss Phillips? I suggest you go home and think carefully about taking up a job like this. Teaching is serious business. Only education can keep most of these boys out of trouble and give them some kind of future. Mr Forrest and I will have to speak, and I'm sure he will let somebody from the office get in touch with you—if he wants to talk with you again."

My second interview was over. Mrs Riley's back disappeared through the door. Embarrassed by my lack of information and preparation, and feeling half my height in the presence of this teaching giant, I slinked along the wall past the smaller room, sensing the dismissive eyes of each woman now busily gathering up her accoutrements to head to whichever classroom she would be in for the after-lunch session. My shoulders drooped as I headed down the stairs and paused on the grassless path, glancing over to the chapel.

"It's okay. You don't need to worry. Her bark is much worse than her bite, and she's an outstanding teacher." The hurried words of encouragement came from the woman who'd sat at the far side of the table upstairs. She'd paused next to my shoulder to whisper her reassurances. Before I could answer, she resumed her purposeful strides, disappearing faster than I could thank her.

Three days later, the phone woke me from the stupor of unemployment. Mr Forrest wanted to see me; I needed to bring in documents. The Ministry of Education had forms to sign. *I might be the new English teacher*—me, rescued by four little boys tending roses under Mr Forrest's wing and by music from an ancient gramophone. I was still intrigued by the words of a man who, I later learned, spent all his waking hours at KC, this place that would unearth secrets about itself and about me. It was the opening of a door to a future I'd never considered before that day when I walked, with zero conviction, from the Number 22 bus stop on South Camp Road into the world of Clovelly Park.

What! Those Boys?

I could not make many informed comparisons between KC and other schools. Alpha was all I'd known. Immaculate Conception High School was *the other* Catholic girls' school, but it had always sounded like an unreachable world, way up in Kingston on a street we only saw when we left Kingston in Sunday's first light, heading to Port Maria—that refuge of my early life—or on our way back, trying to beat the dusk. In the Sixth Form Association, I'd mixed with students from schools like St Hugh's, St Andrew, Merl Grove, and Wolmer's. And of course there were the sixth-form boys from St George's. All my expectations and fears were born of my experiences with teachers at Alpha—those I admired and loved, the ones I recalled with nothing but anger or fear, and the many who had not lingered a day in my recollection.

Alpha's teachers were women of all ages: some fresh from the University of the West Indies or from Catholic colleges in America, some stalwarts like Mrs Riley, and others middle-aged nuns who made Alpha their lives. Some were more concerned about showing off their knowledge than about whether we understood any of what they were saying. Others were seasoned, pepper-mouthed women who brooked no question or argument from students because these were sure signs of impertinence and lack of home training. Some sent us to the principal's office just for "threatening" to be impertinent by the mere looks in our eyes. I'd always wondered why it wasn't just as much impertinence for them to glare us down to nothing, hurling insults that turned us into "jackasses", "idiots", "nincompoops", and "hooligans".

And then there were the others: warm, compassionate women who treated us as if we were their own daughters, women who were firm but fair in their judgements and decisions. They meted out punishment that suited our crimes. With them, one mistake didn't lead to writing a girl off forever. They were well trained, and they knew what they were about. Their wisdom and discretion provided balance. Most of all, they cared. Their faces flashed across my mind, and a myriad of emotions assailed me as I stepped through my little door, home from my second visit to KC.

The images lingered all weekend in the studio apartment where everything I owned and everything I did fit into one space (twenty-seven feet by sixteen feet, according to the proud landlord) that stretched from the louvred windows at the top of the steps through the sleeping area to the dappled wooden screen behind which the builders had cleverly tucked the tiniest kitchen, one thin wall away from a bathroom the size of an aircraft's. Smiling faces and empty eyes faced me as I tried to watch whatever programmes littered the screen of the eighteen-inch TV set I had rented from Homelectrix, first for eighteen shillings and fifty cents a week, which turned into mystifying dollars and cents when we changed our currency in late 1969. Just maybe, if the next few days went according to the early signs, I would be able to keep both the apartment and the TV.

Careful not to call it a done deal, yet hoping somewhere deep down I could still jinx it, I shared details of the "possible job" with a couple of worried family members and my best friend. No one kept her mouth shut as promised. As they spread the news through a rapid string of phone calls, a chorus of strident warnings grew into a clamour, threatening to deafen me.

"What? KC? How you going to manage those hooligans *down there*?"

"Why not go back to your own school if you want to teach?"

"Don't you think girls would be easier to manage—especially at a Catholic school?"

On and on it went, inflaming my doubts and fears even before the job was a certainty. Others added their own expert social analysis to the equation, all the while stretching the meaning of "down there" beyond the obvious.

"You know those boys down there don't come from good homes, right?"

"Yes, it's only because that Mr Edwin Allen changed up the common entrance rules that most of them are in high school."

They were insistent that KC boys would be completely different from them and from me, but they were obviously and conveniently forgetting where we all came from. My three sisters and I grew up long before "single-parent home" became a modern catchphrase to explain the smallest details in some children's lives— from missing lunch money and brown school shoes to bad behaviour and bad school reports to sermons about prominent public figures who had overcome such homes to reach the heights they had reached. Our parents had been sent from the country to go to Kingston schools and find work. But they also found each other, and before they knew what had hit them, they were married and surrounded by three infants. They had few resources to sustain the lives into which they had plunged, with scant preparation for either marriage or babies.

Like some of the children we knew, our early years found us dispatched to spinster aunts in town or grandmothers in country villages, where they only went to the shop for meat, fish, canned food, and rice. Anyone could rustle up a free meal just by reaching a hand to the nearest breadfruit, banana, or ackee tree.

Whether living in the country, home in Kingston, or by the seaside on long summer holidays, we relished our growing-up years. We played all along the street, supervised by any adult in view. We were never tired or sick except for occasional measles, mumps, or whooping cough—all of which were quickly dispatched with fluids, cough mixture, and tamarind bush baths. We were never hungry, not in Idlewild or Galina, with all the macaroni and cheese Miss Louise stuffed into the old American oven, or the Saturday beef-bone soup and Sunday roast beef dinners she and Grandma laboured over, her mouth a mile long as she pouted and grumbled about all the trouble we gave her.

When we felt for something outside of mealtimes, we just had to climb on the shoulders of a young uncle to reach the lowest branch of a fruit tree weighed down with glowing mangoes, reddish-purplish *otihiti* apples, star-apples, or stainy guineps with seeds that could choke any careless eater to death. Or we could burrow in the ground, unearthing young sweetsops we stored in our individual "sweetsop banks" until they were ripe for eating. During the long, hot days at Above Rocks, we hustled to the riverside and yanked handfuls of slimy silver crayfish from the muddy banks. Grandma Gillis soon transformed them into sumptuous meals. Even in Kingston, we only had to look as if we hadn't eaten and our mother would send us confidently to the kitchen to find "bread-in-the-pan and jam-in-the-safe". Nothing interrupted our weekly dinner routine of stew peas and rice, bully beef and rice, ackee and saltfish with green bananas, hominy corn, and on Sundays, the long-awaited chicken and rice and peas with fry plantain and salad.

Apparently, we were poor, but nobody told us. We knew things were hard because our mother insisted that we didn't have time or money to waste on foolishness. We must keep to "our little side" of any house she could afford to rent. And there were many, for landlords soon tired of children running up and down in their yards, even though my mother spread out her pounds, shillings, and pence each payday and took out, before anything else, the amount to go in the back of the bureau drawer, where it would grow into the month's rent. Although she was soon on her own with us and our new little sister from her second failed marriage, she lashed out with proud protests against the daily insults from the abusive wives of sundry landlords.

Our father too had married again, and our relationship with him was built on visits to his new home and on our frequent Sunday outings, mainly to Hope Gardens. There, he'd spread us out on the prickly grass, the frilly skirts our mother made barely covering our spindly legs. Or he would leave us frolicking before the military band in concert, eating all the peanuts, animal crackers, cheese crunches, and ice cream he could afford before making the long bus trip back home. Who could have known our parents had so little?

Repeating her words like the refrain from her favourite song, my mother drummed it into our heads that if we didn't do our schoolwork, we would end up "pushing a handcart and selling pint bottles" for the rest of our days. That daunting prospect before us, we buckled down under the implacable thumbs of the teaching giants at our prep school, and we "studied our books". With no say in the matter, we mastered the thin little books of intelligence, general knowledge, mathematics, and English practice tests. Whatever we might have thought about school, working hard at Blake Prep became the way to avoid my mother's worst fears coming to pass.

Even after the long hours were over and the yellow HB pencils we used in the exams were gone, the grim reminder of those fears passed our gate regularly, his plaintive wail, "Bottle man, bottle man; any pint bottle today?" breaking through the silence of the summer days as we waited to know our fate. Each time the letter came from the Ministry of Education saying one of us not only "passed the scholarship exam" but would get financial help with uniforms and books, my mother's sighs of relief made us feel we'd built one more wall against the dreaded fate of the bottle man sweltering in the Kingston summer sun behind his handcart full of used bottles.

Sometimes my mother worked three jobs. Sometimes she sat all night at the Singer machine, sewing the full gamut of garments for her girls—from new high school uniforms to shorts for PE to fancy dresses to substitute for store versions we couldn't afford. But there were limits, as one time in my first year at Alpha.

"Mama, can I play tennis at school? Jackie and Beth play after school, and I want to learn too."

My mother believed in exposure to different things, so her answer came without hesitation: "Of course you can play, as long as you do your work."

After a few minutes, I realised she hadn't got the message. "So, Mama, when I can get the money?"

"Money for what?"

"We have to buy a racket and pay for the lessons."

"Oh … well, I suppose you better play baseball, then."

These vivid images of growing up led me to wonder about the people warning me about KC boys; about going "down there" to teach. Had they forgotten that all the children we knew who went to high school had made it there because the Common Entrance Exam had come just in time? Their questions and warnings drove me to distraction.

My own hesitation came from my certainty that I wasn't made for teaching. Although I had reacted negatively to the appearance of one building in the school, and to the thunderous descent of students on the stairs, my reluctance went far beyond that. It had nothing to do with the fact that the school was located at North Street. After all, St George's was just down the road, and Alpha Academy was within walking distance. Neither did my bad memories of Alpha have anything to do with its location.

The naysayers drove me to the library at the university's school of education, to dig up information that I hoped would counteract my extremely limited British history lessons with more detailed records about how schools and schooling had evolved in Jamaica. I found a few slightly different versions, but the crucial facts were the same.

Early Jamaican education was all about what England thought was necessary for the society they envisaged after emancipation. They intended to create a local middle class that would meet the specified needs of the country, without any danger of toppling the elite. Elementary schools comprised the strategy to create this cohort. The few high schools that existed up until the 1950s were established to provide education for the children of the white planters and plantation managers who could not afford to send their children back to school in England. Jamaican students in those schools were the few whose parents could afford to pay the school fees or those who qualified for the twenty-eight parish scholarships awarded each year. A few others made their way through scholarships offered by the government into what later became known as grant-aided schools, which benefitted from government subsidies.

The Common Entrance Examination, modelled after the British system, was the method used to select students from elementary level to enter high school. Initially there were two classes of entry, free places and grant-in-aid places. The latter required parents to pay 50 per cent of the tuition fee.

Despite its significance as a passport to coveted high school places, the Common Entrance Exam system did not have the impact intended. After a decade, any discerning eye could see that government-run elementary schools were woefully underrepresented in the lists published in *The Daily Gleaner* of students who "passed their common entrance" and sailed into high schools of their choice. Critics presented figures showing that more than half of the winners of free places came from privately run, fee-paying preparatory schools. It was easy to see what was happening: parents from better-off homes were paying for their children to go to prep schools, which offered them much better chances of passing the Common Entrance Exam. The figures suggested that only one primary school student in twenty-eight would qualify for a high school place. The selection process perpetuated the relationship between ability to pay and entry to high school.

In the 1960s, Education Minister Edwin Allen sought to address this imbalance when he introduced the 70-30 system, prescribing that 70 per cent of high school places should be allocated to children in elementary schools and 30 per cent to those in preparatory schools. The impact of this decision was felt on the intake of students into high schools like KC and St George's, which had different histories and occupied different positions in the perceptions of Jamaicans. When KC had come on the high school scene in 1925, St

George's, founded in 1850 by Roman Catholic priests, was already well established; so were Wolmer's Boys, St Jago, and Jamaica College. When Bishop DeCarteret and the young clergyman Percival Gibson established KC, it was with the specified intention to counteract the economic and social barriers that restricted the pursuit of secondary education by underprivileged black Jamaican boys.

The irony was that KC's first headmaster, Percival Gibson, was a legendary graduate of St George's. He became the first Jamaican to graduate from the University of London with the bachelor of divinity degree, which he had pursued as an external student. It seemed clear that life in the ministry would be his destiny, but people said differences over doctrine as well as social perceptions of the Catholic church—and by extension, St George's—destroyed his interest in taking the Catholic route. It was to the Anglican Church that he turned, pursuing his studies and laying the foundation for a lifetime of service, in which his work at KC was a highlight.

The warnings I got about KC were based on the fact that under the 70-30 system, most of its students came through primary schools and were from less affluent areas of Kingston. By contrast, St George's, located almost opposite to KC, attracted students from a wider variety of primary and prep schools attended by students from so-called better areas of Kingston.

I wanted to see all the warnings as the expression of genuine fears about my ability to manage, but I knew they were as much a sign of ignorance and bias. Like most entrenched social prejudices, attitudes towards both schools were based on some, not all of the truth. I knew less than half of the story.

On the Edge of My First Staff Meeting

The reputations of St George's and KC were the furthest things from my mind when, on a sweltering Thursday morning in the last week of August, I positioned myself on the edge of the general staff meeting called to start the new school year. Part of me lingered somewhere outside my body; the rest of me sat there like a chicken waiting to get across a busy street. I eyed the seasoned staff members as they filed into the fifth-form block, its partitions open to create one long auditorium.

Men and women (in a ratio of roughly two to one) greeted each other, some reminiscing about their summer holidays, some complaining about how quickly the time had gone. Others murmured their resignation to the fact that another year was upon them.

"Hello, lady. I'm Peter—Peter Maxwell. You look like one of our new teachers. Welcome to KC. What's your subject?"

"Yes, I am, thank you. English." *The fewer words I say, the less likely I will be to make a fool of myself.*

"Oh, one of us. And where have you taught before?"

How many times will I have to answer that dreaded question today?

Mr Forrest's voice rang out as he announced the names of the last of the new teachers. "Stand up, please, new teachers. Old-timers, let's give them a big KC round of applause!" My knees trembled and my ears grew hot. Each time the second hand of my Timex watch moved, I was one step closer to dashing outside and getting on the next bus heading up South Camp Road. Every minute that I delayed was sealing off any exit from this trap that was closing in around me.

The clapping subsided. I made a quick note of the names of three other young female teachers; they looked as out of place as I felt. Mr Forrest gave his motivational speech, and I thought with a brief smile of Tennyson's "The Charge of the Light Brigade". His two deputies followed, their faces as starched and stern as the images of headmasters that had lived in my head before I met Mr Forrest. They rattled off goals, plans, rules, classroom allocations—all Greek to me.

Every other sentence that one of the veterans uttered reminded me how out of place I was. It didn't help that the face of my seaside grandmother kept flashing before me, lined with laughter as, for the umpteenth time, she told one of her favourite stories about me.

"You see this girl Frances? I don't know why she used to hate school. All I know is that she used to wedge her wiry little body between the wall and the old wood stove in the kitchen, a good way down from the back door of the house. She would hide in that spot, taking in the heat from the flaming wood as long as she could stand it. Then she would run inside, crying, her face and hands burning, as she called out, 'Gramma, Gramma, sick with fever.' Until I figured out what she was up to, this little wretch used this game to escape one day at a time from Miss Palmer's rickety little school in Port Maria."

How I wished I could be back in my Port Maria! It was always a welcome sight after journeying forty-six miles from Kingston, through the hills and valleys, where the narrow, winding Junction Road kept our hearts in our mouths close to the bumps of ginger lodged under our tongues to keep away travel sickness. Each time we crossed the bridge in the heart of the congested little town, three sights reminded us we were almost there: the stunning blues of the ocean stretched out across the bay; Cabarita—the dot of an island across from the shoreline; and then the timeworn stone walls of the St Mary Parish Church, which had towered above the landscape for more than a hundred years.

I'd crossed the bridge on countless journeys from Kingston to my grandparents' little district of Galina and back, three miles from Miss Palmer's school in the heart of Port Maria. I always stayed longer and went back more often than my sisters, rekindling the bonds with my grandma, recalling the songs and poems of my infancy: "All Things Bright and Beautiful", "Jesus Loves Me, Yes I Know", "Irene, Good Night", and "I wandered lonely as a cloud".

As I grew older, I'd learned to lodge myself against the wall behind Dadda's piano, its keys yellowed with age, its wooden frame weary from shedding splinters. There, I could feel and hear one clunk after the other as his uncertain fingers found the keys that could change the sitting room into a church or school. Sometimes it was a makeshift dormitory where we slept on fold-up cots and bedding on the floor when too many family members turned up at once. But the next morning, it would be a hat shop where tourists paused to buy straw souvenirs and sip coconut water. In the evening it was our playroom for cards and dominoes, or a theatre for homegrown recitals of song and dance and poems by Louise Bennett.

When Dadda went off to work, Grandma flitted to her workroom across the street, supervising women who came from afar to toil, plaiting and turning sundried straw into hats and mats and dolls. Then it was just me—and the piano in its splendid silence, broken only by the turning of pages and the swishing of Grandma's billowing white lace curtains in the country breeze. Abandoning my body right there in that spot, I travelled the world, crisscrossing vast lands and tempestuous seas to inhabit the exciting worlds of Kipling, Alcott, Stevenson, Lewis, Milne, Blyton, and numerous others. Behind the wobbly piano, my lifelong addiction to books was born.

Speaking of books … Mrs Riley was addressing the meeting now, holding forth about the "importance of getting the boys to write good English in all their subjects". *Maybe she is right; maybe my excitement about literature will help me reach those boys!* But how could someone who manufactured fever to avoid school and preferred to lie behind a piano, chasing made-up lives, be equipped to teach KC boys who hated reading? *What am I doing here, about to take the plunge into being an English teacher at an all-boys' school? What am I doing here with this timetable and this mark book, waiting for someone to take us on the school tour?*

Another story stole away my thoughts. This one was from my mother—one that was a little more consoling. "If any one of my children becomes a teacher, it will be Frances. Her grandmother said she didn't like school too much at the beginning, but back in Kingston, she would spend all her time playing school with her dollies. Later, in our Harbour View backyard, she was always teaching trees and shrubs, using stones to mark out her lessons in the dirt under the almond tree. She was really strict with her children."

Well, I guess it's a 50-50 chance that teaching was always supposed to be in my future.

Burdened with the books and notes distributed at the staff meeting, I made my way to South Camp Road, still asking myself what I was getting into. I slumped into the window seat, and the Number 22 bus groaned past the second stop. My face pressed up against the window, I glimpsed the Glenmore Road sign, then abandoned old houses and others that had been turned into business places. Next came Alpha primary school. Then, the arched metal sign loomed high above the gate: Alpha Academy.

My face almost touching the dust of the bus window, I peered as far as I could see up the long walkway to the grounds I had traipsed across for seven years, sometimes plodding, sometimes charging through the thickets of becoming a young woman. I had walked out of those gates to face life, armed with O- and A-level passes and a host of experiences that had left me woefully uncertain about much of who I was, what I believed, and who I should become.

As the bus struggled past the gate, I saw images of myself wandering from classroom to classroom, slipping from the threats of teachers and nuns intent on straightening me out, kneeling outside the office of my headmistress, and daydreaming at the window of my 4B classroom, where one day Miss Barnett told us what a copywriter did at work.

In the years since leaving Alpha, my visits had quickly tapered off and then come to a complete stop. Unlike some of my sixth-form friends, I'd made no plans to study after my A-levels. My teachers weren't sure I would do well, and I just wanted to forget the dim days of the exams. English and Spanish were my favourites, and I would have gladly read *King Lear* and *Pride and Prejudice* twenty more times, but in my circles, leaving school meant going out to work.

My mother had migrated. I was in line to contribute to the expenses my aunt and uncle incurred because we were boarding with them. My mother sent home what she could, but sometimes money was scarce. So when a friend of the family arranged an interview for me to get a job at the bank downtown, I put on my best dress and shoes, threw on a veil of excitement and confidence, and called on my sixth-form debate competition speech. "Yes," my big sister told my mother on the brief, expensive call to New York, "She got the job." All the sighing relatives gathered around the phone told me I was relieved.

From Monday to Saturday, I dressed in the new clothes my mother sewed in New York and sent down with anyone who was coming back home and had space for an extra package. From Monday to Saturday, I made my way through the doors of the Royal Bank of Canada, Duke Street, walked across the marble tiles, and found my way reluctantly to my cashier's cage, steeling myself for the onslaught of impatient customers and the smell of damp, dirty money.

I learned to cover my ears, shutting out the insistent screech of the woman upstairs, who leaned over the railing, calling out as if her life depended on it: "Teller 4! Who is Teller 4? Teller 4, where is the cash voucher? Teller 4, you have to sign each and every voucher. Teller 4, how can you cash a cheque without a date on it?"

Most evenings, two or three of us paced the floor anxiously until well past seven o'clock as the lock-up officers counted and recounted our cash because our paperwork and the money in our tills didn't balance. At night, I jumped out of my sleep, expecting to see the police at my aunt's front door, asking for Teller 4, grabbing me and dragging me to the station because of the money missing from my till.

"You will not be confirmed after your probation if you don't improve right away," my immediate supervisor said. "You have to make sure to write down every word I tell you, and when you go home, practise how to check the vouchers carefully and count the money quickly without making one mistake."

When three months dragged by and they confirmed me to the permanent staff, the family friend took me aside and whispered, "You know that it is just by the skin of your teeth that they confirmed you? You have to work harder. And just look how you look nice in your new uniform. Your mother would be so proud. Come on, you can do better. Look how hard your mother worked to get you through high school. You know how many girls would be glad for this opportunity?"

After four months, my fingers itched from the residue of coins and filthy bank notes I had to count and hand over all day, every day. The last Friday of the month was always the worst. Those were the days when government workers and construction crews came in, hurrying to cash their pay cheques. The lines stretched through the doors and curled around the corner onto

Barry Street, everybody hungry and miserable. Impatient customers glared as I slowly counted out the fifteen pounds, seventeen shillings, and sixpence printed on each cheque, the notes and coins always causing confusion and miscounting.

"You don't really like this work, do you, Miss Phillips?" The department head's tone was crisp; her Canadian accent seemed as alien as her attempts to probe my feelings. She emphasised "this work" in a way that made it seem one had to be a special kind of person to like it—as if one had to be a special kind of idiot not to like it.

"I do like it; I like it a lot," I said.

The woman knew a lie when she heard one, and she never stopped hounding me to admit that I lied. But I wasn't making all of it up; it was exciting to be earning my own money and becoming a "big woman". The feeling that I was a burden on my sister, my aunt, and my mother had begun to slip away as I saw myself becoming established and independent. I admired the efficiency and confidence of some tellers and the many other competent workers at the bank. But I knew I couldn't be a bank teller forever, and I doubted I had the temperament or the skills to move into any other aspect of banking.

After I couldn't look her in the face and deny my lie any more, the head of the department brought in a clipping from *The Daily Gleaner* about the university scholarship exam and left it in my teller's cage. I hauled my cardboard box from under the bed, brushed off my sixth-form books, notes, and exam papers, and stayed up late at nights, going through them. I revised all the notes I could find from another box stuffed with leftovers from A-level Spanish and English lessons.

On a Friday morning that came much too soon, I took time off from the bank and made my way to the university, shaking with nerves and excitement. Hunched over one of two hundred little desks set out in long rows in the university's Old Library, now converted into an exam centre, I filled reams of foolscap paper with miles of words that flooded my mind as I struggled through the puzzles the university professors had conjured to find out who was worthy of a place.

In a few weeks, the results were in my hands. The furore at home over "giving up a good good job to go and study" eventually abated. A university bursary saw me through with the help of funds from my mother and sister.

My transition into and out of university passed without a thought about what would happen afterwards. Obviously, I wouldn't be returning to the bank, but as to what path I would pursue, I had no plan. My exposure to career education and career opportunities remained limited during my years on campus. At home, I was used to people talking about completing school with enough exam passes and then getting and holding a job, not pursuing a career.

A job in television news came after my first application, and I never thought it would be over in just a year.

Now, here I am, about to throw myself into being a teacher. What is wrong with me? Why wasn't I like those girls in Mary Seacole Hall who had known from an early age they would be lawyers or doctors or teachers or librarians? Why didn't I ask the placement officer at UWI to check if there were teaching vacancies at my own old school?

None of that mattered now; at the staff meeting, Mrs Riley had pointed me out as the new English teacher. The introduction to the seasoned staff of KC had left me more daunted, more uncertain of myself and what I was about to take on. In another two days, I would have to step into a corner classroom and become someone I didn't know.

My mind swarmed with a thousand memories of my days at high school and the women who had taught me there. How could I even think I would have the right or the wherewithal to influence boys who might be better students than I'd ever been? *What if they are as challenging as I was to my own teachers?*

The Room with the
Column in the Middle

It was still dark when I left home at 6:10 a.m. on Monday, wearing a bottle-green linen skirt, a pale yellow short-sleeved blouse, and my patent leather pumps, minus the mud stains from Mr Forrest's rose garden. I'd been relieved to see that nobody dressed up for school the way they had done at the bank. Certainly, not many of the ladies at the staff meeting had been wearing stockings.

I'd changed my clothes three times in the half-light. The black skirt seemed too short. The pink dress suddenly decided it needed a slip. My coffee landed right in the centre of the mild red gabardine skirt. By then the six o'clock RJR news headlines were wrapping up, so I dragged on the first skirt I laid my hand on in the closet, grabbed my books and bag, and ran all the way to the bus stop. As I stepped onto the bus, I quickly scanned the landscape for the well-known purple-and-white ties that KC boys wore. Glimpsing two of them near the middle of the bus, I quickly turned in the opposite direction, and tucked myself in the corner of the backseat.

It was 7:45 a.m. Boys were tumbling out of the chapel and into my classroom at the corner of the fourth-form block. A concrete column stood in the middle of the room as if to keep the ceiling in place. *I bet it's a great hiding place for one or two mischief makers and idlers.* How huge the room before me seemed, compared to the classrooms I remembered at Alpha. How small and far away from the desks and chairs I felt, my knees like Jell-O under the teacher's table as the boys rumbled in and took their seats, every face wearing a huge question mark. Staring beyond the rows of eyes to the faded map of Jamaica on the back wall, I was sure every single one of those thirty-seven adolescent boys could hear my heart beating against the wall of my chest. I was certain they could tell from the tremor in my voice that I shouldn't be anywhere near their teacher's podium.

"Good morning, boys of 4A.[3] I am Miss Phillips." I had intended to speak loudly and bravely, but my voice was the squeak of a starving mouse.

---

[3] As in the British school structure, high school during this period started at first form (now grade 7) and progressed through second, third, fourth and fifth forms (now grades 8–11). Students who met

"Good morning, Miss Phillips!" Their voices echoed from the front to the back of the room in a raucous singsong greeting that was soon to become the call to arms on each school day. Too soon, the unholy racket of getting back into their seats broke out—metal chairs screeching on rough concrete, geometry sets scattering on the floor, strident taunts and teasing left over from last term's disagreements, a lost drummer boy beating out his raggedy tune on a wooden desk in the far corner.

"I am your new form teacher, and I will be teaching you English language and literature."

"Yes, Miss Phillips," a few students chanted. Others mumbled and giggled as I wrote my name on the board. Never known for its high quality, my handwriting crawled across the blackboard, the end of my name several inches higher than the beginning. Unaccustomed to the feel of chalk dust in my nervous sweat, I rubbed my fingers and thumb together, trying not to wipe them in my clothes.

"Blow it off, Miss; blow it off," a small boy in the second row said.

"As long as it is not on me!" the one in front of him shouted with a mild threat in his voice.

---

the required standards graduated from fifth form. Some who were very successful in their O-level exams (now Caribbean Secondary Education Certificate [CSEC] came back to lower sixth (grade 12), and most of these stayed to complete the following year in upper sixth (grade 13). In upper sixth, they did pre-university studies and sat Cambridge A-level exams (now the Caribbean Advanced Proficiency Examination [CAPE]).

Do all boys talk so loudly all the time? The laughter and murmuring were turning into a roar. I quickly looked outside to the corridor, hoping no other teacher was passing.

"Yow! Keep quiet and have some respect for the teacher!" This boy's voice came from the third row from the back. His white teeth gleamed like marble against his Cadbury chocolate skin. Though serious, he was not hostile. He obviously had some authority, because the giggles and snickers subsided.

Thank you, whoever you are. But now, can you help me with those thirty-six other pairs of eyes fixed on me?

At that very moment, a boy bearing all the signs that he considered himself a man swaggered in on bandy legs, wearing a devilish half-smile that verged on a smirk. He looked me up and down, taking his own time to walk sideways towards a seat. He pivoted on the ball of one foot and slid into the last empty chair. All eyes followed him, watching and waiting.

"What's your name?" I asked.

I made out enough from his mumbled reply to pick up his name in the register.

His facial expression suggested he didn't want to hear another question, but I knew my audience was on the lookout. A few were already whispering, waiting for one of us to break the tension.

"Why are you late?"

"Me, late? I'm not late; I was with Mr Forrest—Miss."

I had already learned that the *Miss* was always dutifully tacked on to avoid any suggestion that a student was being disrespectful, even when he meant to be.

The glare in his eyes and the twitch in the corner of his lips worked with the gruffness of his words to make it clear he thought it quite crazy of this unknown teacher to question him about being with Mr Forrest. *I doubt he's the type to help with the roses.*

"Well, I'm about to take the register," I said, "so I'll just make a note of that." I said a silent prayer that I didn't sound as feeble as I felt. But what new teacher could question this bold "don't forget I'm a man" assertion that he'd been with the headmaster, especially while thirty-seven boys watched and waited for brand-new Miss Phillips to have her first showdown?

Reprising Mrs Riley's words, but failing to achieve her tone, I gave a one-minute spiel about something or other and then warned them to be on time for class.

I sat down to the task of placing a checkmark next to each name in the register, a faint question mark beside the name of this boy who thought he was a man. I couldn't remember seeing or hearing a guideline for how to note that someone was late with explanation. Nor did I know what kinds of explanation might be acceptable. Clearly, this boy thought his explanation was beyond comment.

I moved on to tackle the tasks on Mrs Riley's checklist. There was a constant rumble: boys walked about borrowing pencils, sharpeners, or pens; whispering; and bursting into laughter. Some exaggerated the scraping of their chairs on the concrete floor, while others leaned back to see how far they could go before their chairs crashed to the floor. Still I made my announcements, gave my instructions, and passed on quickly from one question to another.

I was halfway through the to-do list when a great weariness swallowed me. I opened my mouth to share something else from my notes. Nothing came out. The sudden realisation of where I was and what I was doing—the feeling that I couldn't be more out of place in this room—threatened to suffocate me. *This is it. I am going to fall apart right here in front of these boys. They are going to laugh me to scorn.*

"Miss … Miss … Miss Phillips!"

Why do they always have to scream or wail?

"Yes? What is it?" I answered, almost wailing myself.

"Miss, this boy say if we must use the same exercise book for language and literature?"

"I never say anything like that," said another boy.

"'This boy'? Who is 'this boy' and why are you calling him that in the classroom? Every student in this class must call everyone else by his right name." I made up this ridiculous rule on the spot, hoping the delaying tactic would bring me an answer to his question.

Just as the boy gave me his name, another one was shouting at him. "You are a idiot boy? How you must use the same book for two subject?"

"Is all right. Him come from country. Him soon learn to be a college man," someone else shouted from the other end.

"Stop shouting!" I said, shouting in spite of myself. "They are right—"

I stopped, overwhelmed by drawing a blank as I tried to recall who "this boy" was. *When will I ever know all these names?*

He repeated his name.

"Yes," I murmured wearily. "They are right. You do need two books."

The class erupted with a variety of reasons to protest. "Miss, we don't have money to waste, you know."

"My mother not spending her money on so much exercise book because last year, I didn't use half of them."

"Okay, we'll talk about that tomorrow."

I don't know how many times those words inched from my mouth that morning. They were threatening to emerge one more time when the sound of the bell broke through. *I bet students don't realise they are not the only ones who can be saved by the bell.*

I was sure the boys heard my sigh of relief even though I tried to muffle it as I packed up my stuff and hurried out into the morning sun. Moments after I returned to the staffroom, Mrs Riley quizzed me on the checklist we had prepared. Relief seeped through my bones. I had completed the routine introductions, instructions, and explanations of the syllabi for English language and literature. I'd held up my copy of the formidable *Mastering Modern English*, its hundreds of rules closeted between soft blue covers with a blurb that promised competence in all the required skills of comprehension, summary, vocabulary building, grammar, and composition. I'd skirted around what *To Kill a Mockingbird* had to do with boys who were going to be engineers and doctors. I had steered carefully away from their objections to "all those poems by old white men from England." We'd elected their head boy,[4] who was supposed to become my right-hand man. I'd sent them six at a time in orderly rows to collect their rented books from the book room.

I didn't care that I couldn't remember doing all of that. I just knew I had survived my first foray into the lives of the "hooligans from the wrong side of North Street".

---

[4] Head boy: a male student who occupies the highest position of student leadership in a boys' school or coeducational institution

Settling In

The longer I sat around the table in the small room where I had first seen the English teachers, the more I realised I had stepped into the domain of seasoned experts. Mrs Riley continued her orientation and her hawk-eyed supervision, but I soon discovered her wicked sense of humour and her ability to predict how boys might react to one poem or another.

Her friend Mrs Beulah Reid sat by her side, reinforcing her leadership with equal expertise and firmness, though with a softer demeanour. Mrs Reid had two sons at the school, so she had her ear to the ground for more than one reason.

The other English teacher was the whispering Miss Jasmin Reid, whose sincerity and concern for her students were just two of the hallmarks of this sedate, devoted, and insightful giant of the department. As tall as her namesake was short, Miss Jasmin Reid was as steady as a well-rooted tree and equally refreshing.

The other occupants of the cramped space were a Trinidadian woman who taught Spanish and a Jamaican who taught French. Both had been ahead of me at UWI, but I recognised them as former residents of Mary Seacole Hall, the all-female students' residence at the Mona campus where I had spent my time as a UWI student. All three English teachers were graduates of this university, but the two most seasoned ones had a few advantages that were quickly evident. They belonged to a generation of teachers who had received outstanding preparation for the classroom at Jamaica's famous Mico Teachers' College. They'd headed to the university for further academic exposure after accumulating several years of teaching experience. They were steeped in the techniques of teaching and knowledgeable in the content areas of language and literature. Plus, they seemed to be born teachers. The combination was enviable.

Mrs Riley expected that as an English major, I had mastered the necessary subject matter, so she assigned me to a wide range of other classes besides my own 4A. Students in third and fourth forms pursued standard high school courses. In the fifth form, they prepared for the school-leaving O-level examinations conducted by Cambridge University in England. For most, these exams would be the end of their secondary education. Depending on their results, they would enter the job market or proceed to training institutions or private "extension" schools, where they could repeat subjects they had failed. My senior students were in the lower sixth form, taking advanced classes for pre-university exams.

I was teaching boys between 13 and 18 years old, the latter just a few years younger than I was. I was sure that, like me, those boys had grown up with insistent reminders that education was the way to escape poverty and deprivation—to make something of yourself. The stakes were unquestionably high. I could still remember the agony of waiting at Alpha at the end of each term to discover my own exam results. Seeing them at this stage of their journey made the responsibility weigh on me, often making me shudder at the enormity of what I had taken on.

Midnight found me slaving over the lesson-plan template Mrs Riley had shared, making notes in the margins of my literature texts, coming up with multiple examples of metaphors, similes, hyperbole, prepositional clauses, and auxiliary verbs. I battled with "translating" Shakespeare into both the language and the real-life circumstances of men-to-be in a struggling country.

Some mornings, as I got ready to head to the bus stop, my knees threatened to buckle, my mind assailed by nagging doubts about how little I knew, how well I could impart what I knew, and how I would get the attention and respect necessary to help the boys learn.

To my surprise, I was truly relieved about one thing: there were no cranky teenage girls in this school. I had zero experience with adolescent boys but more than enough with girls—after all, hadn't I been one? Images of what girls were like flashed before me constantly: how moody and vindictive we'd been; how the quarrels between even the best of friends had led to the most caustic verbal attacks in each other's presence and behind each other's backs; how long periods of vexation and silence had followed, sometimes for the rest of our school days.

These boys erupted all the time, called each other terrible names, and even rolled on the ground in fights that broke out in an instant, bringing male teachers hustling to the corridors. But most times, the boys moved on quickly from these conflicts. They were mischievous, even unruly, but not malicious.

Thinking back to my Alpha days, I realised how cruel many of us girls had been towards our mostly female teachers at the height of our adolescent madness. We called them horrible names behind their backs, criticising their noses, their knees, their teeth, their hair, their walks, their speech, their clothes, and their shoes.

"Watch her; watch her buff teeth."

"I can't stand the one they call Miss Williams. Her head look like a wet mop."

"I don't know what she doing here. She talk about she teaching biology and all she can say is, 'No, girls, we are not covering that this term; maybe next term.'"

We huddled behind each other, whispering secret jokes about the nuns, wondering how and why they'd chosen that suffocating way of life.

It was not that I had any illusions about the boys. I knew they talked about teachers. They gave us nicknames (I had a few suspicions about at least two of mine), and they constantly executed pranks to distract us. But they didn't seem as calculated or as vicious as I remembered us girls being. I cringed at the images of what I had been, casting aside some of the anger I'd carried for years about altercations with teachers and administrators, about rules and punishments that I had considered unnecessary and extreme. For the first time, I understood what my teachers had had to contend with.

Eye to eye with the immense difficulty of standing or sitting before thirty to forty adolescents and trying to teach them subject-verb agreement or the difference between main clauses and subordinate clauses, I found myself developing, albeit much too late, a genuine respect for most of my own teachers. I clutched a secret fear that my students would despise me and create trouble for me as divine retribution for my misdemeanours at Alpha. This gave me a special reason to do whatever I could to be as effective as possible, a reason to reach out and try to connect with my students.

Another reason soon began to take shape. At first it was the mere idea of finding some kind of meaning behind what I spent my days and a good part of many nights labouring over. As the boys continued to question why they had to learn what I was teaching, I became aggressive in my search to find answers that would quell their objections. It wasn't enough that I had drifted into the love of reading, or that, despite myself,

I had excelled at language and literature late in high school and found that the world of words and ideas had saved me.

These boys wanted more substantial reasons, and I would have to find them. My teachers had never needed such reasons because we students were never free to ask why we had to learn what they taught, let alone object to it. As my mother had preached relentlessly, "They have the knowledge already; your job is to keep yourself quiet and get it into your own head."

There were other differences too. Boys seemed to lack the ugly side we girls had perfected to deal with our adolescent confusion and anger. These boys were mostly good-natured and pleasant. But they were also more strategic in their management of the classroom and of teachers—at any rate, this teacher. In a school of only girls, I'd learned a lot about defiance, evasion, criticism, and fierce, sarcastic words, but not about the type of manipulation that these boys had clearly mastered at an early age. They knew exactly how to massage situations to avoid difficulties and buy time. Nowhere was this more evident than when certain types of activities were scheduled—like presentations of homework or weekly tests.

One Tuesday morning in 5C, a more vociferous, more singsong greeting than usual threatened to deafen me. "Good morning, Miss Phil—"

"So, Miss, you read yesterday *Star*?" one excited voice shrieked above the rest.

"This is the same thing we talk about last class when we was reading about Cassius and Brutus ... Miss."

I couldn't get a word in. One after the other, the known chatterboxes and even the usually silent boys chimed in.

"Calm down, boys; let me catch my breath. I haven't even marked the register yet."

"But Miss, you say we must notice things going on in the society, and the *Star* report—"

"Keep quiet and make the teacher mark the register!" the head boy shouted, already on his feet. "Miss, mark the register and we can talk about it. We didn't believe you, Miss, but yesterday the *Star*—"

"We will get to that," I said, adding the boy's name. I had become accustomed to the practice of calling all students by their last names. It seemed to come with the territory of an all-boys' school, and it carried no significance. At Alpha, when teachers called girls by their last names, it was always preceded by a frosty and sarcastic "Miss", and it was always a sign of trouble. Not so here at KC. The first names of boys were hardly ever mentioned.

Sutherland, aka Shorty, was halfway up to my desk, brandishing a raggedy copy of the *Star*, Jamaica's scandalous afternoon newspaper. I had to see what they were so excited about, so I set aside the register, along with my lesson plan, and we all listened as Shorty read the *Star*.

Just like that, they won the battle to use most of the class time discussing a story about intrigue and betrayal involving prominent politicians opposing each other for a high position in their party. No one missed the resemblance to *Julius Caesar*. I smiled as I realised the effectiveness of their strategy. Of course, they were relating current events to our discussions in literature. And of course, it was a good thing that boys who were usually quiet had become engaged in the discussion. And of course, they'd had their way.

The real result of this kind of intervention that the boys skilfully and regularly managed to pull off was that the scheduled class time was almost used up, so there was not enough left for them to do whatever I had planned. That was what they were intent on avoiding. I saw the light: it was all about distractions and delaying tactics—schemes to deflect my attention from homework they hadn't done, topics they didn't care for, or preparation they had left incomplete.

Wise to their tactics, I had to develop my own, not just for managing time, but for balancing their expectations and the rules of the school. *You have to stick to the syllabus. You must not infringe on other teachers' class time by ending your class late. Your students must not distract the class next door with noisy outbursts. You must prepare your boys to pass the same school exams as all the other groups, not just the tests you set for them. You must take the register and turn in your attendance figures and grades on time. You must not send the boys out for lunch late or they will be late for their other classes.* A million other similar reminders filled up the remaining pages of the guidelines I was putting together from what seemed like a hundred different sources. But before my eyes, there was always something happening that made the rules seem less important.

Back in 4A, the daily scuffles persisted. The boy who considered himself a man remained sullen, his eyes falling as soon as I glanced in his direction, his responses no more than grunts the few times I directed a comment or question his way. The 4A boys were the cream of the fourth-form crop, according to all the gurus in the staffroom. And yet I was often on the verge of giving up. What would happen when I got to the other streams? How would I manage those boys in 3D—boys now at the same age as I had been during my mutiny at Alpha? Perhaps if I could understand what had led to my own journey into rebellion, it would help me prepare for a classroom of boys who, at thirteen or fourteen, already claimed the title "worst boys ever to come over from Melbourne Park".[5]

---

[5] The Melbourne Park campus was part of an experiment in which KC became a two-campus operation after the student population had grown beyond the capacity of the Clovelly Park campus on North Street. The board acquired the old Melbourne Club's home on Elletson Road, just a few miles away.

Me, the Troublemaker

I had waited the whole evening for my mother to come home to the stack of mail I had carefully tucked behind the clock on the buffet, where she had an equal chance of seeing it quickly or missing it until after I finished my homework and went to bed. As soon as I heard, "Frances, come in here right now!" I knew which chance had befallen.

"What is all this the teachers writing about you and your behaviour at school? If you think I'm going to Sister Bernadette to defend you, you better think again. If they expel you, you know already what will happen to you." Mama plunked the report down on the table. The bottle man's face loomed just above the brown envelope my form teacher had given me, on which to write my parents' name and address "in straight lines and capital letters".

"But, Mama … the teachers and those sisters not fair. They always picking on people they don't like even when we keep quiet and don't do anything. I can't stand them—"

Her right palm bounced off my face, stunning me into silence as the stinging imprint of her four fingers spread out across my cheek.

"Child, don't you provoke me with that rubbish this evening! I don't want to hear any excuse or argument from you. I send you to school to learn, not to get in any trouble with your teachers. I don't care if they are fair or unfair. They know what they suppose to know already. I know quite well that you can be rude. You think I don't see how you look at me from under your eyebrows? I bet that is exactly what you doing at school."

Folding myself down into the chair against the wall, I sat through the rest of her tirade, stunned by her unexpected rage, hoping that hunger and exhaustion would put an end to it. I breathed again when she took off her shoes and stormed into her room. I knew things were beyond serious when my mother didn't go to her evening job. My sisters warned me to stay outside until she calmed down, so I sat under the almond tree with Nancy Drew until the light faded.

On Friday morning at ten o'clock, we all huddled in Sister's office. My 3A form teacher spoke about me as if I weren't there, giving my mother and the headmistress the details they wanted about how I wasted "the whole of the first and second term, spending my time giving trouble". I sat silently, hugging my knees, my rage simmering. I was being blamed for all of it when they were the ones who spoiled everything. *All of you started the problem when you made my friends and me repeat second form. It was your own mistake, and still you punish us for it.* My little brain had taken me back to the year before, when we'd protested as much as a few second-formers could. We pointed out that we hadn't put ourselves in 2A; we were the brightest in that class. But Sister hadn't listened. She insisted that we would stay back in second form because the spaces in third form were needed for older girls. "You all should have been put in first form like all the others who came from prep or primary schools."

Something inside me had exploded. There was no stopping me. I just kept screaming, "It's not fair! It's not fair!" until Sister jumped up from her desk, marched over to me, dragged me up from my seat, and shook me by the shoulders, her face purple with rage.

We repeated second form. My interest in school died like a flower at the end of a broken vine.

The rest of the year had sped by. In spite of myself, I'd progressed to 3A, along with an assorted bunch of 13-year-old girls, most of us balancing on the edge of adolescent confusion and nursing the wounds the administration's decision had caused. I was distracted from the business of learning, and my disappointment had turned into waywardness.

Most of my classmates soon settled down, but not me. Day after day, I coddled the hurt in my heart about being kept back. I couldn't find any answers to my questions about justice. I couldn't reconcile the actions of the principal with the word "mercy" in the name of the religious order to which all the sisters belonged. I made up my mind I would just hate the entire staffroom and be done with it. No one was interested in whether my bad behaviour was caused by my childish resolve to get back at authority or by conflict at home or by the normal schizophrenia of adolescence.

During third form, there were numerous other meetings and notes to my mother. My reputation as a troublemaker spread, and I couldn't bring myself to care enough to change anything. I embraced my downward spiral until school became my nemesis and all teachers my adversaries—that is, until I was demoted from the A-stream. I dragged myself across the threshold into the dilapidated 4B classroom, where Miss Barnett stood at the door, waiting for us to file in.

I continued to wear the sullen mouth and glaring eyes the teachers had written about on my third-form reports—comments that brought the worst out of my burdened, disappointed mother and pushed me farther behind the walls I was building around myself.

Tensions and Tantrums

The daily bus rides to and from KC seemed to set my brain to work overtime, piecing together the realities of the present and the recollections of my past. I wanted to pull the threads together and come to some insights into how I could use my own challenges as a student to help me become this teacher I was supposed to be.

Once I got on the bus, my thoughts drifted all over the place—mostly to my Alpha days and beyond. More and more I made connections between my teaching days and the long-ago times that I had forgotten or deliberately buried. I wondered if the surliness and the aloofness of some boys in my classes were signs that they were struggling as I had struggled. Rushing over to get my second bus to Chelsea Avenue, I watched the Alpha girls sporting my old uniform, and I couldn't shake the images of myself at that age. I recalled my relief and happiness at becoming a high school girl, the betrayal I experienced in second form, the year of rebellion in 3A—and then Miss Barnett's rescue operation.

It had started in the third week of the new school year. My shame about being moved from the A stream to the B stream was still smarting. I had taken up a passive position in the back row, right next to the window, where I could gaze outside and think about better places to be. Through all the trouble in third form, I had remained competent in a few subjects like literature and English language. But the math and science teachers had convinced me I wasn't made for those subjects; those subjects were for bright girls. Still, I didn't want to make this new teacher believe I had any intention of getting involved in her discussions about *Jane Eyre* or *Romeo and Juliet*. I did love reading, but she didn't need to know why or how much.

I felt her eyes on me, watching to see if I was paying attention. I kept eyeing her to see if she noticed me gazing through the window. As soon as the bell rang, signalling the lunch break, I jumped up to leave the room. At the door, her hand fell softly on my shoulder. "I need to speak with you, Fraaynces." She'd told us at the beginning of the term that she just returned from a Catholic college in America; we assumed that was why she pronounced some of our names and some other words like she was American.

I wanted to say, "My name is not Fraaynces, it's Frances", but I didn't want her deciding I was impertinent, as so many other teachers had said just before sending for my mother. Instead, I said, "Sorry, Miss. I have to go to Sister Bernadette's office before my next class." It was true, but I could have stayed a few minutes. *Why you always trying to talk to me? I thought I could actually like you, but now I'm not sure. You just look like you want to get into my business.*

"Well, see me at lunchtime then. Come to the staffroom after you eat your lunch." Her big brown eyes and the space between her front teeth always made her seem to be smiling, but her voice was firm, and I knew there was no way out. I gobbled down half of my patty and coco bread, washed it down with orange juice, and hurried to the staffroom door, praying I wouldn't see any of my third-form teachers.

At the door, I tried to hide as I saw Miss Sarcasm herself—the dreaded teacher who taught us history in third form. "Frances Phillips, look at you! In trouble as usual, I suppose."

"She's not in trouble; she's here to see me." Miss Barnett's firm voice prevented any further comments. Miss Hall rolled her eyes and sashayed back to the coffee pot.

What! This teacher really defended me?

"Come this way. There's an empty classroom right here," Miss Barnett said. My heart picked up speed.

She didn't waste a moment after we stepped into the room and she told me to sit. "I want to talk to you about what happened before you got into my class, Fraaynces. Was something going on at home?"

I knew it! I knew you would ask me about home. And I won't be telling you or anybody else about what goes on at my house. My friend had told a teacher about her parents getting a divorce, and the teacher had told all her friends in the staffroom. I sucked in air and stared at the floor.

"Fraaynces …"

I looked up, then immediately lowered my eyes to avoid hers. They were just too probing, too caring, too whatever they were. I stared at my shoes. "Nothing, Miss."

"But something must have happened. Your second-form reports were extremely good. You went from 2A to 3A. Then, after third form, instead of going to 4A, you are in 4B. I am glad you are in my class, but that switch from A to B stream doesn't usually happen without a reason."

"Maybe you should ask the people who put me there, Miss. I didn't demote myself."

It seemed like a logical answer to me, but her lips quivered. She took that long breath of air that usually ended with "Get out of my class right now" or "You can spend the rest of my class at the principal's office". *Here we go again.*

"Come on, young lady. Don't give me any smart answers. We both know your grades and your teachers' comments must have put you where you are. I have an idea what those were like, and I can easily find out more from the office."

Just as Mama had said, she must have received the lowdown about me long before she laid eyes on my face. *So, if you can find out, why are you asking me?*

"I'm sure you can be a good student again, but you don't seem to want to try. I want to know why."

And I want to know why you can't just leave me alone. "I don't know why, Miss. I'm just not a good student. The good students are in 4A."

"Well, you can't be in 4A, and you know why, *Miss* Phillips." The tone of that "Miss" was no different from when the other teachers used it. *So you are no different from the others after all.*

"But I'm not going to stand by and see you doing less than you can in my class. As your form teacher I will be checking with the other teachers from time to time, to see how you are doing." Her soft voice and comforting tone had disappeared, replaced with a firmness that made it clear she was absolutely serious about her work as a teacher.

In the weeks that followed, I learned what that really meant. It meant she would not stop directing questions at me until I was tired of saying, "I don't know, Miss." She would not give up on the idea that I could produce more than the bare minimum when asked to write a story or an essay. She would refuse to accept that I could not summarise a stanza from a Wordsworth poem or paraphrase a speech from *Romeo and Juliet*. In short, she would demonstrate her conviction, even without clear evidence, that I was putting on an act to suggest that I could not bring anything worthwhile to the learning process.

The things about Miss Barnett that eventually reached me were her dogged persistence and her obvious desire to unearth the better side of a confused and confusing adolescent girl who thought she had a right to be mad at everybody except herself. Miss Barnett was intent on proving that she could penetrate the wall I had been building around myself for an entire year in third form, and that she could get me to care. And she did.

Taking Miss Barnett
to Form 3D

Miss Barnett became my constant companion as I tried to navigate the challenges of 1970s KC. I discovered many boys in whom I saw what she had seen in me at the beginning of my fourth-form year. Like me, they had lost their way and their belief in teachers and school. Some were just going along, waiting for an unnamed force to rouse them from their slumber. And there were the boys who hadn't ever come alive to anything. Could I learn her balance between showing caring and concern and demonstrating firmness in waking them up to reality? Could I sober up any of them enough to help them change, the way she had made me change?

She walked with me into the cramped, dimly lit classroom of Form 3D to stand, with a heavy dose of foreboding, in front of thirty-five faces that mirrored the face I had resentfully presented to my own teachers. At first, the boys in 3D seemed different only because they were my youngest students and appeared incapable of sitting still for more than three minutes. This was their first year coming to North Street from the Melbourne campus where they'd spent first and second form. After KC had grown beyond the capacity of the Clovelly Park campus on North Street, no suitable space adjoining the premises could be identified, so the board had acquired a property on Elletson Road, a few miles away.

The students in 3D had been the big boys at Melbourne—compared only to first-formers, of course. Now at North Street, the bigger boys called them "fryas", the derisive version of "small fry". A few seemed willing to disappear into the cracks without protest at their new status as nobodies, but others were always ready to fight back or even to pick fights— challenging bigger boys at the canteen, getting into trouble, and reinforcing the view that they were the worst boys that ever came over from Melbourne.

By the time I went to them, on Wednesday morning after the ten o'clock recess, most of them looked like they had been to war. I stood at the door, waiting. At least twenty boys crowded around those taking their turns at money football, the game most boys played on the teacher's table during recess, with coins and fudge or icicle sticks.

"Yes! Gwan, boy; your time now."

"Gwan which part?"

"You a idiot boy?"

"Where him can go?"

These remarks rang out from little boys on either side of the table, some supporting and some opposing those involved in each round of the game.

"The teacher is here! Find you seat!" somebody shouted.

"Yes, boys, break it up. It's class time," I said, stepping tentatively from the door, keeping my distance as they broke away from the huddle.

"Go outside and wash your hands and faces," I said to two boys who were leaking sweat.

"Yes, Miss."

"And make sure you come straight back. Now, the rest of you sit down without making a racket and take out what you need for this class—only this class. I am coming around to make sure that's all you have on your desks. No comics, no newspapers, no coins or fudge sticks." I had already been coached to bring my firmest, most hostile tone of voice to 3D. I was learning to match my attitude to all the rumours about what those boys had been like in 2D.

"Miss, Miss, you take Number 22 bus to school, Miss?" The boy who spoke sat in the middle row and could easily have filled two chairs.

Before I could answer, the entire row of boys behind him shouted, as one, "Quiet, boy! Don't interfere in the teacher business."

"OK. Thank you, boys; I will take it from here. What's your name? Yes, you there in the middle?"

The whole class shouted out his nickname, this time on the tops of their voices.

"I asked one boy for his name. Nobody else is supposed to answer. And you … you, speak for yourself," I said, pointing as I approached his desk.

His answer suggested he was quite comfortable with the name the boys had given him, but I wasn't about to encourage him to use it.

"Good. Well, the boys are right. You shouldn't ask teachers questions like that."

"Like what, Miss?"

"Like the one you just asked me, of course. Now let's move on to our work for today. We wasted too much time already. This month we are starting off with analysing sentences and clauses."

The whole class sank into their chairs and let out a prolonged groan.

At the end of forty minutes, numerous incidents had taken place, but none to do with the exciting lesson I'd planned. Two boys fell on the ground, fighting over money. Another one flew a paper plane into the open mouth of his classmate. The whole class laughed uproariously when a boy in the second-to-last row kicked the chair his neighbour was about to sit on, leaving him no choice but to fall flat on his bottom on the concrete floor. A tall, sullen student stabbed at someone with a compass and then said, "Come, me friend, you know me wouldn't stab you, don't it?"

As a colleague from another boys' school had advised, I quietly kicked away the small mirror that a backbencher had deliberately positioned on the floor next to his desk, hoping it would afford him a fleeting look up my skirt. "Anyone missing a mirror, please collect it from me after class, I announced triumphantly. Of course, I kept the mirror. Pantsuits steadily replaced my skirts and dresses after that.

"Are you missing these two boys, Miss Phillips?" Missa Johnno stood at the door, obviously concerned at the uproar. Later that day, I received my first long talk from Missa Johnno (aka Ivan "Wally" Johnson, art teacher, sports master, English teacher, and Mr KC). From him, I learned, among other things, that I would just have to tolerate male teenage sweat; the option was to "lose" boys by sending them to wash their hands and faces. *Now I see it! This is it! This is my punishment for being the devil I became in third form. This is what is going to make me lose my mind.*

Wednesdays and Fridays at 10:20 a.m. became my most dreaded hours. The strategies I tried in other classes fell flat in 3D. In the ever-shrinking rectangle that was their classroom, they were my constantly moving targets, and in my effort to keep track of them, I was their whirling dervish. I left their classes exhausted, diminished, and desperate to reach the doorway, always clutching for air.

The Parent-Teacher Association meeting in week six gave me some answers and even more questions. Fewer than half the parents of 3D students turned up.

I was both relieved and concerned. Walking into the room to face what looked like eleven mothers and five fathers who appeared as nervous as I felt, I wondered how I would explain my failure with their sons. Each one approached the table wearily, perched on the edge of the chair across from me, and leaned in to hear the news from my register and mark book.

"Your son is a bright boy, but he needs to try harder."

"He doesn't pay attention in class; he is always trying to read Batman under his desk."

"Your son can do much better."

"Your boy told me he missed school two Wednesdays in a row because—"

"Listen, Miss, you not to believe one word that boy tell you. I can tell you why he wasn't in school, ma'am."

"What are you saying?"

"I'm saying that the boy is telling lies. It was the same thing last year over Melbourne after him take up with that rascal from down the street!"

"That rascal" was not a KC student, but my student's mother was sure her son missed school two Wednesdays to go with him to watch horse racing at Caymanas Park and "gamble away the little money I give him for school".

The mother of the boy who had asked me about the bus I took was no less distraught. "Miss Phillips, I am sick and tired of the trouble with this boy. Every night I tell him to turn off the TV and do him schoolwork. I come home from work late in the evenings, and I have to wash and cook and clean because the other children are small. And this big big boy won't even set the right example and lift a finger to help me. And now you tell me him not doing the schoolwork either? But you, wait, Miss; you wait until I reach home tonight—"

I could just see this exhausted lady, no taller than my five feet seven inches, and thin as an ironing board, standing up to her son, who was as wide as the door and almost as tall. "I know it is upsetting, but you may have to try something else. This may sound funny, but let me ask you something. Whose TV is it?"

"Mine, of course. Well, I still have to pay for it every month because I buy it on hire purchase. But you know, Miss, is just a little entertainment for the children. They don't have much. The father is a farm worker in Canada, so most of the time is just me and them—you understand?"

"Of course. It must be hard to keep him under control now he's getting older and his father isn't always there. But think about this: the TV is yours, and it has a switch to turn it off, right?" I made sure to use a tone of voice that made it clear I wasn't talking down to her but forcing her to come to the conclusion she had to face.

"Yes, the TV belongs to m—" She broke into laughter. "Ooh … yes, Miss; I see what you saying now. Of course, I can just turn it off. And I promise I will find a way to get him to do the work."

"I will find a way to get him to do the work!" Isn't that my job?

The faces of the mothers and fathers whirled in my head way into the night, transforming into the images of my own mother's face all those years before, when she had pleaded and warned my sisters and me about the importance of doing well in school. I re-lived her frustration over my third-form report—how embarrassed she must have been at the scathing comments of my teachers. And thinking about the parents of my 3D boys, I lived for the first time the panic that had summoned my mother's hand and planted the stinging blow across my cheek. Like my own parents, the mothers and fathers at the PTA meeting were desperate to make something of their children. They handed them over to us Monday to Friday to do our part. *What am I doing, allowing their boys to fall short?*

It was Friday morning, and I was in no mood for any joking. I planned to share the notes I had made during the PTA meeting with the boys in 3D. I planned to emphasise that teachers and parents were disappointed in how they were doing. Without exception, 3D sat silent and stone-faced after having been read the riot act or worse at home. Now they knew I was about to give them my own version. They were right, of course. I intended to warn and threaten and show them that everybody was angry with them and wouldn't tolerate their foolishness anymore.

But I kept thinking about myself in third form. No matter what I'd heard at home or from my teachers, I had simply dug in my heels and lived down to what "they" expected of me. *Maybe that's what these boys are doing!* Why would they react any differently from the way I had back then? Wouldn't they have figured out that I had heard about their reputation from Melbourne? Hadn't I armed myself with special tactics and put on my fight face and my sternest voice to deal with them before I ever stepped into their classroom? How much had I contributed to their behaviour and performance because of my fear, my barely covered hostility, and my low expectations?

The words that came out of my mouth were nothing like what I'd planned or what I figured they were anticipating. "Listen to me, boys. I know you probably got in trouble at home because of what we told your parents. And I'm sorry if you did, but things are serious and they—we—are all worried about you. Everybody knows third form is a difficult year. I imagine a lot is going on inside of you that you don't understand. You are neither little boys nor big boys. The work is getting harder, and we are demanding more from all of you."

My voice and my words seemed to be coming from outside of me. I began to wonder what the boys would make of the unfamiliar tone and this new spiel I was delivering. But if I stopped, I would lose my nerve. I felt I was on the edge of something important, so I let it all out in a series of swift, unfiltered thoughts and feelings.

"Believe it or not, boys, I remember how it felt when I was in third form. I thought I had plenty to be mad about. I was not the best student. My teachers tried hard and my parents too. But I made up my mind to give trouble, and it was a fight all the way—at school and at home. I had to accept the results. And they were not pretty.

"I am telling you all this because I know what it is like to be on the wrong track—and we are definitely on the wrong track in this class. We all can see the bad consequences coming. But you need ... we need to avoid them. If we shape up now and do better in the second month, we can turn around everything by the end of this term. Wouldn't that be good? So ... raise your hand right now if we can do better."

Somewhere in my speech, I'd turned into Miss Barnett through and through. A few boys had shuffled their feet and sat up straight. Now nothing moved—except my left hand, which shot into the air, much to my surprise and theirs.

One by one, the boys of 3D raised their hands. *Thank you, Lord.*

"I am proud of you, 3D. Today we are staying back after school to plan how we are going to do better."

"Miss, I have basketball practice."

"Miss, I have to go to cadet meeting."

"Miss, I have to catch my bus to pick up my little brother."

"We are staying behind to plan how we can do better. Anybody with something better to do will have to come up here and give me the details." My voice was even, and I didn't blink. Nobody came to the desk. I gave each of them a square of blank paper to write whatever they wanted to share when I called them up one by one. We went over their first month's marks.

Each one had to tell me what kind of mark he wanted to get in the coming month. My response to every boy was, "Now tell me what you have to do and what I have to do so you will get that mark."

All These Books We Must Read, Miss?

Not all my students bought in to what I was trying to do. From third to sixth form, every class had conscientious objectors, "bright" boys and agitators who challenged my decisions about how we would spend class times.

"This poem coming in the exam, Miss?"

"My friend in 5B is not reading all these things you give us to read, you know, Miss."

"Why we not sticking to the same syllabus and all of us doing the same GCE?"

The tension sometimes mounted as their insistence that we should "stick to the syllabus" clashed with my efforts to broaden their horizons and make my time with them meaningful and productive.

Many boys did well in English classes because they understood—or had it drilled into their heads—that they must master speaking and writing standard English to get ahead in school and everywhere else. The fifth-formers were supposed to be sharpening skills they had already learned in fourth form, and our emphasis was on practising the skills that would be tested in the exam. But to achieve that end, we constantly had to review the building blocks: expanding vocabulary, constructing sentences, developing paragraphs, and creating different types of content.

Some boys tolerated rules about subject-verb agreement, clause analysis, verb tense, and vocabulary building because they saw the tangible effects on their writing when they applied those principles. The chatterboxes loved vocabulary exercises because new words enhanced their ability to argue and show off. Some struggled through the day, their minds on the cricket, football, basketball, cadet corps, choir, or whatever fun activity or practice session would bring them to life at the end of the day. And there were boys who didn't seem willing or able to come alive to anything, no matter what time of day or what day of the week.

I still followed the examples of my own literature teachers and spent class time reading and analysing selections from set texts. To increase our pace and encourage them to discover reading for themselves, I assigned the boys to read three to five chapters for homework. I gave them guidelines for identifying important aspects of each chapter, such as plot development, themes, character portrayal, and other literary techniques. But that was where the trouble always started! Regardless of which class or grade I entered with the expectation that they had done the reading, similar scenes always erupted.

"Okay, boys, time for our discussion. Take out your books and the notes I asked you to make about the homework chapters." Invariably, my words set off a whispering that soon grew into a rumble as I walked around the room, waiting for them to take out their books and their notes.

"Oy, you read the chapter dem, Star?"

"Read which chapter? The physics homework nearly kill me!"

"Listen, man, is this morning on the bus I manage to read one chapter."

I protested in the most authoritarian voice I could muster, "Well, if you don't read at home, we'll never get through these books in time for the end-of-term exam. In fact, since you won't read for homework, we'll just have to read in class."

"But Miss, I read the chapters, Miss, so what I must spend the whole class doing?"

"Me too, Miss. I read my chapters too. Can I do my chemistry homework, Miss?"

I nearly lost my nerve with the barrage of questions and protests. *Lord, help me. If I don't find a good response right now, this class will be a disaster.*

"Stop! Whoever did the reading, move and sit together in the front row, and we will discuss the chapters. The rest of you move to the back, sit down quietly, read, and write down the notes about what you read. When you catch up, you can join the class discussion."

At first it seemed like a perfect solution. Everybody had something to do. We progressed as quickly as a turtle hurrying across wet sand. I could hardly keep track of how much we were really covering. Leaving the "readers" to talk about short sections, I patrolled up and down the rows of desks like a policeman, grabbing comic books hidden in their laps and removing math exercise books hidden among the pages where they should have been writing notes. After this happened in two more classes, it was obvious to the entire room that we were not getting anywhere.

In our staffroom discussions, no one else complained that boys were neglecting the reading, so I kept my mouth shut—until I walked in on them comparing their progress with the texts. From sheer panic, I blurted out my problem. "I can't get them to read the chapters at home, especially 5C and 3D. I have to spend the whole class on reading instead of analysing. We are way behind," I wailed.

"You just remind them that they have to do the same end-of-term exam as everybody else, and it's your job to make sure they keep up," Mrs Riley said in her dry, no-nonsense tone.

Wait, so what you think I've been trying to do the whole time?

Someone else muttered, "Let them stay back for detention to do the homework. That will soon put a stop to the laziness."

Out of the blue, the Spanish teacher spoke, her sing-song Trinidadian accent reminding me of my days on the UWI campus where we mingled with students from all over the Caribbean. "Quiz them once a week on the chapters they should read. Let them know you will average the quiz marks with all the other marks, and it will affect their final grade. Then, I bet they will read."

All this and more I tried for the next three weeks. I faced the same racket in the classrooms whenever the time came to find out who had read the chapters and, inevitably, to divide the readers from the non-readers and assign them work. So-called "quiet reading" was slow and painful. Detaining non-readers after school was punishment for me as much as it was for them. The number of students who did their reading homework declined. I racked my brain to recall how teachers at Alpha had handled these situations—until it hit me like a rock. *They hadn't! We were girls; we always did more than the reading set for homework!*

That wasn't the only thing that hit me. Two Sundays later, my brother-in-law picked me up to visit my sister, who'd just returned from hospital with my new niece. All along the streets and open lots we passed, I could see groups of men and young boys, just like those at school. Some played basketball on makeshift courts.

Some kicked a football in and out of anything that could pass for goal posts. Others played cricket with makeshift wickets. A few looked like they were just running up and down, not playing any game I could identify.

I turned abruptly to my brother-in-law, who was immersed in his driving and his music. "Hey! How your teachers at school got you to read the literature books?"

"I don't remember reading much. The teacher was from England. Him use to march up and down in the front of the room and act out all the Shakespeare parts with hand movement and sound effects and everything. Same thing with poetry. We had to memorise and recite a whole heap too."

I could just hear the uproar if I got up before my class and acted out a whole *Julius Caesar* scene like some man from England. "But what about the novels?"

"I don't remember reading any novel. I don't think I ever read one. I only read cowboy books."

Monday morning and another dreaded literature class. I watched the boys moving once again into their two predictable groups. The faces in the front group were as resigned to the uselessness of the routine as those in the back of the room. Their shoulders drooped equally, and it was obvious that nobody cared—except me. The disenchantment on their faces mirrored what I felt. This was too much like penance for it to be right. *Isn't this punishing boys who did their homework by giving them extra work to do, while rewarding those who wouldn't read on their time by letting them do it on mine? And what about forcing them to read in detention? Don't I have to stay back with them?* I was wedged in a trap that the boys had set, knowingly or accidentally. We were stuck, and whatever I did seemed likely to make them associate reading with punishment.

As soon as the last bell for the day rang, I was downstairs at Peter Maxwell's table, pouring out my troubles. His voice was calm and steadying. "Boys are not like girls, Miss Frances. Most of them don't like to keep quiet and read. They like to move up and down and do plenty different things. They can't help trying to play and joke around with one another if we don't keep them occupied."

I left him more convinced that I needed to make a fresh start in all my literature classes. But all wasn't lost; in my grammar and writing classes, I was already using some of the methods he had suggested. *Why haven't I thought of using them in literature? How didn't I see the answer before?* I was modelling my own literature teachers. I had completely overlooked the fact that my students were not teenage girls who had mostly grown up on reading!

Armed with the images of boys romping in open fields, my brother-in-law's memories of learning Shakespeare, and Peter's male perspective, I spent the rest of the week and the whole weekend revamping my plans. I scanned through the hefty collection of comics I'd grabbed from boys. These were nothing like the comics called "penny dreadfuls" when I was growing up. The reading material they obviously found much more intriguing than *Animal Farm* or *Great*

Expectations was *Conan the Barbarian, The Avengers, Flash Gordon,* and, of course, Superman and Batman comics.

With this evidence and minimal knowledge of learning theory under my belt, I decided I needed to do four important things. Instead of trying to get them to read three to five chapters, we would focus on action scenes and turning points that kept the stories moving. I would get around the size of the class by dividing them into groups, but definitely not based on who did or didn't do reading homework. I would alternate short bursts of reading with students giving summaries and reports to the class, groups acting out scenes (as we had always done at Alpha), and boys presenting their small pockets of analysis to the class.

Each step of the way, the boys could earn points, but not before groups did their own critiques of each other. Sometimes severe competitiveness made their critiques unfair, ill-informed, and motivated by revenge against other groups for harsh criticisms. I worked on finding better ways to channel what seemed to be much higher levels of competitiveness than I had observed among my classmates at Alpha.

At first, the boys didn't seem to care so much about whether the new methods were working. What seemed to impress them was that I was trying something different because it had become clear the early approaches just didn't work. Gradually, most of them threw their support behind what I was trying to do. Later, as their involvement increased, I could see they were getting the message. The classes were becoming theirs, and they seemed to realise that they could help to determine whether classes were boring and punishing or would help us progress with the subject and get closer to the reading targets that had been such a chore. I was getting the message too: *I can't just do what my own teachers did—not even Miss Barnett!*

I found myself at the library, signing out books about teaching and learning. Many emphasised theories and practices that reinforced approaches I had stumbled upon in my own search for ways to be effective. The biggest lesson I had to swallow was that I must respond to the "real students sitting before me". Their eyes weren't always on the rules or the syllabus or the end-of-term exams. Sometimes, all their attention was focused on getting their own way, avoiding what they hated. *This teaching business is a war of wits and of wills. If I'm going to win, or even survive, I have to come up with my own tactics!*

I began to pay more attention to what the boys said and didn't say; to those who seemed engaged and those who sat with their bodies tucked far back in their chairs, their eyes fixed on things no one else could see, their fingers twiddling with invisible objects or their arms folded across their chests. I left the refuge behind the teacher's table and patrolled the spaces between their desks, hoping to catch a glimpse of their distractions, of the schoolbags under the desks, of the state of their uniforms and shoes. I was looking for hints of where their minds and their souls were hiding, for I knew how well I had hidden my own from my teachers.

My long hours reading behind my grandfather's piano and the impact of my grandmother's animated storytelling on the green-and-white veranda chairs in Galina began to influence what I did in the classroom. I found I could go beyond the textual notes, beyond all I had learned in my university classes, beyond the enlightening English department meetings in which the team delved into the intricacies of the authors, surfacing with nuggets to share with our boys. I was learning to be a storyteller, using my experiences and my words to wake up my students to the world of literature. But I needed much more.

A Whisper in the Clamour

Was there a single boy under age 16 who didn't detest poetry? And yet their textbook *Choice of Poets* was full of it. It was in poetry classes that they came up with the most creative subterfuges to hijack us from the lesson plan. Whenever someone figured out the meaning of a line written by Wordsworth, Keats, or Shelley, the entire class groaned, and the inevitable question followed: "So why him never just say that ... Miss?" They wailed through "Ode to a Nightingale" and exploded with suggestions of what Keats was "smoking" when he wrote "Fled is that music:—Do I wake or sleep?"

As to scanning poems for metre and rhyme schemes, most boys thought this was a crazy waste of time. They had no stomach for iambic pentameter, blank verse, or rhyming couplets. With the end of my rope inches away, I went for broke and seized on "Jabberwocky",[6] the poem I'd found in a model lesson plan in one of the books I borrowed from the library. The teacher had used it to show her students how rhythm worked even with apparently meaningless words. I put a copy on the desk of each boy and waited. After one look, the boys went wild.

"What is this, Miss?" a serious science student said, shaking his head in disbelief. "No, Miss, this is a madman."

"Oy, listen to this!" the boy behind him shouted, rising to his feet and reading the lines in a mocking, overstated style:

> Beware the Jubjub bird, and shun
> The frumious Bandersnatch!

"Wait … what, Miss? 'Frumious', Miss? Any word go like that?"

"What language is that, Miss? Is Latin or Greek?"

"No, no, wait! Hear this! Hear this one!" a lanky basketballer shouted, standing on his chair and waving his paper dramatically. "Listen to this part," he said, dragging out every word:

> The Jabberwock with eyes of flame,
> Came whiffling through the tulgey
> wood.

---

[6] By Lewis Carroll, in *Through the Looking-Glass, and What Alice Found There* (London: MacMillan and Co., 1871).

The uproarious laughter took a while to subside, and I quickly tucked my point in. "I know, I know. It does sound like some other language. But didn't you hear how your classmate read it with spirit?"

Turning to the reader, I pleaded, "Come on, tell them how you knew which words to emphasise and how you guessed the right tone to use." I had planned to speak convincingly, but my words shivered in the air.

The beaming boy obliged. "I know some of the words, and some of them sound like you should say them a special way, Miss." His thumbs were under his arms and his fingers waved as he looked around the class and giggled, a response that the boys usually used when they were demanding and acknowledging praise.

"Yes! Like 'frumious Bandersnatch!'" his friend shouted. "You know that can't be anything nice."

"But what that prove, Miss? The whole thing is still rubbish!" It was the boy who had come in late to my first class, thinking he was acting like a man. He wore his usual smirk like a stamp on his face.

"It proves that sound and rhythm convey meaning even if the words are strange. It shows us that the poetic features we have been using, like metre and rhyme scheme, create different effects even when we don't know the full meaning of the words." I knew my explanation might wear thin, but I hoped at least one boy would get the point.

Luck was on my side. A usually quiet voice emerged from near the window and proceeded to explain calmly and concisely. "Is true. See, all the sections have the same four lines and some of them rhyme. Quatrain is what you said last week, right, Miss?" Noticing that the other boys were listening to him, he picked up speed and confidence. "And listen to this: 'Came whiffling through the tulgey wood/And burbled as it came!' Miss, that is onomatopoeia, right, Miss?" He captured the rhythm and the action perfectly.

His friend sitting next to him couldn't contain himself. "Pure foolishness. I bet you that won't be in the exam. I bet you only this class is reading something like this. What about the syllabus, Miss? When exam time come, how we going to pass if we spend our time on this?"

And so it went on from class to class: a battle to win over some, and a secret satisfaction with the growing number of those who were beginning to see some sense in what I was trying to do. Some boys accepted and even responded to my "outlandish" approaches. With others, the battle continued—boys who considered themselves "serious" students, intent on maintaining their high performance records, questioned a lot of what I took into the classroom.

But the number of believers grew whenever I decided to use music. Armed with my little tape recorder, we listened to different music styles and worked out rhyme schemes, rhythmic patterns, and the meanings of lyrics in songs by the Beatles, Simon and Garfunkel, and various Jamaican artists making headway with the transition from Jamaica's indigenous ska music to reggae. *Choice of Poets* became less and less like bitter medicine. With the help of students who were tuned in to music, others began to let go of their overt hostility to poetry.

The day we turned the pages to the war poems, "Dulce et Decorum Est" by Wilfred Owens and "The Soldier" by Rupert Brooke, 4A and 5C sat up straight. The words were about dying young men, just like the ones they saw on JBC News or stretched out on the streets where many of them lived.

No Jamaican poem appeared on the syllabus or in *Choice of Poets*, but when I saw the effect of bloody words of war and death on my students, I took our own Jamaican poet Mervyn Morris to the classroom. We read "The Day My Father Died", and every boy lowered his eyes in deep thought and then chimed in with his own insights. The poem described something they could relate to, and the poet was a living, breathing Jamaican who looked like someone who might live next door to anyone of us.

I no longer questioned my students' capacity to experience the power of words. Emboldened, I veered further outside the syllabus, broadening their exposure. After reading "If We Must Die, Let It Not Be Like Hogs", a poem by our own Claude McKay, every boy knew what a simile was and could write one of his own.

Writing essays was another story. After a steady diet in the lower forms of writing stories about "How I Spent My Summer" and "A Day at the Beach", fourth- and fifth-formers fidgeted and groaned when they had to write stories. They relished the controversial topics that we dissected in stormy debates before they settled down to write their own persuasive essays. Often, the arguments brought out their adolescent passion along with the best of our Jamaican language, which was usually tucked away carefully until they erupted on the playing field, along the corridors, and in the canteen.

"Yow! Is rubbish you chatting. You don't know nothing about police badness, after police not showing badness to people that look like you." The passion of the boy in the back row was evident in his expression as he shouted at one of the few light-skinned boys in the class. His opponent was a vocal lawyer-to-be who took his nickname in stride and laughed off other taunts about being "a half-white uptown boy with money". He knew the teasing was in good humour and meant no serious barrier between himself and his classmates.

On one of the days when the newspaper headlines screamed about violence in West Kingston and carried letters to the editor from concerned chamber-of-commerce types, church elders, and academics, most of the boys didn't want to write their follow-up essays. They wanted to extend the debate and "tackle what is going on in our country—Miss". It was a moment that tested my resolve to stick to the lesson plan.

I was about to shut the debate down and do just that, when I spotted animation on the face of a confirmed gazer through the window. He was shifting his gaze from its resting place on the windowsill, where he often took refuge from being called upon. A star footballer and captain of a junior team, his nickname was based on his agile movement on the field.

Learning the origins of the boys' nicknames had been an education in itself. Some (like Jacko, Smithie, Bello, Frankie, Fitzie, TC, Wilko, etc.) were just affectionate versions of real names or initials. Others were based on physical or personality characteristics: Smiley, Droopy, Cranks, Midnight, Half-Pint, Peas-Head, Shorty, Fat Man, and Bigga. Then there were those handed down through the years from father to son or brother to brother. In this tradition, Ugly's brother was Double Ugly, and all the McLean brothers were called McDirty.

The footballer got into a heated exchange with a classmate about whether uptown people had any right to judge the behaviour of poor people living in shanty towns all over Kingston. What he had to say amounted to twice the number of words he'd spoken all term and three times the significance of anything he'd ever written. It was enough for me.

"Okay," I said. "Let's make a deal. We will continue our debate if each of you will make your own contribution to the class by coming up and speaking for one minute about the topic. Then you will each write an essay for homework."

The class erupted, each boy shouting his own version of "Yes, Miss!" "Irie, Miss!" "That is how teacher must run class", "Keep quiet", "Mind she change her mind", and "Shut up". All the admonitions fell on deaf ears. The metal chairs assaulted the concrete floor and more voices rang out. I couldn't hear myself think as the noise surged. Panic rose in my throat. *What if Mrs Riley or Mr Forrest or Missa Johnno should walk past the room at this moment?*

The form head boy got up on the dais beside me, calling on everybody to settle down. It was the kind of uproar that would often cause a teacher to walk out of the class and wait in the staffroom. The head boy and other concerned students would hang around Hardie House with apologies and pleas to prevent the headmaster or his lieutenants from discovering the students had behaved badly enough to cause a teacher walk-out.

I was reaching for my bag and books when it occurred to me that walking out would be an admission of failure. *And what if they behave badly in one class after another? How many times can I walk out and still come back without looking stupid?* I stood in the middle of the room and contemplated my options while the noise continued.

Suddenly, by some unknown force, my hands flew up above my head and a stream of unexpected words came out of my mouth in the softest, most steadfast voice I'd heard myself use in a class. "Listen to me. We are not in Coronation Market. This is our classroom. We are supposed to be better than this. If those who know better don't behave better, what is the point of learning to write good essays?"

Rows and rows of stunned faces glared back at me.

In that instant, I learned the power of the whisper amid theclamour.

After a suitable period of quiet, in which I hoped they realised what had just happened, they flooded the room with stern admonitions and apologies.

"That is all well and good, but this is not my classroom. It belongs to all of us. So you all decide what kind of classroom it's going to be, what kind of environment you want to learn in. Sit quietly and think about that. And think about what kind of exchange is worthy of every person in this room."

This was a double period (two forty-minute sessions), which we often had for English. So even after all that, we still had time to carry on our self-styled debate, every boy pitching in with his one-minute speech, everyone impressed with the newly discovered passion and ability of his peers. For homework they wrote their argumentative essays, their knowledge and views of the topic enriched by the sharing. Almost every boy turned in the best written work he had ever done.

After that incident, I sought other ways to make students in my classes set some of the rules for our activities and take charge of different aspects of our classroom interaction. I had come to believe that my effectiveness depended on creating a sense of shared responsibility for whatever happened in each class. It was not that I had been exposed to any formal theories about the value of a democratic classroom. It wasn't even anything I'd heard or read about classroom management. My response was born of an instinctive understanding of myself and my own limitations.

I couldn't stand the noise or the pressure as the smarter boys tried to chip away at the image I was forcing myself to portray. On days when I left school dissatisfied with how my classes had gone, I was anxious and depressed—feelings that stayed with me long after I reached home. I didn't have the personality or the stature to act the role of the strict authoritarian disciplinarian. I had tried it a few times and I couldn't sustain it. The role took too much out of me and the battles wore me down. I had to find a different way.

Showing that their behaviour left me hurt and disappointed may not have been textbook strategy, but at least it was sincere, and I felt more like myself after doing so. *Why shouldn't I show them I'm a human being with feelings just like theirs?*

As my approaches to managing different groups seemed to improve slowly, we got through more of our work, and many boys began to feel a sense of progress. I stopped confining our reading to the books on the syllabus and our writing practice to the required, formulaic, exam-oriented essays in the book and on past exam papers. I knew those were the ultimate goals, but I began to believe that by enriching the process, the end results would take care of themselves. I took everything I could find into the classroom.

I didn't know then that there were theories about teaching English to speakers of other languages. What I did know was that most, if not all, Jamaicans were bilingual—at least we all spoke some version of Jamaican in our homes and informal settings, even though we wrote English and used versions of it in business and education. Naturally, the boys were not as willing or able to share their real thoughts in English class as they were when my back was turned. Then, there was no question that they were fluent, expressive, and creative.

Anyone could know this by listening to them on the corridors, on the field, or wherever no teacher was present and money football or box football reigned. Then they said exactly what they had in mind, found the right words without hesitation, shared moving stories, and engaged in intelligent debates. I had learned when doing high school Spanish that it was hard to think and develop ideas in a foreign language, which was why we wrote our essays in English and then translated them to submit to our Spanish teacher.

It occurred to me that I needed to give my boys the freedom to gather their thoughts and talk through ideas using the language we were all comfortable with. I figured that if they could do this without constantly worrying about English grammar, sentence structures, and pronunciation, they would realise that they did have something to write or say. It seemed obvious that this would make their work easier than trying to get them to think and discuss their ideas in perfect English sentences, which I knew didn't happen naturally for most of us. I decided that as a precursor to writing in English, I would encourage them to express their ideas in the Jamaican language with which they were naturally more comfortable and proficient.

By this time, most boys were usually willing to try anything, and they were soon on board with my two-stage process. They discovered they could write lines of poetry, they could generate ideas for their written exercises, and they could explain their observations about our literature texts. We all saw that with practice and guidance, they could use these ideas to develop paragraphs and then essays with structures and features that were closer to standard English. We were soon writing episodes for a weekly "serial" using Jamaican characters speaking Jamaican. With the content under their belt, most found it much easier to do their follow-up exercises by "translating" and applying formal rules and writing in standard English. For many, interest in writing increased and their word counts multiplied. English class was no longer a drudge—at least not every time.

"Big-Man" Debates

As challenging as fourth- and fifth-form teaching was, there was even more to come—twice a week when I entered the sixth-form room and stood before young men who towered over me and spoke with authority about the realities of life in parts of Kingston about which I knew very little.

Some boys entered lower sixth riding the hope that the still-awaited O-level results would earn them the right to stay for the two-year pre-university programme. But this was not always to be. Shortly after replacing their khaki uniform shirts with the white shirts of seniority, some had to withdraw when the results arrived from the Overseas Examinations Office, showing that they had fallen short of the number of subjects required. Those who remained were usually the cream of the academic crop, destined for university programmes that would prepare them to step into the professional worlds they chose.

Some boys at this level were already in charge of their households, following the departure of one or both parents to "make life in America". As the "big sons", they managed the meagre dollars sent home to keep the siblings going. They negotiated with landlords, prepared for hurricanes, and cleared barrels of food, clothing, and other supplies sent from the US—an activity that led the social workers to label thousands of Jamaican children as "barrel children". They maintained discipline at home, supervising wayward younger brothers drawn to the attractions of street life and gangs. They were men, and my job was to prepare them for exams in general paper and advanced-level literature.

Sixth-formers also comprised the school's student leadership team. From among them came prefects, leaders of extracurricular activities, and captains of sporting teams. They were also the official critics of administration, curricula, and above all, teachers. They represented the school in public forums, and one would eventually be chosen as head boy, not for one class of thirty or forty boys, but for the entire school—the ultimate position in the student hierarchy.

Sixth-formers were past the stage of learning in order to please teachers they "liked". They had enough experience to discern the differences between substance and shadow, between "nice" teachers and effective teachers, between teachers who entertained and those who helped them learn.

I knew all this because Mrs Riley said as much; but I also knew sixth-formers well because it was at this level that I had come into my own at Alpha. I too had languished in lower sixth, hoping my O-level results would allow me to continue. When that hurdle was crossed, and I had put my head down to become a student leader, I too had become a brash and harsh critic of everything.

In lower sixth at Alpha, we had been instrumental in getting the school to acknowledge our maturity by allowing us to stop wearing "baby-girl" tunics and the horrible felt berets, citing how inappropriate it was for an independent tropical country to be aping European headgear. We had stepped proudly onto the McCauley Hall stage to model our creative new design: adult pleated skirt, white shirt blouse, and gold tie, topped off with our Jamaican-made jippa-jappa straw hats trimmed with gold and blue ribbons. When other schools followed our lead into distinctive sixth-form uniforms, we knew for sure we had taken up our positions as social activists. My own sixth-form experience prepared me to be an unofficial advisor when the sixth-form boys planned strategies for tackling aspects of school life that concerned them.

At Alpha, my sixth-form classes had been some of the most controversial, exciting, and challenging times I experienced at school. Those were the classes led by the most articulate and experienced teachers, with the greatest depth of knowledge in their subjects. We waited five long years to sit at their feet, and when we got there, we found that their caustic tongues could be as sharp as their expertise. They opened our eyes and our minds to new ways of seeing the world. They shut down our immature whining with withering glances and the gems of the masters, hurled with dramatic relish at a chatterbox or someone who turned up without doing the homework.

"Out damned spot—Out I say!"

"Frances Phillips, don't you forget what Winston Churchill said: 'Attitude is a little thing that makes a big difference.' I suggest you watch yours."

We accepted the caustic tone and words of these women who seemed to exist on a different plane and to have, at their fingertips, knowledge of the world that ordinary people didn't have. Affecting the same superior air as our teachers, we used their words liberally on our opponents in inter-school debates, ending our propositions and rebuttals with the flourish that was expected to make us win even if we never became the lawyers, politicians, and judges some were practising to become.

Remembering the drama of those days, I tackled my preparation with zest before every class with my "big men", gathering reams of quotations, debating topics, reading lists, and essay topics. Our studies opened doors to both excitement and awe. Some of the set books were as intriguing as they were dense. Where was I supposed to start with explaining lines from Milton's *Paradise*

Lost? How was I to untangle the density of *Hamlet* and the intrigues of Lady Macbeth? Line by line, we grappled with the strange language and made our way to the familiar universal truths. With sixth-formers, I was rid of the challenges that sometimes arose among less mature, undisciplined students. I could turn my energy entirely to teaching and learning. It brought a new type of exhilaration.

Then there was general paper! This was the subject that the Cambridge University Examinations Syndicate prescribed to prepare students to think critically about topical issues and write mature papers about them. Both science and arts students were required to take this class and pass the exam to qualify for university by demonstrating the required versatility across topics from history to social sciences to natural sciences to the arts. This was the class in which I stood before students whose knowledge of economics, physics, chemistry, math, zoology and other subjects far surpassed my own.

My bookshelf began to burst at the seams, the space on the floor littered with *Time* and *Newsweek*, which I read and passed over to the library. Sixth-formers were assigned to read specified articles and lead class discussions about them. My research and preparation time multiplied. The boys were budding radicals, ready to tackle the world, and general paper classes opened the door to discussions of serious, controversial issues. The students probed my views and experiences on the university campus. They canvassed my opinions about local politics and other topical events.

Coming from the innards of Kingston, many of them found it impossible to leave outside our classes their growing disaffection about the state of affairs around us. If the class was exciting or the debate heated, it didn't matter when the bell signalled lunchtime or the end of the school day. They were always willing to stay behind to settle the issue or press me for details of my experiences, especially on campus.

"Miss, tell us the truth: they really preaching communism up there?"

"So, you stopped going to church when you went up there, Miss?"

"You were in any demonstrations up there, Miss?"

They got a brief recap of the most controversial episode in our lives on the Mona campus of UWI: the debates and eruptions that led to our march from the Mona campus in our blazing red undergraduate robes down through Liguanea, Cross Roads, and Slipe Road to Duke Street. It had been an infamous demonstration against a government ban imposed on our lecturer Walter Rodney.

"So, you got tear gas, Miss?"

The question brought back the memory of noxious fumes and the hijacking of our peaceful protest by lunatics, criminals, and the randomly disaffected.

"I did, and we were devastated at what emerged from our actions. We were doing what university students do—protesting injustice and standing up for what we believed in. But we were naive, and we weren't prepared for any of what happened. When the violence erupted and people were starting fires, we just had to run. The next day, everybody was cursing us, calling the university a 'hotbed of anti-government propaganda, communism and even racism'."

Their eyes never left my face.

Our discussions stoked the old passions that had lain dormant inside me, quieted by the realities of navigating the working world and paying my own way through life. But my worries in the lower grades about sticking to the syllabus never surfaced in the sixth-form classes. The types of essays students needed to write demanded that we explore everything, that I treat them as adults and open their eyes to even my own issues and concerns as a young citizen. Still, I was conscious that I had special responsibilities. It was not my job to tell them what to think. I must be cautious about influencing their views, especially about controversial matters to do with politics and religion. They were almost grown men; my responsibility was to help them find their own way.

It was a philosophy that would guide me through all my interactions with students. I was their teacher, not their parent or spiritual guide. I could lead them to information and elicit their unique interpretations of events in our country and even the world, but I was certain that I had no right to shape their beliefs. It was my job to teach them assigned subjects, to use the experience of literature to help them understand human behaviour and relationships, and even to clarify concepts of right and wrong. But I could not tell them what they should believe.

Anyway, I was in no position to be definitive about what anyone else should believe. At that point, I was on my own quest, and clarity was often elusive. Events in our country were forcing me to question my own values and convictions. I was careening on the roller coaster of young adulthood myself, grappling with questions that had no easy answers. Even if I found them, my answers could not be theirs.

Gathering Myself

I soon realised that teaching was affecting me in ways I hadn't even thought about. The work had begun to consume me. I had no choice but to spend evenings and nights marking papers and hammering out plans for the next day. As a teacher, you enter each classroom full of intentions and hope. For forty or eighty minutes at a time, you must manage a slew of rapid interactions. You must arrange lessons to ensure that high activity is followed by short periods in which the students do their quiet work. You must call them up one by one to the desk to go through the results of their efforts at sharing what's in their minds. Keeping a close eye on what thirty-five others are doing, you must help the one sitting with you to work out sentence and paragraph construction, to dislodge his mental blocks against the lines of a poem by Yeats, or to navigate the dynamics in a scene from *To Kill a Mockingbird*. You handle the unanticipated outbursts, the arguments, the distractions, the missing resources, the barriers to accomplishing the objectives of the lesson. You leave each classroom alternately drained and exhilarated, immediately questioning and rethinking what you have done, so you can begin to hammer out more and more strategies for next time.

The process kept me busy mentally and emotionally, leaving me with too little time to become wrapped up in my usual ruminations about issues in my personal life that I was nowhere near resolving. Often, I found myself sorely tempted by my natural inclination to retreat into silence, but the boys simply didn't allow it. If I didn't greet them with at least a semblance of enthusiasm, a couple of voices would break the tension with their uninhibited enquiries.

"What happen to you this morning, Miss?"

"Yow! Boy at the back, is you get Miss vex yesterday; see what you cause now?"

"Shut up yu mouth! You don't know nutten!"

What could I do but laugh? My laughter pleased them, and it pulled me from whatever darkness might have been settling over me, spreading light across the face I learned to wear into their space. They were forcing me to manage the silences and moodiness that my mother had long complained about.

At my previous job, I had been able to cater to my moods and nourish them by limiting contact with others, relishing the solitary nature of writing and editing news stories or promotional notes. I could wrap my troubles in a bag and keep them well hidden, free from questioning or interference.

In teaching, there was no opportunity for solitude or moodiness. But sometimes I worried that students seemed to want something else from me—something I had been warned against giving and my years at Alpha hadn't taught me how to give. Our teachers had always been closed books; they gave us what they knew and thought, and they returned to extract it when the time came for us to prove we had learned. But they hardly ever showed us who they truly were as women. They operated from behind an invisible curtain that blocked our view into what and who they became once they were out of our classrooms.

Since becoming a teacher, all the guidance I had received seemed to reinforce the idea that this was a necessity. The combined message from my experience and advice from others was that a teacher's success lay in one's ability to wear a coat of armour and keep one's real self firmly behind its confines, never being "too open" with students, never admitting one's ordinariness or letting them know who one truly was.

Yet, despite the fact that my students often tried to use off-topic questions and conversations to avoid tests, homework, or topics they disliked, I could see that sometimes their apparent ploys were actually signs of a genuine interest in learning more about my life and the person I was—not just about the teacher they saw in the classroom.

In the early days, I embraced the notion of closing the invisible curtain and hiding myself behind it. It was part of who I had always been. Lately, I had begun to face the temptation of responding to the boys and pulling that curtain back a little at a time. But I wasn't always sure how much I should share about myself. I wasn't even sure if the "Miss Phillips" in the classroom was really me. If she wasn't, I wasn't sure how I could narrow the gap between us. Until I sorted that out, I had no choice but to follow the advice of those who knew better and to make sure I kept my students at a safe distance.

The Christmas break gave me a chance to breathe and try to get in touch with all these contradictory thoughts and feelings that I didn't have time to think about during the twelve-week term that ended in what seemed more like six. In the first two or three days of the holidays, I walked aimlessly around my apartment, starting and quickly abandoning the numerous chores that had piled up while I marked exam papers. I was soon surrounded by clothes washed and waiting to be folded or ironed and put away. I left the dusting and cleaning halfway through. Books all over the place were waiting to be re-stacked on my home-made bookshelves. Half-filled garbage bags waited for other odds and ends to be thrown in. I couldn't finish anything I started; it was something beyond physical tiredness.

It was as if being away from school robbed me of the ability to see or think anything through. I didn't want to remember what being in the classroom was like. I didn't want to think about the fact that one-third of the year had gone and I hadn't had time to consider what would be next. I didn't want to think about options, which seemed to be few. Movies, shopping, and meeting friends held no interest for me. I just wanted to thaw out, to rediscover myself and find out what was really happening inside me as a result of the work I was doing.

The registered slip in the mailbox was a surprise—a package from my favourite uncle, who was making his own way as a parson and teacher in Halifax. He had scribbled the words *Reading Matter* on the space for details about the contents. The next morning as I stepped through the door at the Half-Way-Tree post office, tearing at the small package, a man called out, "You shouldn't open your presents until Christmas."

And who asked you? I thought, impatient with this type of casual interference that Jamaicans were so good at. Sometimes it was funny and endearing, but not that day.

I hurried outside, tearing more furiously at the package, ignoring the man's advice. I peeked at the covers of the two slim paperbacks: *To Sir with Love* and *Up the Down Staircase*. I peered through the bus window into the crowds gathering in the streets for another busy Christmas shopping day. *Of all the books to send me when I'm trying to forget about school! What was he thinking?*

Back home, I tucked both books on top of the pile growing on the floor, realising that my inability to focus on reading was now added to the growing list of things I couldn't do.

Before I could remedy whatever malady was upon me, the Christmas and New Year celebrations had gone by without leaving any impression. After valiant efforts to get me involved with the celebrations, my friends and family concluded I was in one of my stubborn bad moods and left me to my own devices.

I was nowhere near ready, but it was time to face my second term at Clovelly Park.

Downstairs Hardie House

From September to December, I'd headed from the original little staffroom and down the stairs on the way to my classes, stealing past the "men's table", where, among others, Peter Maxwell and Missa Johnno seemed to be always waging fierce debates. Although Missa Johnno was sports master then, he was also an "adjunct professor" in the English department. In our planning meetings, he and Peter could be counted on to bring novel, if unsubstantiated, perspectives to our discussions of *The Rime of the Ancient Mariner*, "Ode on a Grecian Urn", *Julius Caesar*, *Great Expectations*—everything the examiners from the Cambridge Syndicate in England bestowed on us as we sought to excite the mostly unwilling minds of our charges. The men brought equally radical perspectives to our department meetings, always urging us to adopt new approaches and methods. All of us shared what we knew, and together, we fudged out the most challenging lines from Keats, Shelley, and Shakespeare, determined to make the language of their time more accessible to our students.

In January, I migrated downstairs, eager to sit next to the single-minded intensity and creativity that Peter exuded as he harnessed multiple resources to enrich his classes—crossword puzzles, newspaper articles, "manly" stories like *Shane*, *The 39 Steps*, and *Twelve Angry Men*. These texts were prescribed for boys in third form to build the foundation they needed to move on to the more advanced books set by the Cambridge examiners for fifth-formers. I quickly got my hands on them, eager to bring myself up to date, to become more familiar with books that boys might find more intriguing. Peter was also using poems that people like us had written.

I also went downstairs to be near to the energy and excitement with which Peter tackled everything, whether he was setting off to his next class or bouncing back into the staffroom after successfully rousing his students from their pre-lunch stupor or their post-lunch slumber. I began to absorb some of his excitement without even being aware. Missa Johnno kept us afloat with his wit and humour while lending his exceptional understanding of the KC culture and mentality to my many questions and concerns.

Downstairs Hardie House was an enormous square, each of the walls broken by huge windows and doors that allowed the breeze to flow through easily, cooling the temperature and the tempers of teachers who sometimes stormed in from classes that had been confrontational or unpleasant. From my new position, I observed the other teachers from close range. They arranged themselves around long mahogany tables and intermittent leather couches or chairs, according to their disciplines, their allegiances, or just by accident. From time to time, an outburst from one or the other would start a debate about some problem that was brewing or had just occurred.

"I'm sick and tired of that wretched 5C. They are the worst set of fifth-formers I ever taught. I don't believe more than two or three of them care one iota about passing math!"

"As for those 4JT boys—they don't belong in high school at all. How can they learn chemistry when they can't even read and write properly?"

It was nothing like sitting in the serene, orderly atmosphere of the small room upstairs. It opened my eyes to the realities of the staffroom in a typical Jamaican high school. Their unfiltered conversations about a wide range of topics echoed across the room. I could observe the disgust on the faces of students who repeatedly came to the door, complaining to Missa Johnno.

"Sir, is ten minutes gone from the class now and the teacher don't come all now. Every day she come late, Sir, and we not keeping up with the work."

"Hey, Missa Johnno, our teacher is here today, Sir? Is two weeks now we don't see him come to class."

Invariably, Missa Johnno shooed them back to class, encouraging patience and tolerance. But in staff meetings, he and Peter Maxwell were strident in their criticism of teachers who drove into the school twenty minutes after their classes should have started, or remained in the staffroom drinking coffee or marking papers long after boys had come to remind them where they should have been.

The reasons were as varied as the characters involved. A couple were just terrible timekeepers and were late for everything. One or two had other jobs—selling insurance, tutoring private students, or travelling in from well-known rural areas, stopping at several districts to offload huge boxes of green bananas, oranges, or vegetables they sold from small landholdings to supplement the meagre income that was leading more and more men to walk away from teaching.

One teacher regularly fell asleep on the soft brown chair behind the far door, not budging until someone hurried past and tripped over his black loafers or until his own snoring woke him up. Tall, beautiful women who looked more like models than teachers often floated downstairs in billowing skirts, having lingered in the upstairs washroom to perfect their makeup.

The brilliant science specialist was never late for class. Her old vehicle chugged through the gates every morning at seven o'clock, even though school started at seven thirty. She sat sedately and primly in her corner, using her red ink pen to mark huge *X*s across pages upon pages of lab reports while complaining to any English teacher within hearing distance. "It's just impossible, I tell you. They can't even write a sentence. As for punctuation—it's a lost art. Look at this: This one can't even spell *titration*, much less *anhydrous*. What I want to know is how you folks manage in English class."

Not everyone was concerned about punctuation and grammar and spelling. Some teachers of math, history, and science argued that it wasn't their job to decipher the meaning of what students submitted, nor were they going to waste time correcting grammar. "If I can't read what they write, I just draw a line through it and give them a big fat zero."

I timidly joined Peter and Missa Johnno as they tried to counter such views, pointing out that if all of us consistently demanded correct use of English, the boys would take it more seriously. It was like talking to the wall.

In the far corner, one teacher took frequent naps, waking up every few minutes to reach for a fly or mosquito that threatened to perch too long on his shiny forehead. But when the bell rang and he knew he had to teach, he jumped to attention in an instant, grabbed his blackboard eraser and a slim collection of math problems, and strutted across the campus to his sixth-form gurus, stroking his beard every few steps of the way.

Across the passage from the armchair, our artistic colleague spread out reams of sheet music, covering his portion of the table and encroaching on a grade supervisor's miles of paperwork. He walked slowly round and round the table, hands, head, and feet mimicking the sounds he rehearsed silently for the next performance of the choir, of which he'd been a member since his own years as a schoolboy. Only an impatient summons from the door could bring him back. "Yow! Sir! Class time now, Sir. Later for choir practice. Exam time soon come."

And then there were the teachers who stood for discipline and made no bones about expressing disgust at those whom they saw as slackers. These higher-level old-timers, who were officially the senior teachers of chemistry, economics, advanced math, biology, zoology, and physics, seemed to be on another plane. They spent little time in Hardie House, taking only occasional breaks from their labs or the sixth-form block. Gradually, the proof came that these men really were on a different plane. One by one, they moved on to jobs as headmasters at other boys' schools, taking the leadership and administrative skills they had honed at KC.

Always, there were enough teachers in the staffroom to carry on at least one lively debate at a time, on topics ranging from the West Indies cricket team to rising crime and social disaffection to politics and world affairs. Drawing on their subject-matter expertise, gurus rose to the floor to berate the ignorance of others, laughing them to scorn, to collect on bets placed, or to rue the moment they had embarked on an ill-fated discussion.

Some days we erupted in jubilation about the school's exploits in one sport or another. Other days, we succumbed to the gloom hovering over Kingston and the increasing dangers of being located near downtown, where political turbulence threatened to spill over from neighbouring communities that had become known for political tribalism and frequent confrontations between adherents of the opposing parties. Teachers sang the praises of outstanding students and tore their hair out about those who would "never amount to anything". New directives from the Ministry of Education agitated us, and we railed against the growing bureaucracy that distracted us from teaching and solving real problems in the classroom.

Most of all, Hardie House, with its architectural style and old-world charm, was my laboratory. It was the place where I rejected bad examples and absorbed all I could to help me through the remaining days of what I was now sure was a world in which I should not linger.

Mr Forrest loomed across the campus. He picked up paper in the hallways and huddled with groups of young men, discussing matters of great weight—history, politics, music, French, art, literature. He taught senior students and gave extra lessons to weak students. He stood outside my class, watching and listening while I worried about what he might be thinking. He captured boys during lunchtime and force-fed them classical music until some were converted and others learned how to escape. He worked with the choirmaster during countless hours of rehearsals, chugging along to regular Sunday morning services, special performances at school functions, and annual carol services at churches and chapels.

And he tended his garden of roses.

Before I knew it, the academic year was nearing its end. I began to feel there was something important about what I was doing. This brought both satisfaction and fear of not being up to the task. Some boys were clearly progressing in their performance as well as their attitude to my classes. Mrs Riley, Mrs Beulah Reid, and others had given me the support I needed, including positive feedback about how I was doing. Every chance he got, Mr Forrest praised and encouraged me, whether he made up stories about hiding in the corridors and "spying" on my classes, or whispered, "I do have my own detectives, you know, Miss Phillips." His eyes sparkled as he spoke, and his smile found its place just off centre below his moustache.

Beyond that, it was hard to define what the "something" was. I had forced myself to read my cousin's Christmas gift books, and each had brought me many useful insights. I did identify with some of the challenges that first-year teachers Mark Thackeray in *To Sir with Love* and Sylvia Barrett in *Up the Down*

Staircase faced. But beyond the basic characteristics of typical classrooms filled with confused and confusing teenagers, their schools in London and New York were quite different from KC.

True, we suffered from similar resource limitations and an excess of bureaucratic processes. Decisions took forever to be made and longer to be implemented. Our classrooms were drab and badly furnished. But in Jamaica, there were no visible knives or guns at school, and even though they didn't always show it, most students valued education and showed basic regard for teachers—at any rate to our faces.

Some boys were what my mother and Alpha teachers often called "silently impertinent and insolent", but few ever progressed to overt or sustained hostility. They never openly jeered or disrespected teachers. Unlike the teacher in *Up the Down Staircase,* I certainly hadn't been confronted in any darkened classroom or staircase by a menacing student, his eyes roaming all over my body as he uttered terrifying words about his immediate intentions.

The social and racial factors that affected those schools in their foreign inner cities were part of life in Jamaica, and those factors affected how some schools and students were perceived by others. Still, by and large, they hardly intervened in relationships at school.

Although the fictional teachers faced all these challenges and more, the stories depicted them as making dramatic inroads very quickly in their journey to becoming effective teachers. By the end of their first year in teaching, both had changed their minds about leaving their schools. *So this is why my uncle sent me these books. He knows I intend to stick to my plan and leave the job at the end of the academic year.*

Nothing in the books made me rethink. I couldn't claim anything dramatic in my own first-year experience, and I could honestly say that none of what I read or felt had toppled my conviction that a year of teaching was all I could manage. When I reminded Mr Forrest of our agreement, he didn't ask me about my assessment of the year or the outcome of my "trying" to make it work. He didn't argue with my decision or challenge me when I said I'd found the job I always wanted. And this was exactly what I felt. The new job would involve writing, and I would be earning twice as much. So why was my excitement muted?

The Job I Always Wanted

After two weeks' break, I turned up for work in my new upstairs offices on Duke Street. Dwight and Hugh greeted me warmly, reinforcing the arguments they'd used at lunch a few weeks before to attract me to the advertising agency they had joined after leaving full-time jobs at the same television station where I'd worked briefly. As I waited for the receptionist to show me to my new boss's office, I saw immediately that the quiet, sanitised corporate surroundings were a far cry from Clovelly Park. Suited executives and their snazzy, well-dressed secretaries strutted in and out of the offices with an air of self-importance; they were nothing like me or my KC colleagues in the staffroom at Hardie House.

Members of the creative team glided in and out of their glitzy cubicles, shouting out potential product slogans, copy headlines, and jingles everyone apparently found hilarious or exciting. I smiled at the memory of the waiting area at KC, where Mr Forrest had failed to turn up for my interview a year before. I recalled the images of sixth-form boys stampeding above my head and then down the stairs, two or three steps at a time. I could still hear chairs scraping against concrete floors and boys shouting across the classrooms or laughing raucously as they escaped to the canteen for long-overdue lunches. Duke Street was a stone's throw from North Street, but the worlds could not have been more different. Duke Street was the site of corporate offices, banks, and spanking lawyers' suites.

As my new boss beckoned me into her office, I put behind me all the doubts that had assailed me during the last weeks of the academic year. My students had learned of my decision to leave the school and tackled me with unanswerable questions. *Why wouldn't I find all my answers here? Isn't this my dream job?*

"So you are here, Frances. That's good. We have a million deadlines, and you'll have to hit the ground running. Tell me all about you," my manager said, proceeding to fill me in on everything about herself as stridently as if I stood a hundred yards from her. She punctuated her sentences with bursts of laughter at nothing I could see. She jumped up from her chair to point to plaques, posters with advertising slogans she'd created, and certificates of membership in service clubs and private sector organisations. The adjoining wall sported numerous photographs of her smiling with clients, advertising colleagues, politicians, and sundry dignitaries at product launches and ribbon-cutting ceremonies. Only the window in the middle of her off-white surroundings offered refuge, with its view of the Caribbean Sea rippling calmly at a safe distance from her excitement.

Searching for a distraction, my eyes fell on her framed bachelor of arts in communication diploma from New York University perched on the wall behind her. She threw her head back and laughed loudly. "Oh Lord, I've done it again; I've done all the talking. You'll get used to it, my dear; it's just me. Come on. Let's go to the creative team meeting. I'm dying to introduce my brand-new copywriting assistant to everybody!"

I didn't get used to it, and I never felt like her "dear". She chatted incessantly when we were together, and my word count was never more than 15 per cent of hers. In meetings she was aloof and cool, as one would expect a posh Jamaican from upper St Andrew to be. She exuded an air of superiority, questioning almost every statement anyone made about anything. A flurry of client meetings and departmental meetings filled my first week, during which I met the art director, media manager, public relations manager, and clients whose products and services ranged from bottled soda through razor blades to printing.

I longed for the blessed intervals in my own office. I had no view of the sea, but just the thought of its nearness brought me peace as I struggled to distil the substance from all the streams of unending chatter that threatened to engulf me. It took me hours to write one headline, more to come up with an original slogan.

Within a few weeks, it struck me that stringing ideas together for advertising copy, marketing slogans, and news releases was an outrageous waste of writing. The words I put on paper rebuked me for abusing them, for turning phrases and sentences into the slaves of people who had no appreciation of their worth, demanding only "whatever is catchy, whatever people on the street will sing along with, something that will make them buy what we're selling".

The weariness I felt at the end of each day was nothing to do with physical exertion. And it was nothing like the tiredness I'd felt at the end of a day in the classrooms. It was mental exhaustion that overwhelmed me just because of the effort it took for me to feel interested in the cellophane and glitter of this world I had been longing for. But I didn't dare allow the yearning in the back of my mind to make its way to the forefront. *Who will ever take me seriously if I say I am not comfortable with my third job in three years?* I didn't dare own the sense of loss I felt after a few weeks away from what I'd found, but could not yet name, in the corridors and classrooms at Clovelly Park—not until a friend badgered me about being in a bad mood for weeks and wouldn't stop until I admitted what was going on.

"But what's wrong with me? It's a fancy place, and I have the tools to do the job. My pay cheque doubled!" I told her, trying to spice my words with enthusiasm.

"Well, now you can stop complaining about stretching your pay every month to cover the bills. And look, you have your little Vauxhall Viva; you couldn't afford that if you were still at KC! And I bet you the bottom of your brown paper grocery bag will never drop out again while you walking home and scatter your food all over Holborn Road."

If I thought it was hard to fit in at the office, I was in for even more discomfort as my manager announced I would have to attend all sorts of social events to launch new products, celebrate the milestones of the agency's established clients, and woo new ones. These activities usually took place in the evenings, requiring us to wear dressy clothes to work or to rush home and change before heading to one sophisticated venue or another. In any case, it was always too much mingling with a variety of people who hugged and kissed strangers and friends with equal zest. They seemed to love the glamour and the glitter, the endless babbling about nothing, punctuated with laughing into each other's faces, reflecting the emptiness in each other's eyes.

I was snatched from my musings at one such event when my manager shouted across the room, "Come on, Frances! Come and have a drink. Cecilia will show you everything. She's a media manager, and you'll have to work with her on that detergent campaign coming up."

"Yes, that's me for sure," Cecilia echoed. "So what's your drink?"

"Ahm … ah … I'll have a bitter lemon, thanks," I said.

"Bitter lemon, girl? That's not a drink; that's a chaser."

"It's okay. I haven't found any alcoholic drink that I like."

"Well, if you are going to stay in this business, you better find one that you like, because you going to need something to get you through these long evenings."

Cecilia was right; the evenings were long, and I could see why alcohol was a useful companion on such occasions. But the world of cocktail parties and media events was also a tempting one for a young woman like me. It could force me to learn to be more sociable, but in a way that was different from what the boys at school had seemed to expect. My friends said it was a better place for me. They said that while teaching, I had become too serious, always worrying about what was right or wrong for a teacher to be seen doing. Those who had been at university with me said this new job would help me get back to being the party girl I had been on campus—part of a crowd that could spend our entire day "lyming" in the soda fountain or hanging out at the students' union.

They were right. I had missed that part of myself sometimes while teaching. A prospective boyfriend had disappeared after I told him too many times that I was busy marking papers. But now that I was part of an environment that could bring him back and start a new round of socialising, I had no appetite for any of it.

It wasn't just the length of the evenings that turned me off; it was the emptiness of the conversations. It was the string of older corporate types, usually on their way to being tipsy or drunk, who constantly leered at us younger women, making suggestive comments just a short distance from their wives or established girlfriends. And then there were the unattached younger men who always seemed to be sizing us up, weighing their chances, and making overt advances when they could. Everyone seemed to assume I was looking for someone to connect with, but I knew from the beginning that these were not places to find anyone I could stand around me for more than five minutes.

The days stretched out, empty and long. I yearned for the excitement of searching the eyes in one of my classrooms and finding them lit up by the discovery of meaning in a line of poetry, an intriguing new word, the key to Hamlet's confusion. I'd kept in touch with my friends from KC, and they took great pains to remind me of what was going on. My 4A boys had done well in all their subjects and moved en bloc to become a 5A that was expected to get outstanding external exam results. My lower sixth students had become good leaders in upper sixth, and their new literature teacher was impressed with what we had covered.

I dug for more information and relished all I was hearing. A few boys from 3D were now in 4C and doing much better. The rest were still together in 4D—none had been kept back in 3D as we had threatened—and they were growing up. I wondered if the boy from 3D who could fill two chairs had lost any weight, if his father was still doing farm work. And what about the unfriendly latecomer in my first 4A class? How much more swagger did he have in fifth form?

I shoved the images from my mind, put my head down, and concentrated on giving my manager what she demanded. I convinced myself I had no choice but to stay in this world and make this job work. *Why don't I ever seem to have a choice?*

With this in the forefront of my mind, I became thankful for my manager. She was an excellent copywriter; she had no illusions about the relevance of elegant writing to the work we were required to do. Clients needed clever, not sophisticated use of words. She knew how to give clients what they wanted, and she knew what would appeal to the Jamaican buyer. I settled down and learned all I could from her. But even with three successful campaigns under my belt, I detested the world of advertising and public relations.

Every morning I walked through the foyer, down the corridor, and past the boardroom to the last office on the left, imagining the cost of the plush carpets, mahogany desks, and swivel chairs of executives; the lavish paintings on every wall; and the clothes and shoes all the ladies wore. Expensive potted plants shot up in every corner. Flowers in elegant vases adorned sideboards and corner tables. But there were no mud-spattered rose petals.

Back to the Classroom

When the new academic year started, I was back at North Street. This time it was no accident, no act of desperation foisted upon me by the need for quick money. I was going back to a place I felt would give me a reason to get up every morning, a reason to overcome my own weaknesses and find something within myself that could make a difference—for the boys who had opened my eyes to what was meaningful, and for me.

I went back with new expectations, but the landscape had changed. Mr Forrest had stepped down, and another up-and-coming Anglican priest—an old boy of the school—the Reverend Don Taylor had taken up his position as the new headmaster. Now Mr Forrest roamed the corridors and the grounds without the shackles of leadership, his energies directed towards teaching

French and math. Relieved of administration, he seemed to flourish: tending his rose garden, exposing captive boys to the joys of classical music, preparing others to perform in the French drama festival in which KC had an enviable reputation, and supporting successive choirmasters in the continuing exploits of the chapel choir.

Dotting the landscape at North Street, he huddled with groups of young boys enraptured by his storytelling, often inspiring them with tales of the exploits of former KC students who had excelled and were now occupying important positions in the country or overseas. He chastised those he found lurking in inappropriate places at inappropriate times. Every chance he got, he dropped his nuggets of wisdom and wry humour into the ears of teachers plodding back to Hardie House after losing faith in yet another group of distracted boys.

As often as I could, I paused in his company, remembering how he had induced me into his world with his multicoloured roses and the strains of Ravel; how he had planted the seed that I could be a teacher, albeit one with no conviction at the start; how he had allowed me to leave and facilitated my return, never exerting the slightest bit of pressure.

"So good you came back, Miss Phillips. This is where you should be. The boys need you."

"Thank you for recommending me. And Mr Forrest ... I'm really sorry—"

"Don't be sorry for doing what you needed to do." The twinkle crept back into his eyes, and the sideways smile found its usual place. "I knew you would be back, you know. I saw it in your eyes when you told me you were going. And you will be a better teacher, now you know what you want out of it."

"Yes, sir, and I hope I can stay for a good long time."

I watched the twinkle in his eyes, marvelling at the influence he'd had on me—at how effortlessly and without even being aware of it, this gentle man had taken me down a path that would change everything.

"I think you will, Miss Phillips; I think you will. Go on now. Go and excite them. Most of your old 4A boys are in lower sixth now. I bet they will be glad to see you."

The second time of orienting the boys to a new term's work was very different from the first. They were more mature now, and they, along with boys from other fifth forms, were embarking on A-level literature. They were taking the subject not because they had to, but because they had chosen it as one of the subjects considered most likely to get them into university to study law, arts, or social sciences.

"So why you come back, Miss?" Shorty asked. He was at least a foot taller than I remembered, but the name persisted. His voice was steady and his tone more serious than I recalled. A barrage of questions and answers followed, all going pretty much in the same direction—surprise that I'd left and that I was back, predictions about whether I would stay this time. I decided to come clean. These were no longer little boys; they would see through any attempt to fool them.

"I left because I wanted to see if I belonged better in a different kind of job," I explained. "I wasn't sure if I could be a teacher. I had to know for sure."

"So, you are sure now? This is sixth form, Miss— two years' work before A-levels. We need teachers who will stick with us and get us ready for university." This boy's voice came from the third row, just as it had so many times in 4A. His tone was a reprimand and a challenge, and his face told me he wasn't joking.

"I am sure." My own voice shook a little, not because I didn't believe what I said, but because I wondered how certain I could really be.

"So, this term, we are doing *Hamlet, Paradise Lost*, and *Pride and Prejudice*. It's a lot of reading, but more than that, you'll have to think deeply and analyse situations and people."

In the corridor between my 6B arts and the 6B science classroom, I found myself inches from my first 4A latecomer, now six feet tall.

"But wait. Miss Phillips? Is you that come back?" His voice sounded less like a boy trying to be a mature man, and his chin revealed traces of a potential goatee beard. But the smirk on his face was just the same as the first day I'd seen him in 4A. Like his peers, he had graduated from the khaki shirt to the white shirt that set sixth-formers apart from the other students. And his swagger was more pronounced now that his uniform marked him as a senior "college man". He was studying physics, math, and chemistry—and he was in my general paper class, where he alternated between vociferous outbursts against everything, and days of sullen silence and preoccupied eyes. As always and inexplicably, he seemed to eye me with suspicion, much as I had regarded some of my own teachers years before. Convinced he wanted to keep a barrier between us, I kept my distance too—until a Thursday a few weeks after I had returned.

"Good morning, Mr Forrest. Can I help you with something, sir?" I asked, happy to see my favourite person, but a little surprised by his hand on my shoulder just as I turned the corner to head upstairs to my general paper class.

"I need just a few minutes, Miss Phillips."

His face told me it was something he was finding difficult to talk about. So I stopped the basketballer on his way to my class and asked him to tell the boys I would be a little late joining them.

"What is it, sir?" I asked, turning my attention back to Mr Forrest.

"It's one of your students—" He quickly added details that identified the boy I had continued to treat with caution ever since he had acted like a man on my first day in 4A.

"What happened?" I asked. The answer would shed light on the boy who had been a mystery from the start.

Mr Forrest explained that he had been helping the student ever since he'd discovered that the boy had been sleeping at school for weeks. He had been on the verge of dropping out so he could increase his odd jobs around the community and support his ailing grandmother.

They lived in a derelict room in a tenement yard on Barry Street.

Mr Forrest had arranged for the student to meet him early every morning, when Mr Forrest would give the boy a small meal and get his help with roses. *There goes my assumption that he is not the type to help with roses. How poor has my judgement been about other things?* The boy's late arrival and absences had recently been increasing, accounting for a deterioration in his performance.

"Mr Forrest, I am so sorry. Is he okay? I would love to do something, but …"

"He told me he doesn't get along too well with you," Mr Forrest said without a trace of judgement.

I was awash with guilt. I had failed to see and to probe the reason for the boy's disposition, and he'd concluded that we didn't get along.

"No, it's not really that, Mr Forrest. The truth is it's my fault; I just assumed he didn't like me or my classes." *Idiot! This has nothing to do with you. You should have tried harder to reach out; you could have helped him.* "So what's his situation now, sir? What should I do?"

"He and his grandmother got shot in crossfire between some bad boys and the police. He is not badly hurt, but his grandmother didn't make it. We need to find somewhere for him to stay tomorrow when he leaves the hospital. He is going to need help with the burial, and the landlord wants him out now his grandmother is gone. I'm working with some old boys to help out."

No wonder the boys loved their headmaster!

"I am really sorry. But will he accept help from me, though, sir? The truth is … Well, I haven't ever tried to reach out to him, not once."

"It's okay; he won't know who contributed. I need something more important from you. He is really worried about his schoolwork. I need you to get all his teachers on board with setting him some work and marking it for him so we can keep him on track for his exams. I would appreciate it if you could organise that for us, and we will get it to and from him."

In that instant, I was sure that, although I'd failed him, this boy had walked into my class for a special reason that first day. It had taken me almost a year away at Duke Street and the last few weeks back at school to find out where I really belonged. Now, Mr Forrest and this surly unfriendly boy had made me certain.

He had lost his closest relative, but with the help of Mr Forrest and all of us whom the headmaster had rallied to give him support, he was back at school in a few weeks. His swagger was less certain. Every once in a while, the look in his eyes allowed for the possibility of trusting life to give him a break—but it was only a possibility.

Back in Hardie House, some of my colleagues became my friends. Our associations strengthened over patties and bun-and-cheese from the canteen, long debates about teaching, and payday Chinese dinners every now and then. Our days were filled with exciting undertakings that sped us through the year: pageants, plays, debating competitions, student council activities, and school magazines produced on deadline adrenaline.

Taking our cue from the new government's declaration of Labour Day as an occasion for community work instead of the traditional holiday activities, we organised students to clean up the school and its environs. In the summer, we continued the project by repainting and refurbishing the fourth-form block. We grappled with boys who could not be rescued from bad choices; we stood up to the challenge of wayward students, exceptional students and ordinary students who could be motivated to achieve extraordinary results.

I was on the brink of becoming a real teacher.

Every Rose Garden
Has Its Thorns

During my first stint at North Street, my determination to simply survive the year had acted as a kind of insulation against too much involvement. It kept me on the margin of what went on in the school, my eyes fixed on getting through my classes, leaving my students unscathed and myself untouched by the experience. Now that I was back, I no longer wanted to remain on the outskirts; biding my time for a year was no longer my overriding intention. This time, I would immerse myself in the school's activities. This meant consolidating the encounters that I believed I would find most exhilarating, but it also meant confronting those that would be disturbing. It meant taking the thorns that come with every rose garden.

The "thorns" I became aware of soon after returning were not all new, and neither were they entirely due to internal changes in the KC landscape. True, the transition from Mr Forrest to Reverend Taylor demanded adaptation as the new headmaster sought to create a new leadership culture. Inevitably, there were pockets of resistance to his efforts at change. Managing an enterprise that consisted of third through sixth forms at North Street and first and second forms at the Melbourne campus a few miles away was no easy proposition.

The student body had grown to an unwieldy size, with almost two thousand students occupying the two locations. These students included those at "the extension school", which had been introduced to provide an avenue for boys to attend evening classes. There, they could re-sit their exams to qualify for a high school diploma or increase the number of GCE subjects they'd obtained. The administrative and academic resources were stretched, and no one could deny that lack of discipline and underperformance among students were becoming serious problems.

At the same time, there were massive changes underway in the wider society. A new People's National Party government had won the February 1972 election, following one of the most divisive campaigns ever waged in the island. Mr Manley's victory over the Jamaica Labour Party (JLP) ushered in a period of renewed excitement generated by his catchy promise that "Betta muss' come" and by his threat to wield his "rod of correction" to remedy the litany of social ills he identified during his campaign. Half of the society was mesmerised and excited by Mr Manley's early declarations about social change and development.

Disappointed supporters of the opposition party, bolstered by strident opponents of the new government's vision for social change, declared that the new government should have followed the previous JLP government's growth path instead. To their consternation, Mr Manley promptly declared he would restructure the economy to achieve greater local participation in successful industries. The campaign divisions took hold, and arguments raged about the appropriate path forward. Waves of dissension soon erupted, based on the belief that the government's newly espoused democratic socialism was a thin cover for communist intentions. The opposition labour party stoked the uneasiness. Economic pressures from overseas and the withdrawal of support by the business sector had a negative impact on the new government's ability to deliver on its promises.

Dislocation, confrontation, and rampant indiscipline on the streets turned the school into a refuge for students, but school was also a microcosm of the social upheaval that became part of our everyday lives, especially in Kingston. Nobody could travel any distance in the city without noticing the hostile, destructive, and antisocial graffiti daubed across every available fence, wall, or neglected building. The school's offices were regularly robbed, and on more than one occasion altercations between police and citizens turned into chases through Clovelly Park, causing growing fears for our safety.

While school life seemed insulated from overt political disputes, gang warfare between politically divided communities seeped into relationships among students from various schools. Many became concerned about their own safety, leading to a proliferation of students arming themselves with the infamous ratchet knives. We became fearful onlookers whenever we saw the occasional fight break out, because we knew that at any moment, the "safe" traditional fistfight could turn into a violent altercation, and somebody might draw the menacing weapon of choice.

Tension and anxiety prowled along the corridors of Clovelly Park.

Inevitably, the breakdown of discipline in the wider society permeated our walls, and as teachers, we found ourselves distracted from the business of teaching and learning by the need to address inappropriate, even threatening behaviour. For the first time, I was afraid of what might happen if I intervened in a dispute between students or if I insisted on compliance. Staff-student conflicts multiplied as some of us redoubled our efforts to maintain order. Conflicts arose between teachers who struggled to maintain the right atmosphere and keep on teaching, no matter what, and others who threw their hands in the air and stormed back to the staffroom, leaving their charges unsupervised.

Reverend Taylor and the school board, which was strongly influenced by Anglican doctrine, became embroiled in a dispute over church policy, leading to his resignation after just two years. Despite the void in leadership that followed, we buckled down to the business of keeping the school on its path, many of us overwhelmed by the growing signs of a society in crisis and a school without adequate resources to provide a stabilising influence in the lives of nearly two thousand boys.

My friends and relatives who had been vociferous in their warnings against my decision to return to KC soon rediscovered their voices and stepped up their efforts to convince me it was time to leave. As news reports covered a series of disturbances in the area, I faced a barrage of questions and complaints from relatives and friends.

"I don't know how you can see what's going on and still go down to North Street every day to work."

"You don't watch the TV news at night? You don't see that KC is right in the heart of Mr Manley's constituency?"

"You don't think that when police raid down there or JLP people decide to storm the area, the school will be a target or a hiding place?"

"What if the police cordon off the area like they're doing every day in one place or the other? How will you get out?"

My ears rang. I could find no good answers, even in the silence of my heart. From overseas, relatives called my sister and me more and more often, always pointing to my mother's blood pressure going up every time she heard news from Jamaica. In our conversations with her, we could feel the anxiety behind her warnings. An eruption among crash programme workers and JLP activists on the avenue where my sister lived made the US news, and that only made my mother's pleas more urgent, her suggestions more explicit.

"Just get a visitor's visa and come away from that place, even for a few months," she wailed, her voice cracking over the distance.

It was a time that caused many of us to question where we stood on issues that were crucial to our sense of who we were as a nation and as individuals. My political leanings had been shaped largely by my family's inclinations and solidified by my involvements at the university, which many Jamaicans claimed had turned us into "half-baked communists who forgot that taxpayers paid" for our education. I was among thousands of young people who had become eligible to vote in the recent election, but we were never registered. So we were left off the voters' list, leaving us disaffected with the entire process.

The government sought to redress this situation by promising electoral reform and by actively courting the disenfranchised, appealing to us to become more involved in political affairs. Many of my UWI peers took up the challenge. But I had never been overtly political, and I considered that my role as a teacher dictated that I should keep my political opinions to myself. Nevertheless, I was not inclined to follow my mother's appeals and leave the island.

Added to the political divisions, debates about colour, class, and the right to be viewed as "a real Jamaican" began to creep into the national dialogue— if one could use such a term to describe the poisonous arguments that prevailed. Rhetoric about Mr Manley being a "born Jamaican" (versus the JLP's leader, Mr Seaga, who was not) spawned hostile debates about who had the right to lead, who should assume public roles, and even who could speak legitimately about social issues.

Controversy morphed into open disputes about class and colour, which had always simmered just below the surface, despite the interracial harmony that we were brought up to espouse. The politics of the seventies exploded that myth, freeing long-held hostilities and resentments that found expression in declarations like "I Man Born Ya" and "Sufferer Time Come".

The situation brought me face-to-face with questions I had not previously addressed in any serious way. Growing up "brown" in Jamaica, I hadn't always been conscious of realities of race and colour. My extended family was multicoloured. At Alpha, the staffroom and classrooms had been filled with all skin shades, but looking back, I had to face the fact that friendships and cliques had mirrored the status groupings and relationships in the wider society.

Daughters of white, upper-class parents mixed with "high-brown" girls as long as the latter met additional status requirements, such as the "right" home address, family history and economic background. Chinese-Jamaican girls tended to stick together, but they also moved among the first group more readily than they did among those with a skin shade between brown and black. Some of us were difficult to place, because despite our accidental light skin and "good hair", we lacked money and social connections. We stood in a kind of no man's land where better-off students were "above" our level, and those with darker skin, regardless of their own signs of status, eyed us with something like suspicion.

The signs were always evident at school events that brought family members together, or when we had to make donations to school projects or sell raffle books for fundraising ventures. My sisters and I could never donate enough or sell all the raffle books that our better-off classmates could get rid of, merely by having their parents distribute them to their well-placed colleagues and friends.

At the time, not a word was spoken about race, colour, or money. But after leaving school, I could look back with a mature and more discerning eye. Then, there was no denying that the signs had always been there.

On the large university campus, where students came from schools and locations across the island and the Caribbean, I had thrived on the circumstances that allowed me to choose alliances and friendships that matched my image of myself. Even though my light skin brought misunderstandings, teasing, jokes, and sometimes criticism about my choices, I was free to make friends as I liked.

Student activism and the influence of the fledgling Black Power movement solidified my awareness of the illogical and revolting nature of class and colour relationships in a Jamaica that was 98 per cent black and yet had its affairs dominated by white and high-brown political, financial, and social leaders. I delved into the evolution of my country through books written by our own people, and they toppled the entirely skewed version of our origins that some high school teachers and books had fed us. I cringed at the memory of what I was able to define as blatant signs of class and colour prejudice that characterised many of the people among whom I grew up. I vividly recalled the unsubtle attitudes and glaring signs that I had witnessed in my own family, at school, and in other Catholic circles, without having the awareness or the words to call them what they were.

Later, I saw it all through the new and critical eyes of early adulthood: how some members of the family had spoken about relatives with darker skin, how they had treated household helpers, "yard boys" cutting grass, and young black men seeking to court our close relatives. I replayed whisperings behind nervous hands about aunts, uncles, and friends who'd slipped away from Jamaica and were passing for white in America and England.

A strange kind of guilt and shame settled inside me when the mirror reflected my pale skin, which I had originally believed was no more than the accidental outcome of intermingling across generations of my family, with its numerous shades of brown and black. I now understood how much more it might have been—our passport to unasked-for privilege and special treatment unwarranted by anything we did. But light skin had worked both ways. When we were on the good side of the formidable women who seemed to lurk everywhere in Galina, we would be warmly greeted as those "nice brown children". But if we did or said the wrong thing, descriptions could change in an instant, transforming us into "the rude little dry-foot red pickney dem over Miss Gwen yard".

Prejudice had lurked at every level, each group looking down at the next, separated by shades that were often just barely distinguishable. As the time came to explore dating and settling with one boyfriend or the other, my sisters and I had faced a new reality: boys with our kind of skin and hair did not look in our direction. In terms of colour, they may not have needed the age-old "lightening" process by which many Jamaicans chose companions who had lighter skin shades that their own. Still, we could see that our male peers went after girls who came with other trappings—upper St Andrew addresses, "high-class" family names, or parents with the right professional status and financial wherewithal. Of these we had none, and it showed in the appearance of boys who sought us out for dates.

By the time I left university, it was painfully evident to me that the wounds of our "real" history had never healed. They'd festered just below the surface, smelling of a lingering self-loathing that manifested itself in rejection and belittlement of one another without recognition that we were all belittling ourselves. The overt social clashes of the mid-seventies were only a new expression of the same old disease. Now, it seemed the very character of the country was at stake. The battle among the contending forces unearthed layers of hate and resentment among many who feared the demise of traditional social relationships. There was no less hate and resentment among those who believed the political promise that the long-elusive redress was at hand.

It was easy to understand the genesis of it all and to argue that those who proclaimed their time had come were fully justified. Why shouldn't large sectors of the society see some of Mr Manley's initiatives as the rescue of many who had lived for too long on the margins? A new law declared all children legitimate regardless of the nature of the union between their parents; it sought to end discrimination against children born to unmarried parents (who comprised most Jamaicans). A slew of initiatives wrested control of national resources and put them in government hands. Introduction of a national minimum wage, along with moves to strengthen trade unions, protect the rights of workers, and promote worker participation, astonished many who thought they alone had the right to resources and power.

Detractors railed against these and other signs that the new government was intent on "destroying the social fabric" and putting opportunity in the hands of those who hadn't earned it. Special employment projects were quickly labelled "crash programme work", designed to benefit only political supporters. Introduction of the national housing trust tax began to make a difference by enabling Jamaicans who were not well off to acquire their own homes.

The national youth service, the literacy movement, the national students' council, Labour Day community projects, and other programs that mobilised communities, volunteers, workers, and students instilled fear in the hearts of thousands. The government introduced these and other programmes as evidence of its commitment to socialism, but detractors smelled communism everywhere.

How could anyone be objective about the messages that were being blasted across the widening gaps between factions? Despite being naturally laid back, I found myself bristling when people spoke about skin colour and questioned my ability to relate to the new wave of social and black consciousness that the rhetoric of Mr Manley and the "new nationalism" unleashed. When many white and light-skinned Jamaicans took up his offer of "five flights to Miami" in droves, onlookers hurled insults at those who didn't leave. Caught in the crossfire, I learned to attack those who questioned my commitment and treated me like a bogus Jamaican who had no right to speak or get involved.

I hurried to the other side of the street when no-good idlers jumped out of nowhere and called me awful names describing my skin. I timed the traffic lights so I could get by without stopping for the sickening insults spat out by uneducated street urchins when I didn't want my windshield cleaned or I didn't pay enough to have it done. Invariably, their attacks included derogatory comments on my skin colour.

"Watch dey! Look how she red ... but wait ... is a teacher. After she don' have no money!" one or two shouted, pointing at the exercise books and teaching paraphernalia strewn across the backseat of my dishevelled Fiat. *How dare you judge who I am or what I have?*

It was against this background that a pivotal incident with a student blew up in my face. He was a star footballer, and I was a senior teacher and supervisor of his grade. The Manning Cup football season was in progress, and he was in trouble for serious breaches, including missing several tests and classes and threatening another teacher that if she reported him to the football coach, "bad things will happen". I spoke to him several times, advising him to apologise to the teacher and serve his suspension quietly so he could resume his matches as quickly as possible. Faced with the possibility that he would be unable to represent the school in a crucial match, the coaches and several old boys intervened. The headmaster found himself caught between his staff and the old boys, who argued a compelling case for waiving the suspension and allowing their rising star to play.

The boy got it into his head somehow that the final decision was up to me because I was the grade supervisor. His desperation was discernible, and I did feel for him; it was his last year in school, and some said he was being eyed for a football scholarship overseas. At the same time, he clearly considered himself above the rules, and he felt that the backing of some powerful old boys also gave him power.

When he turned up at the staffroom door two days before the match, I thought he might be on the way back to his senses. "Why are you here?" I asked.

"Coach send me, Miss," he said, speaking from the side of his mouth and avoiding my eyes.

"I told you what you need to do. Have you spoken to your teacher?"

"Coach say I must talk to you." He looked past me as he spoke, and something like a smirk suggested he didn't intend to follow through on any advice I might offer him.

"Well, he sent you and you're here; what do you want to say?"

"Coach say you want to talk to me."

The coach and the boy were hoping to wear me down with all this back and forth. I was tempted to give in as I saw the game they were playing. The boy's face wore a blend of desperation and defiance. *I just want to go to my class. Why should I even be fighting this battle?* "Listen to me. I said everything I can. It's up to you to do what you need to do if you want us to look at the situation again. Sorry, I have to go to my class now."

I got up slowly, giving him as much time as possible to show even a hint that he would give in. He leaned against the wall, standing on one foot, the other one tucked up behind him. He said nothing as I gathered my books and bag. I approached the door as slowly as I could. Still, he said nothing. I stepped past him and moved along the corridor, feeling the anger in his eyes as the distance stretched out between us. I was never sure whether he thought about what was about to come out of his mouth or if he even intended me to hear. His words hit me like a stone flying from a massive slingshot. For the first time at school, my skin colour became an issue.

"You see you, Miss Phillips?" My name came out as an insult. "You see how you red?" You go on like you care, but you is just another one of them uptown people, always fighting against black youth-man—"

"Boy! Stop it at once! How dare you talk to a teacher like that! Get in here, now!" I turned just in time to catch the shock and fear etched on the boy's face in the moment when he contemplated whether to run past me or rush straight back into the apoplectic grade supervisor, who was one of the strictest teachers on staff. He must have been approaching the staffroom from the opposite direction and was just behind the boy when he exploded.

I was caught between my own anger and my unexpected compassion for the young man, now confronted with the rage of one of the most feared people on the campus. I was used to facing hostility when I insisted on compliance. I was used to resentment from boys whom I chastised or punished. I had been resentful myself when my own teachers chastised me, so I knew it came with the territory. But the desperate footballer had taken it to another level. This was the first time that a student had attacked me personally, and the fact that he brought colour into it was devastating.

Of course, it was all part of the bigger social upheaval that was making some of us feel despised and alienated. *How much worse must it be for the mass of Jamaicans who have been made to feel this way all their lives? For boys who have every reason to believe "people like me" are always fighting against "people like them"?* I reasoned that history favoured his interpretation and that I was just a symbol, albeit one with the label of "red skin".

It was true that I couldn't fully understand what it felt like to be in his shoes or in the shoes of the thousands of Jamaicans who had grown up in a world they assumed I couldn't relate to because my skin was a different shade from theirs. But all that analysis belonged to my left brain; on the right, the sting of his rage burned, fuelled by the cumulative anger I'd felt towards the boys at the traffic light, the urchins in the plazas, and the leering crash programme workers resting on the sidewalks all over Kingston.

Even after the matter was resolved and I received overwhelming support from staff and students alike,

I felt a deep and lingering hurt. I could feel myself pulling back, wanting to protect myself from the venom I had seen in my footballer's eyes and the bitterness I had heard in his words. I longed for the safety net that the detachment of my first year of teaching had provided—that year when I'd had no plans except to get through the period and move on to my glamour job in advertising. The simplicity of that world dangled itself before me again as I winced at my footballer's rage. *Why should I subject myself to this abuse, when I can find opportunities to work and live in another world entirely?*

It was too late. KC had fingered my heart; I could no longer be detached and uninvolved. I wanted to be there. I wanted to become steeped in the excitement and intrigue of watching the light come on in the eyes of every boy, to keep even one from ending up at the traffic lights. But I needed something to dull the memory of the footballer's harsh words, which charged me with something I did not associate with any part of who I believed I was.

Discovering the "Fortis" Phenomenon

The incident with my footballer was the worst, but it was only singular because in snapping, he had taken his rebuke too far. It touched on my growing fear about the society's mood. The volume and stridency of the outcry from the upper classes about Mr Manley "mashing up the country" and letting criminals and hooligans (i.e., poor black crash programme workers) loose on the streets had increased. Television broadcasts of political meetings revealed a new kind of hostility. Outside the supermarkets, scraggy little boys hovered, their faces wound into tight balls of bitterness as they hurled obscene racial slurs at "red people", who hit back with their own colour-based insults.

At school, we watched it all from a relatively safe harbour, and gradually, the pain from the footballer's incident dulled. But it had sparked my interest in how being a star athlete could influence a student's behaviour, and I'd begun to probe the issues. Most athletes who represented the school were known to be as disciplined in the classroom as they were in their chosen sports. Though many were not as successful in academics, they did their best and stayed out of trouble. Most sports coaches and old boys upheld the rules that required athletes to conform, just like all other students. But there were always those, like the enraged footballer, who lost their heads and overplayed their "star" role, paying scant attention to the rules of the school and neglecting their schoolwork. Boys like these always believed their coaches and old boy supporters would prevail on their behalf if they encountered problems with the administration.

This was partly to blame for the view widely held in the society that KC was nothing but a sports school. As an insider, I knew this to be false. Those comments showed no awareness that despite the many constraints, the school had always held its own academically. It also had an enviable record of performance in drama, music, debating, the cadet corps, the French Drama Festival, and other activities that took place without fanfare and away from the public's view.

My increasing involvement in some of these extracurricular activities opened my eyes to the existence of a unique quality with which KC boys appeared to be endowed. I became aware of it in dribs and drabs. I saw it when I helped Peter coach the debating team and when we worked with the boys producing the school magazine. I heard it in Missa Johnno's descriptions of athletes who outdid themselves in various sports. It was the same with the cadet corps as they prepared for their inspections, and with the choir—whether in Christmas recitals or a massive production of the musical *Oliver* that they performed to sold-out audiences in Kingston. These activities revealed that it was not just sports that could ignite the passion of KC boys. I became intrigued by this characteristic that I had never seen before.

Everybody I asked attributed the fierce school spirit to Bishop Gibson, and later Mr Forrest. They explained that both headmasters had given new students regular, inspirational lessons about the history of their school and the legends who had put its name on the map. Their constant reminders about the school's mission to uplift boys from deprived backgrounds inspired students with a unique tenacity and will to succeed.

Students spoke of receiving detailed lessons about the history of the school during their first weeks at Melbourne. Some could name teachers who used classes to talk about KC's origins and shared stories of legendary old boys to inspire them to work harder and turn out for sports. Outsiders associated the fierce school spirit of "old" men who had graduated ages ago with the early exploits of KC in longstanding sporting competitions. But some old boys lauded the achievements of academic legends as well.

On the inside, we saw it in everything. It was as if almost every boy who stepped through the school's gates inherited a terminal passion for his school, a passion that continued wherever graduates went in the world, manifesting itself in an unshakeable belief in KC that many detractors called arrogance. What became obvious to me, now that I was conscious of it, was that the boys always wanted to be involved and to do well. Their labours and their commitment were not always as extreme or as visible as those of the sportsmen, who trained way into the night and ran miles on Palisadoes Road before dawn on Sunday mornings in the weeks leading up to important competitions. But they were there nevertheless. Whatever activities we undertook, the boys were not satisfied with just participating; they always wanted to excel. If there were prizes to be won, they firmly believed they had a right to claim them.

I became so preoccupied with observing this dimension of my involvement with boys outside the classroom that I took every available opportunity to discover the source of their spirit. There was no question that during these activities that took place beyond the syllabus and the disciplinary codes, students and teachers enjoyed less formal interactions, showing sides of themselves not possible within the dynamics of the classroom. They fostered a different type of relationship that paid dividends when everyone returned to formal settings.

A new question plagued me: Would my footballer have reacted to me in that hostile way if he had known me better? He knew me in one role only—a dispenser of discipline who, he believed, had the power to destroy his stardom. And I knew him only as an offender. *What if he had known me as his teacher as well, and moreover, as someone involved in an activity that excited him and allowed him to see another side of me, and I of him?*

For KC boys, participating at the highest level, winning, or at least fighting to the end of every competition seemed to be part of their sense of who they were as people. For some reason that was passed on from one generation of students to the next, they believed that fighting hard and winning was an integral part of what it meant to be KC boys. Nowhere was this more evident to me than at the next staging of the annual Boys' Championships, when I became a witness to its highest expression. I was severely chastised after admitting it was my very first time attending the event. Teachers and KC old boys around me expressed disbelief. "What! First time at Champs? Girl, you missed half your life. Where were you all those years?"

As the Saturday afternoon sun blazed across the stadium and the competition among athletes got into high gear, I saw the reason for their consternation. It really was something not to be missed.

From our perch in the bleachers directly across from the finish line, I could feel the place throbbing with excitement. Students from numerous high schools occupied blocks of seats surrounded by their fans, creating a rainbow of pulsating purple-and-white bodies screaming for KC, green and black for Calabar High, blue and red for Camperdown High, blue and white for St George's, green and yellow for Excelsior High, and countless other colour combinations of other schools. By Saturday evening, the racket grew deafening as students and their supporters beat their drums and blew their whistles and horns, accompanied by raucous singing and chanting of vociferous cheering songs— then falling into sudden silence as their athletes fiddled with their starting blocks and everyone held his or her breath for the starter's gun.

The excitement and intensity were enthralling. For the first time, I experienced at close range the power of the exceptional devotion and pride that seemed to come with the purple-and-white tie and to live in the soul of students, old boys, and many who proclaimed themselves as such, even though they had never stepped through the gates. I feared for the hearts of young and old KC enthusiasts as races were won and lost. Some athletes exceeded expectations; others fell to the ground, writhing in the agony of strains, cramps, fractures, pulled muscles, and dashed hopes. Missa Johnno went through pack after golden pack of Benson & Hedges as coaches and sports masters huddled together, consulted their programmes, calculated points, and matched them up against their detailed plans and forecasts.

In the distance, the frantic gesticulations of Head Coach Foggy Burrowes punctuated the counting of points and the confident predictions of who would come out on top. KC legend had it that Foggy planned the participation of the KC team down to every point, charging each boy with the responsibility for bringing home the results "he owed the school". And every boy believed that he must do what was expected of him, no matter what—whether he owed one point for a low place in a final event, or maximum points for clutching his baton and carrying it safely to the finish line in a relay final.

At the end of my first experience of the championships, KC boys had outperformed their arch-rivals Camperdown, Jamaica College, and Calabar. Amid screams and whistles, they raised the trophy above the heads of their heroes as night fell on the national stadium. Chants of "Fortis, Fortis" rang in my ears as the crowd thinned and we made our way from the stadium. This chant was coined from the school's motto, "Fortis Cadere Cedere non Potest". It was the only line of Latin that most KC boys knew, and the tiniest one could translate the words: "The Brave May Fall but Never Yield"—even though his elders would warn him that only the Latin was to be described as the motto.

This was the school's twelfth consecutive victory, and I saw, at a much higher level, that quality I had been observing in my other school activities. It was the spirit that came soon after entering Clovelly Park, wearing purple, and being heir to something Bishop Gibson and Mr Forrest had instilled. Generations of old boys felt compelled to pass it on to younger ones. It was something which made them believe that, despite their circumstances, they could achieve exceptional results.

Despite mixed fortunes or the taunts of detractors, they could prevail.

It didn't matter whether individual athletes won or lost; they were all "Fortis" warriors. I saw in their eyes the moment when the joy of the school's victory displaced the agony of even the harshest individual loss. The sight took me beyond the charges I'd always heard about KC people being "too boasy and full of themselves" and the accusation that KC "think dem can't lose" and "think winning champs is everything". I began to understand the reasons for their sustained achievements, as well as the school's impact on thousands—from the smallest boy wearing his purple-and-white tie to the "oldest" of bald, greybeard old boys—and it left an indelible impression on me. *What if we could get students to channel this spirit into academic effort?*

On Monday morning, the athletes entered the chapel, pride etched across their faces. Small boys in the benches stretched their little bodies beyond their height, leaning out to touch their heroes. Some limped in wearily, dragging their heavily bandaged ankles, thighs, and knees, but they held their shoulders square and their heads high, for they too had battled for their school, whether winning or losing individual events. I knew that this scene was being replicated in several other schools which, despite having lost the ultimate prize, were celebrating their participation.

A glimmer of what I was looking for began to take shape in my mind. It was the seed of what was to become a deep conviction about the power of commitment and motivation and the value of building both through extracurricular activities, including sports and healthy competition. If these activities taught students discipline, commitment, determination, and the importance of putting the team ahead of themselves, were they not a valuable part of the educational process?

Yes, there were undercurrents and whispers in Hardie House about the coaches and some old boys who took over the lives of athletes in the months of training that led up to competitions. We all grumbled from time to time about boys being allowed to stay in school even after failing to meet academic targets, just to represent the school in various sports. Did being a star athlete make up for neglect of academic goals, inappropriate behaviour, or absence from school in times of competition?

Another question I asked myself was whether the boys who limped along the corridors after being injured, or who left school with few or no passes in their school-leaving exams had been misguided by sports enthusiasts, coaches, and old boys into believing that prowess in sports could compensate for failing at school. I wanted to find out this and a great deal more about the role of sports and competition in the lives of these boys.

I stepped up my interaction with students and old boys who were dedicated to maintaining the school's dominance across many sports. I badgered Missa Johnno who, as a father, English teacher, old boy, sports master, and the most significant liaison person between the school and the old boys' fraternity, had a unique in-depth perspective on the issues swirling in my head. The more I learned, the more my interest congealed into my bigger questions. *How can we promote a level of interest, commitment, and dedication to academics that will even approximate the interest, commitment, and dedication shown by the boys involved in sports? Can "Fortis" be a battle cry to bring out the best of our students academically?*

Nobody could deny that the contrast was stark. Students who excelled academically received quiet admiration, usually when end-of year results were announced, school-leaving exam results were published, scholarships were announced, and prizes were awarded at annual prize-giving ceremonies. But students who excelled in sports were permanent rock stars. Little boys followed them around the campus. Their names and pictures streamed across the newspaper. They had followings in girls' schools. Their parents strutted with pride. Their names fell from the lips of prominent old boys in important positions across society. Scouts came to Jamaica every year to look into the possibility of awarding athletic scholarships. Every year after being spotted at the Penn Relays in the USA, a few outstanding athletes packed their bags and their spikes, heading for colleges overseas.

The question nagged me for months: How could the pursuit of academic excellence compete? How could we get students to aspire to excel in schoolwork and see it as an opportunity for both hard work and fun? Could those who achieved exceptional results in academics become stars too? As teachers, we assumed it should be obvious to students that doing well in school was the primary purpose of being there. As teachers, we all preached this; we knew our job was to motivate students to do their work, while providing tools and opportunities for them to achieve their goals. But we often forgot that achieving academic excellence involved studying hard, doing homework, reading, slogging away at demanding essays, practicing math problems, and writing up tedious lab experiments.

These activities require the same commitment, discipline, and effort that excelling in sports demands—but there is a huge difference. Academic exercises tend to be solitary activities that take the student to an isolated place, away from the camaraderie and excitement of training with a sports team. Was it any wonder that in a boys' school with such strong traditions in sporting excellence, boys gravitated towards achieving in sports or became ardent admirers of those who excelled at it? It seemed to me that we were overlooking a huge barrier that stood against getting students as excited about their schoolwork as many were about sports, even just as spectators. How to assess the impact of that barrier and then to get around it presented bigger puzzles than I could solve, but maybe I could make a small difference. I began my search for the ways to do it.

Forward to Schools' Challenge Quiz!

At first, I could come up with nothing beyond diversifying my teaching methods and trying to transplant my own excitement about learning into the hearts of my own students. Knowing this would not be enough, I tackled this as the first phase of my mission, still searching for a more tangible method.

Then, out of nowhere, I saw a glimpse of an answer. Ironically, it came from JBC, the television station where my ill-fated career in television news had come to an abrupt end. A few years earlier, the station had launched the *Schools' Challenge Quiz* (SCQ), a television competition to showcase the knowledge, dedication, and sportsmanship of the island's high school students.

SCQ was no boys' championships, but it was where I would start my search for a way to create excitement about knowledge and learning. In the third year of the JBC competition, the York Castle High School team from St Ann made history by becoming the first rural school to take home the prize. The coach was one of my closest friends, and I didn't hesitate to test my theories on her. I was full of admiration for the experiences and lessons she shared about her involvement in coaching the team.

Beyond that, her answers to my numerous questions about the significance of the experience for the students increased my conviction that their participation had strengthened their interest in academics. It had also brought something unique into her teaching, her life, and the life of the school—something that went far beyond being able to hoist a trophy on TV and at school assembly.

The experience went to the heart of how the students saw themselves. It cemented ideas about their worth and proved they could be successful on a big academic stage. It proved that "big city" location and reputation weren't everything, that access to the resources of Kingston schools wasn't all. What really counted was the energy and excitement that their participation generated, their recognition of the relationship between hard work and success. They learned the extent to which self-esteem is intimately linked to one's own efforts and achievements.

Of course, when I shared my insights with my colleagues, the doubters said all this depended on "winning", and only one school out of thirty or more could win. "What about the impact of not winning?" they asked. But everything I'd heard and read about the impact of competition told me that many of the gains would come even if participants didn't win. I believed that just the process of preparing for the competition and participating in it would have a major positive impact.

This echoed the comments of KC boys who had participated in many similar enterprises and who, despite losing, confirmed the value of participating. Small groups of KC's sixth-formers had done well in the JBC competition every year since its inception.[7] In the first year, Missa Johnno had organised activities. Another teacher, Mr Simpson, accompanied the team to the studios. Geoffrey Madden, Cecil Taffe (deceased), and Brian Grant, captained by Clive Goodall, took to the JBC studios and demonstrated the usual KC determination and spirit. They'd reached the semi-finals, only to be pipped by sister school St Hugh's High, the only all-girls' school ever to win the competition.

Through their performance, the boys gave early notice that the quiz would be another competition on which KC boys would steadfastly set their sights. Head Boy Selbourne Goode and his prefects sought to build on the foundation by conducting a third-form quiz

---

[7] I am deeply grateful to the dozens of SCQ alumni who contributed details of quiz matches and their unique memories to my description of our years of participation in the programme.

as part of their outreach to the youngest students at North Street, and in their own effort to foster interest in academics.

A year later, Missa Johnno tackled the project again with significant help from Mr Simpson and other staff members. Our squad consisted of Selbourne Goode, Warren Blake, Clifton Smith, Paul Smith, and Geoffrey Madden (captain). In a great show of team spirit, Clifton gave up his position to Paul, who showed a little extra potential in some areas. In doing so, he embodied a principle that became established among aspirants to positions on KC quiz teams: the goal of selecting the school's best team superseded all others. The school achieved its best results, reaching the finals and losing to Wolmer's Boys. The captain pointed out, "We have the material and the spirit to win. What we must do is harness these two and point them in the right direction."

The third KC team consisted of Carlos Escoffery, Dale Walcott, Vernon Edwards, and Rainford Wilks (captain). We lost to St Jago by one point, leaving the way clear for the eventual winners, York Castle High School. Again, the team members shared the results of their experiences in the competition, warning their successors to "have many practice sessions together to ensure smooth teamwork" and to be "quick on the buzzer".

All this meant I wasn't starting from scratch. Our predecessors had created a strong foundation and fuelled the school's belief. They had sparked the ambitions of others. At the start of the 1973 academic year, I set out to build on the foundation they had laid. I was about to test my growing theories about the role of extracurricular activities in fostering interest in learning. My deliberations about the competition merged with the theories that were congealing in my head about the ways of channelling that special quality of KC boys into the academic arena. But I was also looking for something to broaden the kind of relationships that could exist between students and teachers. And I had not forgotten my painful experience with the star footballer. I was still looking for answers to some of my questions about the incident with him and other similar incidents that had made their mark.

Heeding the lessons shared by the previous years' teams, I assembled my first group of sixth-formers early to begin training for participation in the 1974 competition. The early start was critical because it made the point to everyone that the burden of building interest and participating in the competition would not be left to a small group of enthusiasts, like those who had set us on such a positive course in previous years.

I learned from Missa Johnno and the football coach George Thompson that they never started out with a football team; rather, they assembled a squad—a large number of interested boys who would train together for months before any competition, without knowing who would actually play when the first match came. This strategy ensured a constant supply of players who would be fit and ready for selection to the final team.

Since one of my many goals was to capture the imagination of students and plant seeds of commitment and excitement by holding up knowledge and academic excellence as something worth pursuing, I had to find a strategy that would attract a large squad of "quiz men". With the help of the sixth-formers who first showed interest in competing, we started with a series of quiz competitions to whip up interest and encourage students to show up for training.

I had moved from my one long room in the small Holborn Road apartment building to Mountain Terrace by then. Soon all my extra space was overrun with back copies of *The Daily Gleaner*, *Time*, and *Newsweek*. I dragged my faded copies of *The Students Companion* and *The New First Aid in English* from dusty old cardboard boxes. Numerous general knowledge books from the library found their way into my living room. I scoured the shelves of bookstores for everything I could find—from general knowledge books and games to the *Guinness Book of Records* and numerous collections of "cool facts" and trivia.

I read these from cover to cover, searching for facts and compiling questions and answers for practice sessions. But I also roamed through fifth- and sixth-form syllabi, past multiple-choice questions, and my teaching notes to make sure we would also cover material the boys had to know for their exams. Every afternoon after school, I trekked from Hardie House to the sixth-form block, where a growing number of boys turned up to train for SCQ. Students and teachers contributed information and questions, suggested strategies, and dropped in to peek at how things were going.

On any given afternoon, a fly on the wall could have become an expert on numerous subjects by eavesdropping on dozens of boys perched on chairs, backs of chairs, windowsills, and tables, observing keenly as different four-man teams auditioned— acquiring new knowledge, sharpening their answering skills, heckling each other, and just having a good time. The room overflowed with boys from my original 4A and 5C, science and math students from my general paper classes, and boys I had never taught. It was a motley crew, including the "big man from 4A" who regularly took a seat among the challengers. Since the loss of his grandmother, he had lost some of the sullenness in his eyes, settling well into his senior position in the school.

As potential team members established their claims, others challenged them, egged on by the growing audience. Some of them joined in by bringing in new material, trying their best to come up with questions that would stump the leading contenders and call attention to others who exhibited unexpected knowledge.

By December, the news had spread. Upstairs in the sixth form block in "Big Yard" or "Cassava Piece" was the place to be after school. KC had a brand-new source of excitement.

Down to the Wire

The format of the television programme dictated our approach to practice sessions. After sharing general discussions, observations and news of what competing schools were up to, formal practice sessions followed. Senior boys who saw themselves as potential quizmasters took turns with me at the head table, facing the two teams who sat across from each other, their desks lined up to simulate the JBC studio.

Throughout each practice session, we kept enthusiasts engaged in shooting impromptu questions at the teams, clarifying and adding new information and rotating in and out of the contesting line-ups. For the first seven to eight minutes, questions were posed to alternating teams, with a stated amount of time for answering. The objective was to accumulate as many points as possible for answering correctly.

In the ensuing "minutes section", teams had to answer as many questions as they could in the space of one minute, learning to save time by answering as quickly as possible (sometimes without waiting to hear the entire question), or by declaring "pass" and moving on. This continued until each team had completed three minutes. In the third and most heart-stopping section, students had to indicate by the rapid press of a buzzer that they wanted to answer a question posed. The risk of losing points was high, as was the reward of gaining two points for each correct answer.

Each afternoon, we simulated the entire quiz process, with the quickest team member to hit his desk winning the right to answer in the final section. In time, this created a racket and was difficult to police. One member said he had made a home-designed buzzer to practice on but confessed that with so many loose wires, nails, metal sheets, and batteries, it had twisted itself into an unholy mess and he had abandoned his efforts to bring it to school. Soon after, a crew of science students took on the task of working with their teachers to create our own buzzers.

We were now in the big league. Our practice sessions took on the drama and excitement of the real thing, complete with students playing the roles of timekeepers, scorers, fact checkers, and, of course, cheerleaders for the contenders of their choice. At intervals, we rested from the gruelling practice, telling stories, reading and reciting poetry, listening to music, discussing current affairs, and just enjoying a new kind of interaction that dismantled traditional barriers between the boys and their teacher-turned-coach.

At the same time, we could see team spirit and friendship mushrooming as students from different grades, subject areas, and social groupings got to know each other better and became united in the pursuit of a new, common goal. Though not quite like training sessions for sportsmen, our practice sessions took on the atmosphere of athletic training as the boys approached their tasks with both seriousness and amusement. We spiked our humour with images from the world of sports, joking about strengthening the brain to avoid "pulling a muscle". We dubbed exercising the thumb to press the buzzer "thumb push-ups". Boys heckled each other about having a brain injury when someone was guilty of successive wrong answers.

As the sun crossed the sky to late evening, we packed up the buzzer and the books; cleared away orange juice boxes and cellophane packages emptied of bun, biscuits, and peanut brittle; restored the room to order for the next day's classes; and tumbled down the stairs. Invariably, the last four or five boys tucked themselves wearily into my green Fiat, and we laboured through the gates, heading for South Camp Road, Tom Redcam Drive, and Cross Roads—brain-dead men-to-be trying to get home before sudden death from hunger or mental exhaustion. I dropped them off one by one to get their buses and then made my own way back to Mountain

Terrace. Though this was never spoken, everything was part of the bonding that reminded us we were involved in something important—an enterprise bigger than any one of us.

Two big challenges faced me. The first was how to create a balance between fuelling the desire to win and helping students appreciate the experience for its own sake. More importantly, how could I channel the excitement about preparing for the quiz into everyday schoolwork? They were the questions that became the hum in the background of all my quiz activities.

By the end of the year, with the real thing just around the corner, all that remained was for us to select the final five from the large number of boys who consistently displayed the enthusiasm, commitment, disposition, and diligence to represent the school. As a group, we mulled over the criteria for selection and reminded ourselves of the fortunes of our predecessors and the advice they had passed on. We knew the importance of having the most well-rounded team, and we debated what this should mean to our selection process. Having seen the unquestionable maturity, supportiveness, solidarity, and team spirit that the months of practice had fostered, I doubted that anything in my role as an adult or my position as a teacher made me more qualified than the entire squad to name our team. I was convinced that everyone understood what was at stake. What better way was there for me to show my confidence in them than to turn over the selection to those who had invested themselves in the process just as I had?

The gravity of the task was etched on their foreheads as they settled into a hush. I distributed small squares of paper for each boy to name his recommended team by secret ballot. Not surprisingly, most of us concurred in the selection of Michael Fitz-Henley (captain), Ian Jackson, Audley Jones, Orett Campbell, and Ivor Nugent (reserve) as our 1974 team. The first three were boys from the 4A group I'd taught during my first nervous year in the classroom. Now I was a far cry from the edgy, unprepared teacher who had circumscribed my relationships, ensuring that I would not become too involved. I was thoroughly invested, and everybody knew it.

Armed with the certainty that we had done the work, our gladiators stormed the JBC television studios from January to April, challenging all comers and setting new standards. In the process, we dispensed with highly touted competitors. In the first round, we defeated Hampton 60–29. Our second date was the emotionally demanding contest against York Castle High School from St Ann, the team that had inspired me to get involved.

My friend was still that team's coach, and we sought to soften the blow that would inevitably fall on one of us and our team by making a fun-day of the whole affair. Mountain Terrace was the venue for a day of friendly practice matches, punctuated with food (fish for the brain), lemonade, and orange juice, as well as bouts of heckling, banter, and horseplay, before heading for the match. This became the model for practice matches between many competing schools, maintaining the spirit of healthy rivalry that the competition was introduced to promote.

We made our way to the studio together. Once there, we temporarily assumed the game faces of serious contenders, knowing even then that what we had shared went far beyond those limits. KC led all the way to the third and final round. York Castle drew level at 33–33, aided by a few incorrect answers from KC. The teams were still level at the end of regulation time and had to go into extra time. "Fortis" persevered, and we came out victorious in the end. Phew! That one had been close.

We marched steadily and purposefully through the competition, securing victories against our North Street neighbours, St George's College (37–32), and Ardenne High School (50–24). In the final match, we faced Jamaica College, the previous year's beaten finalists and one of our legendary rivals in sporting competitions. No doubt JC had visions of taking the title this time around, but the KC contingent was full of confidence, and by this time we were regarded as the favourites.

The match was a tense affair, with KC leading by two points at the end of the second round. In the buzzer section, JC drew level with us at 20 points, but this was their only moment of glory. KC accelerated to an emphatic 40–20 victory. It was done: the KC team of 1974 would deliver the coveted JBC Schools' Challenge Trophy to Clovelly Park for the very first time.

The newspaper photograph of the prize-giving ceremony told many stories: There were not six but seven KC people in it. The three team members held their miniature trophies, and the captain held the big one. The coach still clutched her tightly rolled notes in one hand, the other barely touching the trophy. Vice Principal Carlton Bruce received the cheque from Dwight Whylie, a KC old boy and the former colleague who had ushered me into the world of advertising, one that he too had abandoned to become the general manager at JBC.

The leading character from another story crept out with me as I stepped from the studio, his small voice materialising out of the darkness just at my elbow. "You really build a good team, Miss Phillips; the college lucky to have you."

I looked to my side, but the face was not where I expected. The whisper had come from a head perched uncomfortably above broad shoulders that were now way above mine. This was a working man, and the afro he'd sported on the football field was gone, but his purple-and-white tie hung proudly around his neck. His voice was not the one I remembered.

"Is that you?" I asked.

"Yes, Miss. Congrats. The team murder JC, Miss."

The star footballer who had attacked my skin colour turned to walk away before I could answer. From a slight distance, he barely got the last words out. "And … sorry for what happen that time last year, Miss."

"Thanks" was all I could manage. Maybe it was all that was needed. Wasn't it only right that the boy who had helped in his own oblique way to put me on the road to the quiz experience had found his way right next to me in that moment?

Yet another purple-tinged KC face loomed in the victory celebration. It belonged to someone who had surfaced from a quiet stream of the KC river and had lately begun meandering into my life. Weeks before quiz training had approached its final phase, I had been seated at the long table facing the open door of Hardie House late one evening, diligently marking exam papers. I'd turned suddenly to face the door as two heavy footsteps landed on the wooden floor.

"Good evening, Miss. Any idea where I can find Wally Johnson?"

I noticed only the striped shirt, purple tie, and thick glasses framed in dappled brown.

"His car is right there under that tree, so I guess he's somewhere around."

"Okay, thanks. I'll take a look."

In a few minutes he was back, this time lingering without any obvious reason. "You don't mind if I hang around a bit, do you, Miss?"

"I'm sure he'll turn up soon. He's always here. You can sit if you like; we are definitely not short of chairs." *Imagine, I stayed back to finish marking my papers, and now this!*

"Thanks, I think I will. And you said you are Miss—"

"I didn't say." After a long silence, my words felt unnecessarily harsh, so I mumbled, "Miss Phillips."

"Pardon me?"

"I said it's Miss Phillips."

"Oh … Hi, Miss Phillips. I'm Dickie—Coke, not Cooke; Coke as in Pepsi. We have a meeting with Wally. Some of us old boys are helping out with Champs preparation." Then his "twenty questions" cascaded from his mouth, with only brief pauses for my one-word answers: What was I doing at KC? Why was I in Hardie House so late? A young lady like you teaching boys? How long? Where? What? Why?

Our involvement brewed slowly at first, but by the time my work with my quiz team had gone into high gear, he'd found enough traces of purple in my blood to become really curious, and the rest had taken care of itself. He had journeyed to the studios in time for every match, sweated profusely when the going got rough, and erupted just like one of the boys when the final score showed we had won. After every match, his rust-coloured Dodge Avenger had transported half the squad to Burgerman, where he regaled them with jokes and old-time KC stories like the one about a famous contest. "So, this is how it happen. A whole group of us was standing upstairs the fifth-form block, seeing who could spit the greatest distance—"

Their attention suddenly stolen from their hamburgers, two boys broke in, "What! You mean a real spitting contest, Sir?"

"Of course; how you mean, man? That was everyday business," he said, his face lighting up at their obvious engagement. "So, this day, after a whole heap of practice spitting, it was time—time for the final shot! Every Jack man was doing his perfect swirl to make sure he was gathering the biggest spit missile possible. I was ready. I position myself and hold my stance. No way I was goin' lose this time. The starter call out, 'One ... two ...' Everybody draw in breath and ready to let loose. 'Bruce a come!' ring out from behind us; it was the voice of the lookout who did jus' spot Missa Bruce himself, bounding 'round the corner. That was the end of that spitting contest—and nearly the end of us!"

It was the same thing after every one of the numerous stories and jokes that he peppered our conversations with. The boys forgot their exhaustion and roared. Mr Coke took up the bill for dozens of hamburgers and gallons of fruit punch, kept us in stitches, and then drove behind me as we transported the boys to their homes all over Kingston. He had made inroads into the lives of my quiz boys, and by the time the competition ended, he had cleared the path into mine.

With their final exams behind them and my school responsibilities complete, we headed for Trinidad to enjoy "the big prize" for winning the competition. From our base at Canada Hall, the male residence at the St Augustine campus of the UWI, we carried out our official duties as Jamaica's Quiz Champions at the university, the Jamaican High Commission, the Texaco Oil Refinery, and Radio Trinidad.

Then it was time for me to set the boys free to make "their best use" of the visit. They established contacts with select "ladies" at St Augustine's Girls School, explored the cinema at Tunapuna, and lounged at the beach at Maracas Bay. We sat glued to the television, and the boys defended their respective teams vociferously as Germany and the Netherlands battled in the World Cup football finals. Despite heated arguments over the football and endless heckling among the boys, anyone could see the strong bond that the quiz experience had built. They looked out for each other and saw to it that nothing with the slightest resemblance to Trinidad's dreadful iguana found its way anywhere near to me or my plate.

It was easy to see that, by way of organisation and preparation, KC had brought something new to the competition. The team members functioned as a disciplined and integrated unit, using eye contact, well-rehearsed hand signals, and techniques to quickly identify questions. Highly developed group responses helped them overcome weaknesses that had always been evident in the performance of students who operated as individuals and tripped up each other under the pressure of the studio. In our own practice sessions, blurting out the wrong answer before consultation had become a cardinal offence, and those guilty of doing it repeatedly found themselves in Coventry until their colleagues thought they had suffered long enough.

JBC's dramatic quizmaster, Dennis Hall, had acknowledged our unusual team approach, but detractors came up with less complimentary interpretations. When the boys tried to hurry him through the "minute section", which demanded speed as well as accuracy, they accused us of aggressive tactics to control the process. When the boys consulted each other in a split second before answering confidently in a unified roar, some accused them of setting out to intimidate their opponents.

On some occasions, Mr Hall would start to ask a question and the KC buzzer would shriek before he was through. He would always stop at once, rightly demanding the answer. To the amazement of everyone, the boys would whisper for a second, and then the entire team would produce the correct answer.

Sometimes, anxiety silenced all of us, and then one voice came out with the answer. A prime example of this occurred when Mr Hall announced, "This will be an audio question. Listen to the tape and identify the music." My heart almost broke through the wall of my chest when KC's buzzer sounded before I had picked up a few bars. There was no consultation. Jackson's answer was swift but sure: "Chi Chi Bud, O!" Somehow, he had made out the traditional Jamaican folk song from the version used by JBC as their station identification.

When our strategies worked, some, including those in the studio who saw it first-hand, acknowledged that our team worked like a well-oiled machine. Those more inclined to find negative explanations for everything came up with devil theories. But these were really signs of how the boys approached their responsibility to the team. Each one took special pride in mastering his own trove of unique subject matter that he kept hidden until it was needed. Jackson had plucked that answer from his secret stack of information about everything Jamaican, from folklore to history to popular music. He seemed to take special pleasure in annoying our hearts as he did by pressing the buzzer when the quizmaster intoned, "What fabric—" and coolly provided the correct answer, "Calico", which had been chosen as the fabric for that year's independence celebrations.

Fitz-Henley's treasures included details about classical music that delighted his music teacher, making up for the evenings when quiz practice kept him from guitar or piano lessons. If anyone had awakened Fitz-Henley from his deepest sleep and asked the name of the bandit from Greek mythology who had a special bed, he would have answered "Procrustes" in his clearest voice because this man, who had a bed that stretched the bodies of his captives to fit it, was Fitz-Henley's favourite person of all the mythological figures we met in our explorations.

From his bottomless bag of world affairs facts, Jones had plucked little-known answers to questions about outstanding figures in the history of the African continent and other black countries. He was our expert on revolutionary Jamaicans like Marcus Garvey and African leaders like Julius Nyerere of Tanzania. Campbell knew secrets about Greek and Norse mythology that we had not covered in practice, and he had been a member of Mr Maxwell's book club, so his bag of secrets yielded unexpected answers about Caribbean literature.

Of course, my blood pressure had skyrocketed during every match and by the end of the competition, I had a dozen new grey hairs to go along with my frayed nerves. I'd chewed my fingernails down to nothing in those moments when my boys pressed the buzzer before the question was out of the quizmaster's mouth. But neither the money for the school (a mere fraction of what the prize money later became) nor the defeat of our historical adversary JC nor the trip to Trinidad was what stayed with us long after the immediate euphoria of becoming champions. The ultimate prize was the certainty that we had put in the effort to achieve our shared goals. We had opened the door to our own version of student-teacher collaboration. It was a story of welding students together to put their efforts behind a collective goal that supported academic effort. We had set out to create a culture in which students aspired to learn more and admired one another for seeking and sharing knowledge.

For me, one of the prizes was that I had proven to myself that we could create extraordinary excitement around something that was based on the pursuit of knowledge. For our critics, we had presented proof that many KC students were interested in more than sports. I had seen the evidence that—win, lose, or draw—I was onto something that would infect my entire approach to teaching. I wouldn't have missed it for anything!

Back to the Mona Campus

I had made up my mind upon returning to KC that I would need to pursue formal studies to acquire the knowledge and techniques that trained teachers had at their fingertips. My interactions with the SCQ squad added a new and exciting dimension to my teaching experience and cemented my intention to spend the foreseeable future in teaching. The competition filled me with the desire to see that light of discovery come on in the eyes of more students—not only in the quiz room but in all the classes I taught. It also convinced me that I needed more tools to tackle the tasks ahead, more validation of my hunches about what else I could do to infect students with a commitment to learning.

Having accomplished my immediate goals with the quiz, I faced October 1974 as "back to school" time. There were two established paths to becoming a qualified teacher in the Jamaican education system. One was to pursue teacher training without first pursuing a university degree. Our teacher training colleges had played a massive role in national development by providing the avenue for this. Anyone could identify numerous senior educators and other public figures who had been moulded into intellectual maturity at Mico, St Joseph's, Shortwood, Church, and Moneague teachers' colleges. The graduates of these institutions, especially the long-established Mico, were known to be outstanding teachers, administrators, and achievers in other professional endeavours. I had experienced the impact of two of them right there in the small staffroom upstairs at Hardie House.

The other path was to pursue a first degree in one's chosen subject matter and then get training via postgraduate studies in education at the university. Since I already had a degree, the latter would be my route.

As I drove through the gates to "my" Mona, memories of days in Mary Seacole Hall and of roaming carefree all over the vast surroundings immediately overcame me. Going past the chapel and left along Ring Road, I smelled the fresh fragrance of my valley, nuzzled in the protective arms of the glorious Blue Mountains. New buildings had sprung up since my departure a few years before, but nothing could take away from the lush, comforting ambience of what had been my special and favourite place in the world. I rolled my four windows down and breathed in the aroma of damp, freshly cut grass, spreading out like a carpet broken intermittently by giant, superficial roots of ancient trees that had withstood parching drought and hostile hurricanes. Nondescript poui trees, slumbering in the nonchalant October morning, were still waiting for the time to burst into the splendid yellow-and-pink blooms that would announce the exam season in another few months.

I inched my way past the natural sciences block, the administrative block, the social sciences block, and the grey-and-red cut stone of the aqueduct. The Taylor Hall buildings, the library, Chancellor Hall, the road to Irvine Hall, and the old house of our former warden punctuated my path around Ring Road. Except for the fact that I was now behind the wheel of a tired old Fiat, I felt as if I had never left.

I turned in to the Mary Seacole Hall parking lot and eyed the parking situation quickly, remembering how few cars had been there during my years in residence. Now, finding parking spaces on campus had become an obstacle course. I almost gave up the search before I spotted a red Lada backing out of a space near to the porter's lodge.

Although I would not be living on campus, I had the right to park there because as a graduate student, I was attached to this hall of residence. In fact, there was a pile of university mail waiting for me in the same antique wooden mail sorter that had been affixed to the wall at the porter's lodge years before my time. Turning away with my stack of brown envelopes, I paused to take in the sights and sounds of the quadrangle that had been so central to my existence during my three years of being one of the Seacolites, as those of us who lived in Mary Seacole Hall on the Mona campus were known. The dining room doors were thrown open, just as they'd always been at that hour of the morning, releasing the aroma of a hundred fried eggs spread out across a huge, oily metal tray, their soggy yolks leaking across the borders into their frilly whites.

Young women poured out of the numerous exits, hustling to their classes. Others scooped up the last remnants of breakfast, or went to meet eager young men waiting to grab their hands and walk off into the excitement of undergraduate romance. I could almost hear the giggles of the scores of girls who had swarmed with me into the porter's lodge years before to check mailboxes for letters from home, or to collect long-awaited phone messages and hastily scribbled notes from male visitors who'd turned up at the wrong time.

I hurried across Ring Road to the school of education, my heart racing with anticipation of the experience that would clinch my decision to stay with teaching for the long haul. I made my way upstairs to the small seminar room where the coordinator of the diploma in education programme stood waiting to usher us into our adventure.

The formal studies were quickly underway— philosophy, sociology, psychology, history—along with educational assessment and methods of teaching language and literature. It was an intense and exciting experience that provided the theoretical framework for some of what I had been trying to do and all I should have been doing. At times, I was astounded that I had been allowed—and more to the point, had dared—to enter a classroom without being equipped with the information and experiences that the programme provided.

But I was also consoled by the evidence from my studies that some of my instincts had been right. I didn't have to be a slave to the syllabus or the end-of-year exams. It was more important to focus on the students before me than on the rules. I learned that noise was not always disruption, that chaos was often creative, and that integrating the Jamaican language in the classroom experience was not a mortal sin.

Though my studies brought stunning insights, especially about the potential of education to be subversive, some aspects also frustrated and annoyed me because they offered very little that was specific to the needs of my country. The models and the gurus and the textbooks were mostly imported from the US and the UK, perpetuating the outward-looking preoccupation of Jamaica's search for solutions. This disconnection and the inevitable tension between theory and practice dominated some of our discussions.

The lecturers were capable and highly qualified, but many of them had never set foot in the classrooms of Kingston, except in their roles as examiners supervising the teaching practice of their own students. Many of them had sat for first degrees at the university and progressed through their academic development to the

PhD level uninterrupted by work experience outside the academy. It was easy to spot those lecturers who had taken a pause and ventured out to get a taste of real teaching in real schools. They understood our concerns and related to our experiences in the 1970s classroom. They were able to draw on their own experiences in similar schools. They accepted our impatience with the tardiness of the Ministry of Education in moving education policy to address the realities that we faced.

Truthfully, I had little or no appetite for educational administration. My interest was not in policy making or the paper-pushing humdrum of office work associated with education. For me, the excitement of teaching lay in face-to-face encounters with students. But the study of administration did reinforce my intolerance of some of the leadership practices I had observed—way back in my days at Alpha and now at KC. Modern leadership theory supported my approach to managing my classes but came up short when I sought answers to some of the problems we faced at KC, where interference from wider social conditions demanded a balanced approach to discipline, punishment, and parental involvement in the challenging business of learning.

At every step during the journey, we challenged the theories and principles that seemed more fitting to foreign environments. We questioned the methods that denied the realities of our own class sizes, the difficulties some of our students had with reading, and the challenges of domestic arrangements that didn't support students' efforts to study. We searched for answers about dealing with the limitations of home environments that provided no assurance of uninterrupted electricity supply, books, or even physical safety. But discussions with colleagues from other schools gave me the assurance that the challenges we faced at KC were not unique to the school; we were all in the same boat.

It was inevitable that I would find it difficult to immerse myself in my studies and separate myself from the realities at North Street. In addition to the fact that I was constantly thinking about how I could apply my learning when I returned to school, almost every day I left campus to go back to KC and continue my work as the coach of the quiz team, now seeking to reinforce its historic win with a successful defence of our title.

Back at North Street, a new principal, Reverend John McNab, had taken up his position and was in the process of putting his own stamp on the school's operations. I was lucky to be away during yet another leadership transition. I stuck to my studies and slipped past the drama of change and rumour, darting straight to Big Yard to continue my work with the quiz programme.

Most of my classmates at UWI knew of KC's performance in the quiz and of my involvement in coaching the team. We had numerous debates about my theories. Some promised to "borrow" my ideas when they returned to their own schools, but others scoffed at the castle they thought I was building in the sky.

The chief objector to dreaming was a woman who looked twice my age and was nowhere near as optimistic as some of us were about making a difference through teaching. After what seemed like a hundred years in the classroom, she seemed incapable of a single hope for education. Insistent as a deaf woodpecker drilling down through a dead tree trunk, she pecked away ceaselessly at every effort we made to see more possibilities than barriers. She ended every argument among us with one version or another of the same cryptic doomsday mantra: "You can keep on wasting your time, my dear. You don't know what o'clock striking in this Jamaica. If you was married like me with four children of your own, you would know which side to butter your bread."

The woman had taught in several schools and never failed to remind me that my exposure was limited. I had been in only two schools for any extended period—Alpha and KC. As our statistics guru and educational measurement professor warned every day in his grim baritone voice, "The biggest mistake every one of you will make is to draw mighty conclusions from your miniscule experience."

His words rang in our ears until the final term arrived, and it was time for the dreaded teaching practice. We would not be supervised and examined in our own schools. We had to choose schools that were different in specified ways. Excelsior High School was mine. Its social profile and history were similar to those of KC, but there were a few significant differences. The most important—and terrifying—one was its co-ed status. I wasn't sure if my unexpected anxiety about teaching practice was caused by the presence of girls or because I would be observed by a professor whom I admired and wanted very badly to please.

Every one of the classes I taught under his supervision felt like a near disaster. I stayed up late at nights planning creative methods to get my students involved, but most of them fell short in the execution. Students who were usually compliant became agitated and distracted in the presence of the "man from the university". Teaching aids and processes I introduced to demonstrate that I had absorbed "modern" ideas about role playing, audiovisuals, and borrowed flip charts fell flat. I had my first bout of real hypertension, along with large doses of disappointment and humility.

As if from a distance, I heard the words of my supervisor giving me his final assessment. "Some things didn't work so well, Frances, but you always had yourself to fall back on. Remember, you will always have that. Maybe you shouldn't plan to try out everything you learn at the same time. There will be time." Not even his half smile, comforting tone, or lilting Trinidadian accent could assuage my distress and loss of confidence.

In time, it was in doing my final study that I found my stride. I knew from the beginning of the programme that I would use the opportunity of my field study to explore and seek evidence for my pet theory. I firmly believed that students' performance, especially in language and literature, was impeded by economic factors that created domestic and societal settings that produced immense disadvantages for many students. I argued in my study that low levels of parental education and interest, along with economic deprivation, affected students' ability to learn. Though decidedly small and tentative, my research produced indicators which seemed to confirm lower levels of performance among students deprived of nutrition, rest, books, educational supplies, and parental involvement. For me, the most significant outcome was that findings about students from two different schools affirmed my hunches about some of my students at KC.

At the end of the programme, I totted up the outcomes and found that I had spent the nine months productively. My biggest gain was in my new approach to lesson planning, an approach that emphasised precise, measurable objectives for each class and deliberately selected strategies to accomplish them. No longer would I focus on the classroom process without duly considering the ends to which it should lead. My instincts were refined by principles and strategies that would make my classes not just interesting or even enjoyable; they would help me set and achieve measurable learning targets. And if I neglected the syllabus in future, it would not be an arbitrary decision to do something that felt more important. It would be a deliberate choice for a specific purpose related to the desired end results.

There was one other gain, albeit unrelated to the diploma I obtained. I sat at the feet of the established Jamaican poet Mervyn Morris, who taught our extracurricular creative writing class and re-opened the door to my old hobby, charging us to "write even one line of poetry every day". I would have an answer when the time came for me to go back to school and face the relentless nagging of those boys who challenged me with "Miss, is time you write you own poems instead of just reading what other people write".

Spreading Our Wings

Back in the classroom, I was surprised at how much I felt the absence of the girls at Excelsior. I missed their softening influence on me and on their male classmates. By comparison, my KC boys now seemed rough at the edges. I set my sights on how I could gently introduce them to the idea of girls in their classrooms.

"So why you went back to UWI, Miss?"

"She did want a break from us and our noise."

"And Miss, how you mean to go and teach at Excelsior?

"And how you used to say you didn't like teaching girls?"

"I was afraid they would be as awful as I was in school, but they were nothing like that. And by the way, maybe if we had girls here, you would be better," I said, testing the water.

"What, Miss? Girls at KC? Never!"

"No, Miss, never! Bishop would fly up from him grave!"

"Bishop never even mention girls when him start this school, Miss."

Clearly, I would have to gentle them myself! But wait—this was not true. I had new opportunities provided by SCQ training. Our interactions with York Castle and other co-ed or girls' schools provided models for associations that could do the trick. I would look to other extracurricular activities to contribute to the process.

Not much had changed in the day-to-day routines, and it was easy to settle into my new classes. Armed with the confidence that some of my theories had been reinforced by experiences in the quiz room and at the university, I tackled my new classes with zest and excitement. Collaborative and cooperative learning activities found their way through my doors. Although cumbersome to handle, we rearranged desks and chairs to form small and large circles in which students faced each other and me. Without physical barriers between us, we talked through issues and concerns that brought greater meaning to writing and reading literature. I had also learned from the quiz experience that competition had its place. My classes became a constant effort to insert competitive activities while balancing all the strategies I was now intent on exploring.

The quiz experience had taught me the value of bringing more of myself into my interactions with students and allowing the kind of self-disclosure in regular classes that we shared in our informal practice sessions. I talked freely about my decision to stay with teaching for the long haul. I shared my high expectations of them and encouraged their aspirations. When they did the right thing or performed well, I praised them liberally. When their words or actions hurt one another or me, or let down the standards to which we'd agreed, I let them have it. I was no longer hiding myself behind the veil of authority and the all-knowing image that I had been led to believe I must project. The weight of pretence was lifted from my shoulders. *Why did I ever buy that nonsense about keeping my real self hidden from my students?*

Wanting them to know me better and to accept and trust me was not just for my own comfort, though. I now believed it would make them share more of themselves, including the problems I knew were often the cause of inconsistent performance and disciplinary problems. I firmly believed that making them see more of me as a person would make them show more of who they were as people. I now understood more of what made Peter Maxwell the "complete" teacher that he was. I had found the term to describe him scattered all over the pages written by the education gurus whose work I studied on campus.

Peter had been a "student-centred" teacher long before those books were written. For him, the concept went far beyond methods and activities he introduced to the learning process. His brand of student-centredness came from the person he was: from his laser-like focus on each boy to the manner in which he brought everything to bear upon his teaching—heart, soul, mind, and blue Volkswagen. He manifested student-centredness in the hours he spent preparing and the special effort he invested in arranging for extra resources, such as the unsold newspapers he got the newspaper companies to donate to the school.

It was palpable in his sensitivity to the special needs of the boys who entered KC in third form after passing the Grade Nine Achievement Test. These boys bore the brunt of another inequity in the education system, another consequence of the multiple types of schooling and the limitations of the Common Entrance Exam. Despite the existence of primary, preparatory, and all-age schools, the Common Entrance Exam was still the education ministry's strategy for creaming off high-performing students at the primary level and placing them in the limited number of high school places available in the system. Although the exam had become less elitist since the introduction of the 70–30 system that brought more primary school children into high school, it did not address the inequities that remained.

One of these was manifested in yet another creaming-off strategy, which was the Grade Nine Achievement Test. This test was introduced to give students who remained at all-age schools after not passing the Common Entrance Exam another chance to get into traditional high schools. Successful students, now around ages 14 to 15, found themselves at schools like KC, some of which placed them in a special third-form "stream" to provide them the opportunity to integrate, catch up, and make their way to the coveted O-level exam passes.

Many did not fit into the high school culture. They already had a sense of their own potential for failure. They often grappled with difficult socio-economic conditions, and they often stood out from other third-formers based on class indicators that operated despite the uniquely diverse KC culture.

I took up the cause of these boys with Peter and other concerned teachers. Together we railed against the discriminatory attitudes toward them, advocating relentlessly for special approaches to help them adjust and derive as much as they should from late migration into a traditional high school.

Well-equipped with the theories, I was ready to be infected with Peter's evangelism. We had no time for pessimists who could see no good in the boys or for placeholders who were constantly waiting for the results of successive job interviews in other sectors. We were unapologetic in our criticism of colleagues who repeatedly arrived at school late or lingered in Hardie House long after they should have started their classes.

A few teachers who had taken up the new Jamaican pastime of "higglering"[8] to supplement their earnings

---

[8] "Higglering" is the practice of buying various items and selling them in public, in offices, in homes, and from cars, usually to

gave us the side eye and quickly scraped up their wares, slamming their car trunks the moment one of us approached. None of these groups had large numbers, but they were enough to distract the majority of us who were committed to doing everything we could for our students.

We became the nemesis of officials who vacillated about critical issues, sidestepped difficult decisions, and displayed a tendency to generalise their complaints about "irresponsible teachers" instead of tackling guilty individuals. We abhorred administrative approaches that elevated the importance of paperwork and minutiae above issues that were critical to the learning process or the welfare of students.

It was a gruelling but exhilarating time.

Naturally, students were the main source of our low and high points. But who knew that parents could be as exhausting as their sons? Nowhere was this more visible than in the altercations that occurred when parents were dissatisfied with the decisions that we made about placing their sons in certain classes and approving their choice of subjects to take in school-leaving exams. Most parents expected their sons to take between six and eight traditional academic subjects in the O-level exams. After all, the number of passes obtained was a prime measure of success or failure in a student's high school career. They were also linked to the preferences of employers, who understood the currency of established courses like English language,

---

supplement income.

math, history, geography, physics, chemistry, Spanish, French, and biology.

On the other hand, both traditional employers and parents doubted the market value of passes in Bible knowledge, technical drawing, metalwork, woodwork, principles of business, accounts, and other recent additions to the curriculum that had more of a vocational flavour. Many parents understood the links between subject choice and employment prospects and further studies, so they became panic-stricken when they believed that their sons were in line to accumulate passing grades in "useless" subjects. The problem arose when the performance and attitudes of students gave clear evidence that their preferences and abilities were not in line with their parents' wishes or with the job prospects they were eyeing.

Faced with these and other issues, we ventured into the field of career guidance. At best, our efforts were informal and unofficial, because none of us had the benefit of special training in the field. My instincts about the need to help students in this area were sharpened by my awareness of my own false starts when I had wandered into the working world with zero preparation. Stumbling first into banking and lurching from there to university, broadcasting, teaching, advertising, and back to teaching, all within the space of a few years, did not make me an expert on career preparation. But it had certainly taught me the hard way that guidance about career choices should be an essential part of the high school curriculum. We were not equipped to make that happen, so we did what we could.

We started by trying to instil in teachers that we should all be helping the boys make connections between learning and working, between the subjects they were pursuing and the jobs and careers that were likely to be available on the local job market. "Bright" boys pursuing the mainstream courses in science, math, and the arts had the idea they would go to sixth form and pursue traditional career paths into the professions. Beyond those, many boys were pretty much plodding along, few giving serious thought to what they would do after completing fifth form—which by then had turned into eleventh grade, following the change from British to American terminology.

With a small group of interested teachers, Peter and I implemented strategies to help us connect our everyday teaching to the career paths available. Career guidance material was not available in ready-made form suitable for the purpose. The office staff groaned under the task of typing dozens of old-time stencils. Hands and stencils alike became sticky and stained with bright pink correcting fluid. We watched and waited with fingers crossed as the protesting old Gestetner machine grumbled, struggling to churn out copies of job advertisements, publications from tertiary institutions, career guidance books and pamphlets, newspaper articles, and anything we could lay our hands on to post on a notice board unimaginatively labelled "Jobs and Careers".

Our intermittent invitations to guest speakers to come into our classes and talk about their jobs developed into major career development events. For between one and three days, we suspended regular classes and staged day-long activities in which speakers from the working world and post-secondary institutions gave talks, showed film strips, hosted discussions, and gave demonstrations about academic, vocational, and business pursuits.

By today's standards, these were small-scale career education efforts, but at the time, they represented significant investment in an endeavour that had little backing by way of official policy or resource allocation. Still, we were opening the eyes of the boys and broadening their perspectives about the future. Of course, we did not succeed in converting all parents to accept new ideas about training institutions and jobs their sons should consider.

One staunch opponent described our efforts as "watering down" her sons' education with subjects that she believed should only be taught in the few remaining schools that bore the label "comprehensive" or "technical". At PTA meetings, she railed against our presentations that focused on giving students career information that would validate their interest in metalwork and technical drawing. "After this is not Kingston Technical School; is Kingston College. My sons must go to sixth form and then university or, at least CAST."[9]

But the worst of her responses was yet to come. Her first son had spent hours with me discussing what he should do with his six O-level passes. He'd spent a few weeks in lower sixth, but he did not feel comfortable doing physics, math, and economics. Like many lower sixth students, he had no clue about economics, but it was the subject that students inevitably chose when they found themselves in need of a third class to complete their programme requirements. Although he liked his other two subjects, he didn't see himself spending two years on them or going on to university.

The boy's eyes flashed and his ears perked up whenever a discussion turned to car engines. He knew everything about how the most popular cars handled Jamaican potholes and reminded me often about putting air in my tyres. As the weeks passed, he stopped me more and more often to ask about notices posted on the "Jobs and Careers" notice board.

"Miss, did you post the advertisement about the new auto mechanics school?"

"Yes, I did. Sounds like your cup of tea, right?"

"Seriously, Miss, that is where I need to be. This A-level business is not really for me. It's fun and all that, and I can get to play basketball, but I don't feel I should stay after this year."

---

[9] The College of Arts Science and Technology which later became the University of Technology

"That's a big decision. We have to look into it some more," I said.

"But what about the people who own car repair companies? They going give jobs to people who graduate from that school, Miss?"

"We can find out more about it, and you can decide nearer to the end of the academic year."

"All the same, Miss, you know my mother, right? She believe I must go to UWI or CAST. All day long she preach that anybody who don't do that will never come to anything."

"I know she believes that. She wants the best for you, and she thinks her plan is best. You will have to try and reason with her. Why don't you let her come in one day and we can talk about it?"

It wasn't a week later that his mother met me on the way to the staffroom after class. I could tell from her heavy breathing that she had marched from wherever she'd parked her car, and she was not in a good mood. "Morning, Miss Phillips. I need a word with you," she said tersely.

"Good morning; nice to see you. Come this way. Let me just get rid of this pile of books."

"But I have to get to work."

"I won't be a minute."

"Miss Phillips, I am not pleased at all at all. You know from the last PTA meeting that I don't like all this talk about technical drawing and metalwork, right? And now I hear my son talking foolishness about leaving sixth form. You please let him know he is to finish up the A-levels to get into UWI or CAST."

"I know that is the plan, but your son has been saying—"

"Yes, Miss Phillips. I know what that boy has been saying, and I am not interested in this foolishness about fixing cars. And moreover, you really believe I could even consider letting my son go down to some auto mechanic school down Maxfield Avenue?"

"I've been looking into it for a few boys. It's a new, well-equipped school with good instructors from a similar school in Germany. It's opening a whole new area of training and you know your son loves—"

"What I know for sure is that you wouldn't be telling your own son—that is, if you ever have one—to leave KC to go and do no trade fixing car." The woman's barely covered jab was typical of many mothers who believed teachers without children (i.e., young and inexperienced) had valid opinions only when we agreed with their point of view. Any sign that we might be going against their ideas was a chance for them to point out that without our own children, we had no right to give advice.

But the problem was much bigger. The fact was that many parents looked down on the non-traditional jobs and careers that were emerging as areas of interest for their sons. Parents believed that by exposing the boys to information or advising them about such options, we were encouraging them to turn away from the paths the parents had planned. The new challenge was how to prepare students for new ways of looking at the future without alienating them from their parents. It was a tall order, but support was growing from employers who took part in our career-day activities. We were on the right path.

Defending the SCQ Title

Back in Cassava Piece and Big Yard, a growing squad of SCQ enthusiasts had gathered since the summer, ensuring that the departure of three members of our winning team and numerous members of our squad did not leave a void. Fitz-Henley, Jackson, and Jones had packed up their miniature trophies along with their GCE A-level passes and made their way to the university to study medicine, economics, and engineering, respectively. Their final exam results contradicted the predictions of naysayers who said involvement in the quiz would detract from their academic work. We knew otherwise. We knew that in terms of both motivation and exposure, involvement in quiz activities didn't diminish commitment to their studies or academic preparation—it strengthened them.

Continuity brought stability, and we were soon secure again in the knowledge that the winning formula was still in our hands. Campbell and Nugent held their batons firmly and took up their positions as potential foundation members for the 1975 competition. But there were no guarantees. Victory had spread the SCQ infection all over the school, and new enthusiasts were coming out of the woodwork. Our practice room was bursting at the seams.

The core members of the squad from the previous year were there from beginning to end. Even though we had won, they reminded us of things that had not gone according to our plans the first time around. They proposed new strategies and brandished new challenge questions, slurping down orange juice, passing around cheese crunches, nibbling on patties, and sinking their teeth into bun and cheese. The buzzer had been restored to use, and old exercises were revamped. Thumb push-ups were passed on from Fitz-Henley through Nugent and Campbell, who were the links between the winning team and the new aspirants, constantly reminding them that "ambition should be made of sterner stuff".

When January rolled around and it was time to select the final five, both veterans had staked their claims, and the competition was really about the other three positions. After weeks of hectic practice sessions in which newcomers displayed their knowledge and grit in equal measure, we reminded ourselves of our process for choosing the final team. The room fell quiet except for the sound of forty brains ticking and forty pens and pencils scribbling.

Orett Campbell emerged as captain, leading Ivor Nugent—promoted from his 1974 reserve position—Donovan "Pip" Shaw, and Barrington Salmon, with Kenneth Vaughan as reserve. We stepped up our practice sessions, more determined than ever to replicate our experience of the previous year. Still, there were new elements, not the least of which was the fact that we had five new personalities who were quite different from their predecessors and from each other. These differences created new dynamics.

Just as in the previous year, the team members established their dominance in their academic subjects and developed special interests in the other areas we needed to cover for the competition. Campbell and Nugent were now in upper sixth and were recognised specialists in the science subjects. The new captain consolidated his position. Aware of his new responsibility, he set about sharpening his knowledge of art, music, mythology, and West Indian literature. Nugent added current affairs, Spanish, and sports to his portfolio, polishing his hidden gems for the time when the team would need them. With experience from his position on the school's basketball team, he infected the room with the special brand of "Fortis" competitiveness bottled by KC athletes, spiking his heroic stories with sporting statistics that regularly seeped from his pores.

Salmon had lived in England, and his experiences as a Jamaican boy growing up there brought not only a unique perspective, but first-hand knowledge that enriched our wide-ranging debates about social and political issues as well as our coverage of subjects like history, geography, and world affairs. He was a master of word meanings. If faced by a menacing interrogator, he could recite, without a blink, all the different meanings of numerous "frequently confused words".

Shaw, the quiet one, took up the mantle as the specialist in French, world affairs, and geography. In the moments when he was not on a practising team, it was easy to forget that he was around, because he hardly spoke. But his quietness was never mistaken for lack of interest, knowledge, or diligence. He was always listening, his brows furrowing as he buried his head in a book of facts or questions. When he did open his mouth, it was with the quiet certainty of someone who knew he had invested the necessary time to master his responsibility areas.

Just as Nugent had done the previous year, our new reserve, Vaughan, threw himself into preparing to provide back-up in as many areas as possible.

Whoever might have predicted that the second time around would be easier was way off the mark. Our 1975 warriors faced the new challenge of having to defend our crown amid constant reminders that no school had ever won the competition two years in a row. It was just the kind of "first" that whetted the "Fortis" appetites. None of us flinched, but we knew everybody was coming after us. "Uneasy lies the head that wears the crown" was no longer just a line from *Henry IV*.

We kicked off our title defence against Wolmer's High School for Girls with a score of 38 to 23 and breathed our collective sigh of relief that we had avoided the ignominy of being eliminated in the first round, "and by an all-girls team at that". Very often, the boys quite forgot that their coach was a "girl", so ill-advised remarks like that one would slip into casual conversation. I reprimanded them instantly, warning them about never becoming "male chauvinist pigs".

Rid of those early jitters, we consolidated our performance, defeating the vaunted Jamaica College 60–30 in the process and falling just short of the highest ever score of 62, set by St Hugh's in the first year of the competition. In the next round, we defeated St Andrew High School for Girls 41–29. The semi-finals found us across the TV studio from the formidable Manchester High, a team that had been touted to win. Our score of 40–28 in that match was a big confidence booster that prepared us well for the final against previous winners, Wolmer's Boys.

The popularity of the quiz had soared, and animated supporters from both schools poured into the cramped studio, overflowing into the yard, where the management put a TV under a tree. Stragglers were able to watch, erupting in a massive roar every time their team inched ahead.

The fortunes of the teams waxed and waned. As tension rose and blood pressures spiked, KC surged ahead, each team member pulling a special treasure from his secret place. Shaw made his mark, cleverly deciphering the English translation of a French phrase pronounced by the quizmaster in an accent that was far from impeccable. Salmon soon chimed in with his identification of a line from Shakespeare and the name of the famous Old Vic in London. Not to be outdone in the team's attempts to send me to an early grave, Nugent waited for his moment, leaned forward, and perked up his ears as Dennis Hall assumed his poetic voice and uttered words none of us had heard: "To begin at the beginning: It is spring, moonless night in the small town, starless and bible-black …"

"'Under Milkwood'!" Nugent cried out simultaneously with the screech of the buzzer, certain that the quizmaster wanted the name of Dylan Thomas's famous play. Relief spread like a mist over his teammates and coach alike, and his smile, fit for any toothpaste commercial, stretched from one side of his face to the other.

The hand of the clock was racing when the quizmaster began his next question with two words, "In 1798—"

The KC buzzer shrieked, stopping my breath. *This is it! Nobody can answer that.* I could see the two points disappearing from our score, heralding certain defeat.

One word from Campbell's lips broke the silence: "Malthus." Our captain had reasoned in a split second that the biggest event in 1798 must have been Malthus's essay on population. By now, "the country boy from Titchfield" had become a star, but he remained calm, his hand nonchalantly at his jaw, waiting for the confirmation that the year's competition was done and dusted.

We hoisted the trophy once again after a comfortable score of 35–20 against the team from Marescaux Road. "Fortis" streamed out of South Odeon Avenue, satisfied we had given a fitting gift to the school, now celebrating its fiftieth anniversary. Mr Coke was again one of our most vociferous supporters, and again, as many boys as possible climbed into his Dodge Avenger to head for Burgerman. The prize trip was to Trinidad, but this time Missa Johnno would escort the team. It was Mr Coke's fault; he had done the job of convincing my family (and me) that he was "the right one". We planned a wedding for the summer.

Mr Johnno and the Crew Versus Dreadlocks and Smoke

By the time we returned to school in September, the social and economic changes in the wider society had continued unabated—and not all were for the better. The worsening economic woes and social unrest brought many challenges to parents, teachers, and school administrators, often spawning conflict and arguments about traditional values and assumptions.

Signs I had missed while away from full involvement in the classroom greeted me at full strength. It was as if all the forces that were set on transforming the society were coming together to create a giant push for a new reality. Conflict over the influence of the American-based Black

Power movement had escalated. Now, under the impact of worldwide developments, opposing perspectives emerged. Among the progressives, the belief took hold that Jamaica belonged in the forefront of any movement to strengthen the identity and culture of black people.

The opposing forces were equally strident in articulating their views: Jamaica's history and social structure, bolstered by our motto "Out of Many One People" rendered this "American foolishness" irrelevant and divisive. But many maintained that race and colour still separated Jamaicans—that despite Mr Manley's proclamations, there was still no visible change in the complexion of the society. Lighter-skinned (and usually better-off) groups continued to dominate the country's leadership as well as the opportunities for advancing.

Some accused university students and foreign faculty at Mona of importing the "alien concept" of black power onto the campus and infecting "innocent" Jamaican students with foolish ideas. Similar debates had already come to a head with the Rodney Riots of 1968. But the rhetoric leading up to Michael Manley's election, and following his determination to effect social change, caused increasing concern about the direction in which the country seemed to be moving.

At the same time, the influence of Rastafarianism was mushrooming, partly spurred by Mr Manley's engagement with the Brethren during the campaign. Impetus for the movement also came from the inroads Rastafarian performers were making in popular music. Though not yet an international star, Bob Marley had affixed his name to the infant reggae brand, and along with the Wailers released the *Natty Dread* album, giving another fillip to the movement with songs like "So Jah Say" and "Rebel Music".

Even the rise of Marley brought controversy: Some Jamaicans called his music (along with all the other emerging protest music) "chaka chaka noise", renouncing leading musicians for loudness and disruptive lyrics. But their complaints came upon a flood of defenders; their music had already broken through the impotent social barricades against it. It was the music of the streets, and the young were absorbing the message.

Most KC boys were old enough for their parents to allow them to wear the popular "big afro" hairstyle. There was no telling how much of this was about fashion and the world of pop culture versus how much was about adherence to the Black Power movement. The height and the thickness of some afros led to new school rules for both girls and boys, sparking protests against the perceived discrimination against the natural hair of almost all Jamaicans. Numerous run-ins occurred between students, parents, and administrators, but these were mild in comparison to what was ahead.

Several new symbols of social change hit the streets, capturing the imagination of Jamaica's young men, and those at KC were no exception. Dominant among these was the red, green, and gold crochet belt associated with Rastafarianism, which emerged as the single most significant cause of consternation and panic among parents, especially middle-class professionals.

The moment a boy replaced his brown or black belt with the offending crochet belt, his apoplectic mother or father (sometimes both) would descend on the premises, searching for the principal or Mr Johnson (parents never said Missa Johnno). If the advent of the belt coincided with the twisting of their sons' hair into twirls that were usually the precursor of the dreadlocks associated with Rastafarianism, parents bombarded school administrators, demanding plans to address the crisis taking over the school and contaminating their sons. Arguments over school policy raged, Ministry of Education officials contemplated every angle of the issues, and storms erupted at PTA meetings.

But nothing could stay the wave of change. The belts proliferated. Many afros that had grown outward turned downward, first into wormy little twirls, then into thickening twists, and, eventually, into full-fledged dreadlocks that demanded the red, green, and gold woollen tams—the final confirmation of "big trouble". Parents and administrators took to tearing out their own hair as their sons dug their heels in and clung to the new trappings of their independence.

The reasons for the new look were as many as the boys who embraced it. Some were rebelling against the rules of home and school, asserting their right to wear what they wanted. Others were actively and proudly embracing blackness, together with Rastafarianism, the new religion born in their own country and promising a magnetic belief system. It was built on belief in a black God, afrocentrism, naturalism, and a rejection of

Babylon, which embodied all the ills of the Eurocentric and American-oriented Jamaican culture. Some were just being teenagers. Still, parents and some school administrators began to see the combination of the Rasta belt, dreadlocks, and woolly tam as certain signs that the end of their son's bright future—if not of Jamaica—was at hand. At the very least, the combination became the bane of parental existence.

The emerging subculture seeping into the schools found its expression in the protest music left over from ska and morphing into reggae. The Wailers declared, "Hear the words of the Rastaman say / Babylon you throne gone down." And Peter Tosh shocked the world with his bold call for marijuana (ganja) to be accepted, "Legalize it / and don't criticize it."

So-called subversive lyrics fell with ease and certainty from the lips of young boys, brimming with a new awareness of who they were—or at least who many thought they wanted to be.

Internal conditions at school were playing their part in feeding the turmoil as well. With close to two thousand students, KC was way past the size our physical and human resources could support. The headmaster bemoaned deteriorating physical conditions, growing indiscipline, and mounting distractions from academic effort as major factors affecting the learning process. Many seasoned teachers, especially men, moved on to jobs that paid more and demanded less emotional and intellectual investment. Inexperienced teachers were unable to fill the gaps immediately, and many did not stay long enough to do so.

In our staff and PTA meetings, arguments raged about falling standards and the reasons for them. As the problems with uniforms, physical appearance, and hairstyles multiplied, we spent hours debating alternative strategies. Some thought we should take immediate and decisive disciplinary measures against the baby locks and the Rasta belt and back-pocket rags before they led down what many believed was the inevitable path to ganja smoking in the far corners of the premises. The counter argument—that we should leave the early signs alone to avoid stoking further rebellion—soon wore thin as we faced the unmistakable evidence of glazed eyes staring from the back rows of our classrooms. What reassurances could we give to fretful mothers and enraged fathers when their sons' end-of-term reports proved that the journey from coloured belts to glazed eyes often correlated with missed classes and deteriorating grades?

I understood enough of the competing ideologies to know where I stood, but the venom spewed by the antagonists warring about who was to blame and what should be done threatened to shut me down. I identified with the new-found self-awareness of the young men around me. I empathised with their passion about the new beliefs and alliances drawing them away from tradition. But I also saw that some boys were slipping towards the edge of a precipice that nobody understood. The agony of parents facing perceived and real dangers became visible. As teachers, we feared the loss of our young men to poorly understood belief systems and practices that ran counter to how they had been brought up.

Some boys were just drawn in by the catchy words of protest and the intoxicating rhythms of the music; it was a short step from that to the changes in their appearance and behaviour. We reasoned that overreacting to them would be both unnecessary and imprudent. Others were bright, diligent students who had set off on a serious quest for new insights and self-understanding. Wasn't it our job as teachers to support their search, even though we were uncertain of how to do this or where it would end?

Between these extremes, there were boys who were being seduced by ideas they didn't understand and drawn in by the new attraction of trying out "a little spliff" instead of the traditional "Craven A" cigarettes smuggled into the bathrooms for a quick smoke. Whether they were prominent athletes, students struggling with personal challenges, or young men wanting to experiment with a new idea, the process was similar.

A few prominent students, known for their heroic performance in one sport or another, also became involved. Seven or eight little boys followed boys like these everywhere. They were stars; they never had to join a line at the canteen or carry their book bags or training gear. Their names fell from the lips of old boys in animated sentences of hope, punctuated with the names of KC legends.

Then, when the season for their chosen sport was over and the attention subsided, they would begin to miss a few classes, especially after lunch. The first real signs were always undeniable: previously well-groomed hair would begin to twirl, and their brown or black belts would give way to the crochet belts.

"What's going on with so-and-so?" I would ask Missa Johnno, who could always rely on me to alert him when a student needed a second look. Sometimes his response would be reassuring. But when he gave an excuse to avoid discussing a particular boy, I knew he was worried himself. In some instances, the twirled hair was no more than a passing fad. In a few cases, the deterioration was swift and merciless. Absences from class multiplied. The twirls overtook an afro hairstyle and turned down into the telltale baby locks. Then Missa Johnno would slowly nod, a grave look creeping into his eyes. We had witnessed quite a few boys who travelled that path, and we managed to do enough to keep them on the right side.

When we seemed to be losing the battle, parents, coaches, and concerned old boys became involved, including some prominent old boys in the medical field, who always took a few boys at risk under their wings. Parents absorbed all the advice these old boys had to give, but their shoulders sagged under the weight of watching their sons transform in ways none of us understood.

Missa Johnno sat for hours with one or another of these boys under the tree outside Hardie House, and he talked until his throat gave out. For those who were most affected, his words echoed without impact. Their visits to school became sporadic; they turned up at odd hours, unclean and unkempt. Their speech and actions became erratic and even threatening, their eyes empty. In the end, we witnessed two or three withdraw into a dreadful silence before they dropped out altogether.

Stories like these echoed through the corridors of numerous schools. Medical experts debated the effects that smoking marijuana could have on adolescent boys. Many thought the scenarios were limited to boys' schools in Kingston, but similar stories about girls soon emerged, and some schools in rural areas encountered the same issues. Researchers argued that the weed had no effect on the brain. Gurus countered with studies that "proved" marijuana caused lethargy, loss of motivation, and inability to concentrate. Psychiatrists suggested the so-called ganja-induced symptoms exhibited by young people were symptoms of undiagnosed schizophrenia.

Social workers pointed to socio-economic conditions that were threatening the stability of parents, disrupting home life, and creating conditions that caused students to seek solace through multiple avenues, including ganja smoking. They produced statistics showing large numbers of "barrel children" who lived without parental supervision. The Ministry of Education stepped up its guidance services and set the framework for guidance counsellors.

Out of the turmoil, Missa Johnno emerged with a new persona captured in "the Beast"—a name widely used across the streets of Jamaica to refer to the police. Determined to stem the tide of loss, Missa Johnno became single-minded about saving boys from themselves, even if it meant acceptance of the ugly nickname or its softer version, "Police Chief". The bubbling optimism and sharp sense of humour which had quick-marched across the grounds with him for so many years still lingered. But too often they were hidden by his knitted brow and his clenched lips as he undertook the most steadfast search for boys on the verge of trouble and those already drowning in deep waters. Those whom he rescued knew the truth. Underneath the new persona, Missa Johnno wore the same old garb of mentor, confidante, problem-solver, father figure, and protector of all things "Fortis".

Except for a few brief years in London, where he developed his talent and passion for art, Missa Johnno had spent most of his life at KC, first as a student and then as a sports-master-turned-dynamo who devoted most of his waking hours to the school. In my first year, I assumed he had been some kind of athlete while at school, because although he didn't seem built for any sport, I thought he could win a walking race in the Olympics. The miles he covered must have at least equalled those covered in training and competitions by all the school's most famous athletes. It exhausted me just to watch him rushing from Hardie House to the canteen, from the swimming pool to the chapel, and from the principal's office to Hardie House.

His role as sports master ran the gamut from hustling to buy limes to mixing a sugary brand of lemonade to peeling oranges for KC's "at home" cricket matches. Weighed down with four or five well-built boys, his green Anglia struggled to the seaside for sand training on Sundays before dawn. His disciplinary strategies ranged from covert visits to the nearby "Miss Pearl shop", an institution as feared by administrators as it was loved by the boys, to patrolling Lissant Road after lunch and hauling would-be escapees back to class.

Missa Johnno's devotion to school activities knew no bounds. Still, he found time to be in our heady English department planning meetings, where he rattled off lines of poetry and spouted his own unforgettable interpretations of images from Shakespeare, Keats, Dickens, and Wordsworth. His anecdotes and gems from KC's history dotted both his literature classes and the pep talks he gave to sportsmen whose courage might be dimmed by injury or defeat.

In short, Missa Johnno was the embodiment of "Fortis". His heart rattled with the same delight for KC's clinching of the mile relay when twilight fell on the stadium at Champs as it did for a fast bowler's run up to take the final opponent's wicket in the Sunlight Cup competition. It throbbed as fervently for victories or losses in basketball, table tennis, or Manning Cup football as it did for the triumphant performances in the French drama festival and the KC choir's soul-stirring renditions of "O Holy Night" and famous songs from *Oliver*.

And when we were all convinced that, regardless of the forces driving them, the triple symbol of belt, dreadlocks, and ganja posed a serious threat to many of our students, he it was who mobilised us to mount a counter-offensive designed to save as many as we could. We saved many, but we ached for every one that we lost

The Worst and Best of Times

Preparation for SCQ had grown into a full-fledged extracurricular programme with objectives that far exceeded the television competition or even my original hope of nurturing interest in the pursuit of knowledge. We counted it as one more avenue through which we could rescue some boys who might fall into the margins of alienation. Many who sat at the back of the room or hovered in the corridors outside the door were not considered "academic", but neither were they particularly inclined to sports. For them, quiz activities provided a haven after school, and they hung out at practice even if they were not inclined to contend for a place on the team.

As the time came for us to prepare for the second defence of the trophy, more boys like these found their way to wherever we were. If nothing else, it was good for them to rub shoulders with the serious enthusiasts and contenders who were outstanding examples of hard work and commitment to something bigger than themselves. But they were also good for us; they were spreading the word about this new "club", and they brought others with them, some who became infected with "quiz mania".

As far as defending the trophy was concerned, the pressure was mounting. Some people had begun to whisper that KC was trying to "hog the competition just like everything else", that it was time for another school to win so the public wouldn't "lose interest in the programme". In our own circles, the danger of high expectations lurked. Even some supporters wondered if we could really accomplish a third straight win.

The growing visibility of the competition as one of JBC's stellar programmes led to an increase not only in the number of schools participating, but in the quality of preparation they undertook. The search for new information intensified. Contrary to what many critics of the programme believed, JBC did not provide anything like a quiz syllabus from which questions were taken. The categories remained the same, but with the growth in the number of schools and matches, the scope of questions was widening and the difficulty level was increasing.

After many weeks of training culminated in the usual group selection process, it was Barrington Salmon, the survivor from the previous year, who emerged as captain, leading Patrick Dallas, Michael Hewett, and Stephen Vasciannie into battle, with Franklyn Eaton as our reserve.

By this time, Salmon had built upon his foundation as the chief wordsmith. Like his teammates, he held his own across school subjects, but also maintained a stack of special, secret answers in general knowledge and art. Hewett took over from Shaw as the quiet one on the team, but like his predecessor, this was only until he seized his many opportunities to pull answers from his jewellery box bursting with literature, theatre, sports, and cinema.

Dallas took care of the buzzers and dug into his deep pocket of gems about physics, math, and chemistry. His addiction to puns brought out some of his most hilarious contributions to practice sessions. We could always rely on him to start a pun war and break mounting tension in the dimming light of a practice session just before a big match.

Vasciannie, the first fifth-former to make a KC quiz team, silenced any doubters who may have feared that a fifth-former would not be ready for the "big man" league. He held his own with knowledge of all his school-based subjects, especially math, history, geography, and a generous helping of Spanish to balance the French answers in which Dallas excelled.

Our process had yielded an excellent team. Our expectations were high.

In the first round, the team set a record for the highest score any school had achieved to date, outmanoeuvring St George's, our long-time rivals in legendary "battles of North Street", with a tally of 69 to 44 points. The second-round match saw us outscoring DeCarteret College 44–24. Things were looking good as we went into the quarter-final.

In the next round, Cornwall College travelled from the west, threatening to take us down, but we sent them home with 25 points and took encouragement from the fact that although each round was becoming more challenging, our 46 points augured well for what was ahead. The match against Wolmer's Boys was a close one, but true to form, we excelled in the buzzer section, eking out the victory with a score of 25–19.

We now set our sights firmly on making history by taking the trophy a third time.

Alas, we were not the only ones with our eyes on the finish line. The highly touted Manchester High School journeyed into Kingston with the full force of the hungry. After a nail-biting buzzer section, KC was left stranded, trailing their 32 points with our 28. We had faltered, and for want of a mere four points, we had cleared the way for the victors to meet Munro College in the all-rural final. When it was over, Manchester High travelled home to Mandeville with their pride intact and the trophy aloft, becoming only the second rural school (after York Castle High) to take home the coveted SCQ bacon.

After the loss, the boys in my regular classes rallied around me. Amid compassion, encouragement, and uplifting quotations, their rough edges were nowhere to be seen. Though some had never set foot in quiz practice, we could always count on their interest and support for our efforts.

Our lively discussions during quiz practice had shown me how engagement with literature (even from an old, faraway world) could excite the boys. Increasingly, I had transported the fun approaches from quiz practice to my regular classes to help overcome the lingering resistance of some students to studying literature.

We no longer slogged away at rhyming couplets, dense imagery, or rote learning of speeches by literary characters. Instead, we focused on identifying enduring themes and images of nature that cut across the borders of time and space. We looked to our own surroundings and culture for signs of these, and we could always find them. We had no host of golden daffodils; no skylarks tweeted in the morning mist. But grass quits flitted through the blazing blooms of the flame tree, and hummingbirds rustled between the blossoms of prolific bougainvillea. And as our study of poetry opened their eyes to our own surroundings, the boys learned that beauty was all around us and poetry was for everyone.

We had no kings or princes fighting over monarchies or queens, but the boys were becoming adept at analysing family conflict and dissecting wars between political adversaries. They connected actions and speeches from the pages of Shakespeare and Milton with the deeds and words of local and international figures embroiled in events of our time. They laced their presentations with memorable quotations, growing more aware each week of the power of the well-chosen word delivered in the right moment. It had worked in the quiz room, and now I was sure it was working in the classroom.

At the same time, the loss unloosed a barrage of weighty warnings from home-grown critics about our emphasis on the quiz competition. Listening to their various versions of "I told you so" and the predictions that the loss would result in withdrawal of interest in the programme, I began to wonder about my theory of using SCQ to achieve all the goals on which I'd pinned my hopes. Would the pessimists be proven right in pointing out that the benefits of the competition came only to the one winning school? Could it be true that all the other participants gained nothing because they didn't win? But what about the scores of boys and girls across the island whose schools had been defeated in the competition repeatedly and yet continued to participate? Surely they proved that losing the competition did not make them losers! I wanted to believe it was more about the experience and the faces of the numerous boys who'd streamed into the practice rooms with fire in their eyes than it was about the outcome. I needed to hold to my conviction that the programme was doing what I intended. But was I expecting too much?

As I made up the announcement that quiz practice would resume, my fingers trembled from anxiety that the number of boys turning up for practice would diminish, that my "knowledge movement" would die an early death. The numbers admonished me for doubting. I fixed my gaze on the faces lined up before me in our first practice session of the new academic year, and I knew the truth at once. Defeat had not shaken the resolve of the committed. We stitched up our wounds and gave solace to the weary. We conducted our post-mortems, made candid observations about our strengths and weaknesses, and pressed forward with plans to return even stronger. We had indeed lost the icing, but we still had the cake.

The "old quiz men" turned out in their numbers. They filled folder pages with new questions. They scribbled their observations about potential team members and pressed them into my hand on the way out the door. They grabbed friends and hauled them into quiz practice to show off their potential. Our quiz programme was open for business.

We motivated newcomers with stories of our record score and numerous other high points that stood out despite our loss: how Hewett had stunned us with his calm answers to obscure questions about sonatas and concertos; how Dallas quelled his nerves and brought the house down with his answer about "coal carriers" on strike in St Lucia; how Vasciannie put his head down, peered through his quarter-inch-thick lenses, and furiously scribbled the calculations for an intricate math problem. And we relished the praise heaped on our captain Salmon, whom quizmaster Dennis Hall had singled out at the final match for his commitment and team spirit. We had been knocked out, but our impact had not been forgotten.

Over the ensuing weeks, we fine-tuned our process, ending up with a team of almost all newcomers. Maurice Bailey, Charlton Collie, and Maurice Haynes took their places under Vasciannie's leadership, with the support of reserve Rodney Edwards. Each worked on his special interests and developed mastery in areas little known by others. Each became an expert in his own right.

We all knew that Francis Ford Coppola was the famed director of *The Godfather*, but Bailey, officially a student of literature, history, and economics, seemed to have studied the inner workings of Coppola's mind. He schooled us about the director's other movies and the characteristics that made his films unique. Bailey was also versed in mythology, Bible knowledge, music, and current affairs. He was the closest thing to this team's "quiet one", but behind his reserve, he brought composure and balance to the team.

Charlton Collie, of the bobbing head and frenetic speech, was the fastest solver of intricate math problems, but in five seconds any member of the team could "integrate $1/x$ with respect to x between the values 2 and 1". Generally relentless in the sciences and well up on current affairs and geography, Collie often got his inspiration from the ceiling, where he deciphered magical writings invisible to everyone else.

Once when he did this in a practice match, his unexpected answer to a math question about a train moving through a tunnel was right on the dot, eliciting cheers from the opposing team's quiz teacher and, more to his liking, from all the girls in the room. Haynes was another cool customer, who, despite being a science student, filled the gap left by Hewett in the areas of classical music, cinema, and theatre.

Vasciannie, the first student to become captain in lower sixth, was now the unlikely voice of experience. His subjects were history, math, and economics. But the compilers of the quiz questions stayed away from economics, so he took on responsibility for West Indian literature, general knowledge, and current affairs. Reserve Rodney Edwards, ever the enigma with a wry smile, brought his own brand of energy and humour.

With the support of the rest of the squad, we journeyed again to the Half-Way-Tree studios, ready for whatever fate awaited us.

In the first round, we met previous winners, Ardenne High, whose reputation preceded them. Our team dug deep, coming out on top with a score of 54–35 points. Bolstered by our early show of strength, we did well in the second-round match against Meadowbrook High, scoring 39 to their 13 points.

In the quarter-finals, the boys from Munro College came into Kingston with the backing of the entire parish of St Elizabeth, threatening to knock us from the perch which was becoming increasingly comfortable. Their record score of 93 in an earlier round had caused everybody to sit up straight, wondering who, if anyone, could beat them.

Munro presented the biggest challenge we faced, but in the end, we found the depth required to post a score of 35 to their 26 points. Relieved at getting past the highly touted warriors, we looked ahead, confident we had passed the worst.

The semi-finals saw us maintaining our pressure in the buzzer section, scoring 39 points against St Jago High's 18. The finish line loomed. Between us and the ultimate prize stood Jamaica College, our age-old uptown adversaries from Hope Road. Their threatening messages about upsetting the purple applecart had travelled through the Kingston streets to our practice room.

But they had fallen on deaf ears. On the night, we put our heads down from the first tick of the clock and set off on our sprint to the final bell. Our score of 30 points to their 10 was as much a shock to us as it was to them, but we grasped it firmly—along with the trophy—and sashayed into the waiting crowd at Burgerman, delighted that we had replicated our efforts and brought the trophy back to North Street.

As the boys and our crew of supporters celebrated, stories were told and retold of the tense, nerve-wracking, and match-changing moments that highlighted the team's foray through every round of the competition. Who could forget the terror on some KC faces (not least the coach's) when Bailey attacked the buzzer as the quizmaster uttered that strange question about the name of some ultimate battle in Norse mythology? Onlookers told of the expression on his face as he matter-of-factly called out "Ragnarok", clearly wondering why anyone would worry for even a split second that he might not get it right. Such was Bailey's composure.

Then there was Haynes, whose moment came with an audio question. After just a hint of the song, he stuck out his left elbow, eased forward with his right thumb, and pushed the buzzer, triumphantly identifying "The Drinking Song" from the famous operetta, *The Student Prince*.

The captain caused our hearts to freeze too, stopping the quizmaster in mid-sentence and taking no more than a second to blurt out with certitude that the motto on the armorial bearings of the Kingston and St Andrew Corporation was "A City Which Hath Foundation"! The young team validated the faith everyone had put in them, and the SCQ trophy travelled home in safety to Clovelly Park.

JBC had upped the ante, making the first prize a trip to Toronto. From our hall of residence at the University of Toronto, KC old boys from another era fetched us and feted us, taking us as far as Mississauga, where doctors, businessmen, and lawyers, still infused with the "Fortis" spirit, fussed over the boys and regaled us with stories and legends from their colourful KC memories. We made trips to the CN Tower, then the tallest building in the world, as well as Niagara Falls and a lake in Mississauga, compliments of an Air Canada executive and his sons. There, the boys showed off their angling skills, dominated by Collie with his single catch.

It was another dimension added to the SCQ experience, taking us all to the cleanest, best laid-out city we had ever seen, with intermittent explosions of flowers of all shapes, sizes, and colours emerging out of concrete niches and crevasses all over the city. Some created a stunning rainbow of colours and textures to mimic the face of a giant floral clock.

The page turned on another stimulating chapter.

A Bigger Picture

Winning the SCQ competition three times did not change my life or the life of the school. It did not change the public's perception that KC was a sports school. It did not cause the school's detractors to rethink their evaluation of where we stood in the scheme of longstanding institutions with more social pedigree than a school founded to rescue poor black boys. These were entrenched perceptions that would not be so easily shaken.

Stubborn supporters of "superior" schools belittled our achievement in the quiz, charging that it was a fluke, that it didn't take away from the essential character of KC as a second-class school when compared to the long-standing St George's, Wolmer's, Munro College, and Jamaica College. Deep-seated social prejudices had not been touched, even though we, who lived on the inside, knew the import of what the school was doing in several areas of school life.

Furthermore, effecting these changes had not been among my most important goals. What I wanted above all was to let loose a virus that would infect as many students as possible with a thirst for knowledge and a willingness to engage in an ardent search for it. Both the process that evolved and the victories we experienced were signs of a dream coming to pass. Still, I was not finished. My search continued for ways to contaminate more boys in my regular classes.

But the bigger picture loomed. The performance of the school in external exams had not improved. We were holding our own in some subjects, but overall, too many boys were underperforming. Administrative and academic resources were stretched as many men abandoned the classroom in search of better-paying jobs, further diminishing the adult male presence in the school. Despite the many effective women on the staff, the boys needed male role models, which were in short supply in many homes. Discipline suffered under the weight of wider social dislocation, and the evidence of poverty and deprivation proliferated.

In his budget presentation, Prime Minister Manley had enthusiastically proclaimed the introduction of free education for secondary and tertiary students. But it soon came to light that at that very moment when so many of us in education jumped up and down with joy in front of our televisions, the look on the face of his minister of finance was not the look of a man inspired. It was the terror he felt from knowing no money had been earmarked for such a mammoth undertaking. The secret was out—Mr Manley had been driven, by a heavy mixture of optimism and determination, to make up the free education policy right there at the podium at Gordon House.

It wasn't long before parents realised that sending their children to high school was as expensive as ever, especially considering their fast-disappearing jobs. The rapid devaluation of the Jamaican dollar multiplied the economic woes, and even working parents could no longer stretch their measly income to meet all the demands of schooling their children. Boys outgrew their khaki uniforms faster than their parents could replace them, and many wore their shoes to school long after their heels and toes could feel the hot asphalt through their threadbare socks. Even the rental fee for books became prohibitive, and more and more boys turned up for class with nothing to read. Some were too hungry to stay focused on schoolwork as the long hours stretched out between mish-mash breakfasts and Ben Johnson day dinners[10], no longer confined to the day before pay day.

Inevitably, reaching out to students with material needs brought evidence of even more challenging circumstances than lack of money. Their confessions about the scarcity at home soon yielded other reluctant

---

[10] Jamaican name for the day before payday when money is scarce and meals are skimpy.

revelations—stories of confusion and emotional turmoil way beyond what young boys should be grappling with. A drunken father habitually beat one boy's mother and younger siblings. A third-former's father went missing in Brooklyn just when the boy's older brother was due to join him and become a second source of remittances back home. Their solemn eyes fixed on their shoes, little boys told of mothers in the US who had given up the struggle of being employed as illegal aliens, falling along the wayside into drugs and hustling. Grandmothers buckled under the weight of responsibility for sons and daughters left behind and turning to waywardness.

A boy with a flawless record of behaviour stole books from the library, only to confess that he did it because his dream was to make the SCQ team. He was tired of his father harassing him to stop staying at school late for practice so he could come home and help with the other children. His khaki pants were so short, I could see his calves between his socks and the hems that had been repeatedly let down, leaving the marks of too much ironing. Someone in lower sixth missed his exam because he had to go with his 17-year-old high school girlfriend to beg her grandmother to take her in. She was four months pregnant, and her mother had put her out of the house.

It crossed my mind that some boys would become convinced of the uselessness of education in the face of their struggles for survival outside the walls of the school. But there was too much evidence to the contrary for me to dwell on such a thought. Of course there were unmotivated students and those who turned wayward, proving the self-fulfilling prophecies about the inevitable destiny of inner-city students. But these were never the majority. Despite the challenges, most boys packed their book bags, donned their sun-bleached uniforms, and made their way to claim their space at Clovelly Park, the place where they could pick up a key that would eventually lead to a different door from the one back in their struggling communities.

And when they got there, they spent the day with classmates, friends, and teachers who paid no attention to where they came from. This was Clovelly Park—the leveller. Boys from downtown, uptown, and every other location in the city and its outskirts perceived the school as their home and took from it all that they needed. Among the flying purple-and-white ties that moved in both directions along North Street and South Camp Road, the boys kept their minds fixed on the messages implanted inside them about what it meant to wear the striped tie. In the majority, they knew who they were and what their business at school was.

So who were we as their teachers to be less committed to doing our best to support them? Despite the ever-increasing needs they presented, and in the face of overwhelming social change, we had no choice but to turn our attention away from the outside forces and give them all we had. We knew just how miraculous it was for some of them to even be at school. Although I felt out of my depth from time to time as I struggled to be a source of support, I had no choice but to bolster my commitment to making my classes and my extracurricular activities as effective as they could be. Still, I couldn't deny that on some days, my certainty about how much I could do wavered.

"Fire Burns Wood but Tempers Steel"

It started as an out-of-place flicker dotting the Kingston night sky on an otherwise unspectacular night in May 1977. Little by little, it ballooned into a menacing ball of orange that announced something unquestionably bad would unfold before morning's light. As the word spread that the location was near to the South Camp Road end of North Street, throngs of KC supporters made their way down to confront the monster. But by the time they got there, it had already struck the main buildings and devoured Hardie House. Hastily plucked from all over Kingston, teachers, old boys, grown men, and little boys stood in the schoolyard, hands behind their backs, hands at their jaws, and hands waving in protest at the destruction before them. Some could not contain their tears; others walked around in circles, kicking away mounds of rubble and wondering.

The bright orange burned itself out and the crackling subsided, leaving the embers to smoulder through the night. The sun rose on devastation. Headmaster McNab gathered his troops to survey the desolate scene. Students trickled in, shaking their heads at the mass of smoking debris that stood in the place of their sanctuary. Final exams were a mere few weeks away, and classes had to go on. Emboldened by Dr McNab's rallying maxim, "Fire burns wood but tempers steel", the entire KC family—school board, staff, students, old boys, parents, and supporters—huddled in groups to hammer out coping strategies. We came up for air only when we had established concrete plans and knew what our tasks would be.

Their purple-and-white ties fluttering in the wind, students of all sizes took to the streets of Kingston, relieved of their classroom schedules to channel their energies into the task of drumming up support for their school. This time, it was not for a sporting team or a march to the JBC studios. It was a horde of "Fortis" believers, heartbroken but resolute, bearing thousands of empty metal cans hurriedly labelled in purple and white, with the headmaster's reminder in bold print. In return for whatever donations they could afford, people from uptown, downtown, and all over town had themselves tagged with purple-and-white emblems.

The tag drive brought not only much-needed funds but new levels of awareness all across the island: KC was in trouble and needed help. In the months that followed, we battled the disarray on our home ground as frustration and dislocation took their toll on hundreds of students deprived of the oasis that the school premises had been. At times, our hearts faltered, but one encourager-in-chief after another rose up to rally the "Fortis" spirit. While administrators, old boys, parents, ministry officials, and volunteers fixed their attention on recovery plans and activities, teachers and students put their heads down and limped through the weeks of preparation for imminent external exams.

Remarkably, most boys kept the focus on their tasks, made their way to school every day, and roamed their favourite haunts as if the outside world couldn't touch them. Under the lignum vitae tree outside the rubble of Hardie House, the younger ones still gathered during breaks and after school, playing harmless pranks, chasing crumpled orange juice boxes made into box footballs, filling the smoky air with their laughter, and hanging on to every minute of the childhood that seemed to insulate them, at least for a while, against the realities around us.

Not far away, members of the cadet corps marched to the rhythm of a faithful old drum, their boots gleaming from Nugget shoe polish and numerous swift strokes of an old wooden shoe brush, their khaki seams sharp enough to cut a careless finger, their eyes averted from every distraction. It was cadet inspection day.

Across the campus, in the chapel, thirty boys raised their voices, eyes fixed on the waving hands of the choirmaster leading regular Thursday afternoon practice in preparation for Sunday service in a neighbouring community church.

It was past the season for boys championships, but another one would come in a few months, and already old boys were huddling with groups of sprinters, quarter-milers, long jumpers, high jumpers, discus throwers, and hurdlers, all intent on making their mark at the national stadium when the time came. Elsewhere, in the usual spaces and in new makeshift ones, strong, agile figures leaped into the air, jostling and falling as they hustled after basketballs, footballs, and cricket balls, their sweat gleaming in the afternoon sun.

The fire had not dimmed the light.

In June, we laid out all the chairs we could find in the quiet areas free from the smoky remnants. Week after week, the senior boys filed in, their faces wearing excitement, anticipation, and anxiety as they sat down to the solemn task of writing their futures onto lines and lines of foolscap paper. The chief invigilators called the start, and all of us patrolled the rows and rows of desks, handing out papers, clarifying instructions, and raising silent prayers that the spirits of our beleaguered charges would prevail against the forces that threatened to distract them from their purpose.

The summer vacation was devoted to massive clean-up and restoration. We started the new academic year in relative stability despite inadequate accommodation. The exam results that greeted us at the end of the summer brought balm to the wounds left by the fire. Some of us had feared that the dislocation that prevailed before the exams had given the boys a perfect excuse to underperform, but once again, most proved their determination and resilience. While some fifth-formers achieved middling results, the majority obtained more passes in more subjects than the national average. Among sixth-formers, there were some outstanding results that led to scholarships to the University of the West Indies, and, for the first time, countries like Hungary and the USSR. The spirit of numerous sporting teams had not flagged in the aftermath of the fire, and they recorded the usual achievements that placed them at or pretty close to the top of the schoolboy rankings.

Following the education ministry's new policy of experimenting with double-shift schools, the board took the opportunity of the rebuilding to implement the long-awaited strategy of merging the extension school with the day operations. This brought our numbers to over 2,400 students, with 120 teachers led by one headmaster (now called a principal) and two deputies (now vice principals). The physical facilities creaked, and the human resources groaned under the weight of fitting two full rounds of administration and learning into the hours between sunrise and sunset.

Wearing white epaulets added to their uniforms, morning-shift students turned up bleary-eyed before the sun was fully awake. Their class hours reduced, they had to hustle out of severely limited classroom space in time to accommodate their afternoon-shift counterparts. Distinguished by their purple epaulets, afternoon students stumbled into school at the unlikely hour between noon and one o'clock. Some parents worried about heading out to work in the mornings, leaving their sons to face the spectre of unsupervised time. Everyone remembered what the devil could do with their idle hands, not to speak of their wandering minds. Others agonised about the whereabouts and activities of boys who finished school by one o'clock and had to vacate the premises to make way for the second shift. Like airport workers, teaching staff policed arrivals and departures and monitored holding areas, eventually turning up weary and distracted to teach our assigned classes.

For the SCQ family, the annual weeks of respite for basking in our previous performance and planning for the future had been quickly hijacked by the fire and its aftermath. New priorities occupied all of us. Many of our loyal supporters and the main contenders for the team had moved into positions of leadership that the school sorely needed. The school's new head boy and some of his prefects were central to our preparations. But they also faced unprecedented challenges trying to provide leadership in a two-shift school with additional classes relocated to the Melbourne campus as a result of the fire. The changes threatened to curtail extracurricular activities and opportunities for interaction with younger students.

Nonetheless, our determination and commitment to SCQ prevailed, and soon we re-established our routines. Although we all recognised the advantages of having a winning team entirely intact to defend the trophy, new aspirants emerged, and the old-timers redoubled their strategies to challenge for places. Ultimately, Vasciannie, Collie, Bailey, Haynes, and Rodney all retained their spots. We sped through the early rounds, living up to our reputation as triple winners. Soon it was time for the quarter-finals, and we set out on the path to the studio, committed and confident of our readiness.

The boys of Munro College marched into Kingston from Potsdam, St Elizabeth, where they had honed their skills and polished their weapons for the battle against "Fortis". The team put up a valiant fight, but Munro was not to be outdone. The remaining schools breathed; the defending champions KC would not be contenders in the final rounds. Our friendly neighbours, Wolmer's Boys, eventually stepped into the void and took home the trophy to nearby Marescaux Road.

We held no post-mortems, and we put off plans for the next season. The year had been an exhausting one, what with the emotionally draining fire and the long period of rebuilding our school and our spirits. The loss had not been limited to buildings and furniture. Prized records of the past had gone up in the flames. Photographs, mementoes, and cherished books that had been strewn across the long tables of the staffroom were gone. And the national treasure that was Hardie House was no more. The breeze coming up from the waterfront, with its whiff of the sea salt, would no longer rustle the pages of exercise books or send us chasing loose papers carelessly left on the cluttered tables. No more would little rascals come peeping through its elegant floor-to-ceiling windows to see what their missing teachers were up to. In place of Hardie House, huge mounds of rubble had settled into the landscape.

This time, no one recorded the details of our SCQ matches in the school magazine.

Relentlessly, social disruption and economic hardship continued to wreak havoc in the wider society, fanning the social and political fires stoked by the government's battles with the international monetary fund (IMF), which originated from loan agreements between Mr. Manley's government and the fund, leading to conditionalities that dictated certain austerity policies. All over the city, graffiti artists daubed walls and fences with headlines that reinforced or contradicted the news of the day. From one side to the other, rebel artists posted slogans attributing blame for the desperate conditions. Some appropriated the name of the IMF, now embroiled in the country's affairs, declaring as its new meaning "Is Manley Fault". The JLP detractors produced their own version of current affairs, linking the name of the leader of the opposition with America's Central Intelligence Agency (CIA), now accused of leading US efforts to destabilise the country. The unholy coinage CIAGA (after CIA and Mr Seaga) took its place everywhere, right next to the IMF graffiti.

Despite protestations and blame sharing on both sides, the political warfare prospered under the patronage of both parties, locked in a protracted battle for the support that would be essential whenever the next election arrived. Newspaper reports of lives lost to violence became the order of the day, culminating in widespread outrage against incidents in which merciless killings reached a new high, including women, children, old people, and babies. Lawlessness manifested itself in horrendous gang warfare, state of emergency raids, imprisonment of politicians, massacres, and fires. Despite the wreckage and the remnants of our own inferno, the school had no choice but to be a place of refuge.

The Blue Room

It was not until the weeks before the summer break that I felt the full impact of what the past year had been. The frenzy of reorganising and keeping the school afloat had suppressed the emotional impact of the fire and its aftermath, robbing all of us of the time to grieve. Escalating social turmoil and the impact of the new poverty brought disenchantment and evidence of new needs among students. Career guidance and involvement with boys needing financial support took a distinct turn in the direction of generalised counselling. I began to wonder at the futility of trying to equip some of our boys to pass exams when they were suffering from so many other deprivations and the society was infected with so many maladies.

By now, teaching had become my first passion, followed closely by coaching the SCQ team; they were complementary activities that strengthened me inside and outside the classroom. Every day, I saw the evidence of how hard most boys tried to fight against the forces that threatened to disrupt their schooling. One would have expected that with the social conditions and resource constraints we faced, we would have encountered rampant indiscipline, absenteeism, high dropout rates, and substandard results.

But this was not the case. There were undeniable danger signs. The school board and the principal repeatedly voiced their concerns about the size of the school and the numerous constraints. But for the most part, the boys attended school regularly. They abided by the rules and made the best of their situation. With that evidence of their commitment and effort, it was impossible for us to abandon hope. For me, it would have been a betrayal, but I knew that more was needed than even the best teaching that we could give.

I began to search for information about what guidance counsellors did and how they were trained. It had occurred to me that I should look in that direction to add another dimension to my role as a teacher. The Ministry of Education's foray into guidance services had occurred some two decades before, but the early focus was on joint initiatives that involved the education and health ministries. These were aimed at addressing the related problems of teenage pregnancies and absence of effective sex education.

During the 1960s, formal training of guidance counsellors had begun, and by the late seventies, programmes were well established, with courses offered through the ministry, at teacher training colleges, and at the UWI. By the time the conditions around me had begun to perk my interest in the field, the ministry, through its established guidance unit, had committed itself to the placement of at least one guidance counsellor in every secondary school. Various strategies were being used to achieve this goal, but it would be a long time before it would be realised. The idea was simmering in the back of my mind.

At the same time, there had been signs of unravelling close to home—signs Mr Coke and I had both tried to ignore by immersing ourselves in our respective jobs. In a sense, the threads of our relationship had emerged out of our common passion for KC. Our involvement in the school had stitched them into a neatly embroidered tapestry that comforted us like a warm old blanket and protected us from the early storms in our marriage. Our individual shortcomings and the defects in the relationship had been showing themselves in small fractures, like the lines across a cracked but not yet broken dinner plate. But we had averted our eyes. Nonetheless, a day came when sudden and unexpected tests were thrust upon us from the wider family circle, and we could no longer ignore the signs. We opted to try separate paths.

Two weeks into the summer holiday, I had no choice but to face the stark emptiness I lived in—no school, no papers to mark, no lessons to plan, no quiz practice, and no roomful of friends bursting into round after round of laughter at a string of my husband's endless jokes. I stood at a crossing where not two but three roads converged, each one threatening to keep me in a world I feared I could no longer manage.

Looking down the closest one, I saw the path back to my home, where I could resume the battles from which I'd hurriedly walked away. Another could take me to my sister's house, where I was the odd one with an empty space at my side. On the third path, I could remain where I'd spent the last few weeks—in the cheap, dark apartment for which my paltry teaching salary could pay. My companions were giant brown-skinned cockroaches that skated across the kitchen sink and crawled up from the cracked bathtub whenever I turned on a light.

Long days without school stretched out before me, and the storm clouds seemed set to hang over for a long time. I hurled unread novels across the room, only to turn around and stare unseeing at the images gyrating across the television screen. Morning after morning, I dragged myself from the sleepless bed, made myself tasteless coffee, and sat in the sun on the tiny back porch, scrolling through the words I'd scrawled across miles of yellow notepad pages, hammering out arguments for and against each of the roads before me.

Then, unexpected as the sun breaking through dark, swollen clouds, a new face paused in mid-air just above mine, bringing the promise of something so gentle, so comforting, so unexpected that I could not help reaching up to it. Turning away from all that I knew to be safe, I took refuge, tossing and turning in the lovely radiance his face brought into the bleak, roach-infested square where I was trying to live.

I unboxed my long-forgotten vinyl LPs, sharing the soundtrack of my youthful years, sprinkling small doses of delight across a landscape of disappointment. Evening after evening, I detached myself from my consolation and watched him step out into the darkness, knowing I should never let him come back into the disarray that was my life. Now and then, the twilight and the music stemmed our restraint, and we made promises spawned by the moment. But we knew very well that the realities beyond my doorstep would make it impossible to keep them.

On a half-hearted August morning, as I pored over the crossword puzzle, a five-by-seven advertisement leaped up from page 17 of *The Daily Gleaner*:

> The British Council invites applications from teachers for fellowships to study for the Diploma in Guidance and Counselling at the Institute of Education, University of Reading, Berkshire, UK.

A feverish few days later, I sank into my broken-down green Fiat after a brisk walk from the Ministry of Education and just breathed. Twenty minutes before the deadline, I'd handed the clerk a manila envelope stuffed with forms, certificates, letters of recommendation, and school documents to support my application for the fellowship that could at least remove me from the nest of cockroaches.

Over the next few weeks, I absorbed the news that I had been selected for a fellowship, and I took the steps needed to embark on that fourth and least familiar road of all the roads before me. The thought of what I was really doing scampered in and out of my mind, but I never allowed it to settle. I was too caught up in the whirlwind of interviews, medical exams, and paperwork to pay attention. And the busyness kept me from feeling anything—not the responsibility of making a unilateral decision that could put the last nail in the coffin of my marriage, nor the failure to discuss my situation with any friend or family member. I felt no uncertainty about the path I was taking.

All I could think was *What a godsend*—a gift that would allow me to escape from everything and get in touch with the part of me that was nowhere to be found. Beyond everything, it was the unexpected opening that could take me where I could obtain at least some of the expertise I needed to tackle the new problems that were forcing so many students to seek help. It was not until a full month later that the enormity of what I had begun really hit me, as my sister manoeuvred her lime-green Datsun out of the stunning maze of Heathrow Airport and headed for the motorway.

"You have to get closed-up shoes. Your toes will freeze in a few weeks from now," Marjorie said, her eyes swiftly sizing up the strappy sandals I had worn from Jamaica.

"I know," I answered, newly terrified at how unprepared I was. "I have to get warm clothes too."

The next morning, we went shopping, the brisk September breeze slapping me on all sides of my face. In the afternoon, I breathed in the aroma of freshly cut grass as my new brown loafers sank into the crunchy blades leading to the Office of Graduate Students' Accommodation, Reading University. *This grass has no smell and no sunshine gleaming between its blades. It's nothing like the carpet that rustled in the wind outside my window in Mary Seacole Hall.*

A woman's voice broke into my reverie. "I'm sorry, we didn't get your letter confirming that you'd be taking up accommodation on campus. All the graduate housing has been allocated."

"But the documents I received didn't say anything about a confirmation letter. I checked the box on the form. This is my first time here; how will I find—" My lips trembled as I spoke. *Why are you arguing? This is it; this is a perfect excuse to get a quick flight home!*

The woman's voice droned on. "You don't have to worry. We can recommend off-campus places. There are people who are happy to have our students as lodgers. I have a list right here."

I toyed with refusing the list and heading for a travel agent.

As we got into the car and headed toward Wokingham Road, I could tell my sister was again fearful that I had just upped and left Jamaica without adequate planning. It was partly true, but I couldn't bear to see it on her face just then. I fixed my eyes on the road signs, dying to spot the ones the accommodations officer had scribbled on a page torn from her notepad. It was one thing to put myself in this pickle; putting my sister in the middle of it was not to my liking. The silence hung between us as we waited for a clue we were on the right path.

"Look! Look!" I shouted. "That sign says Wokingham Road." Up past the cemetery and a strip of small shops with flats perched above them, we travelled about a mile. The trees had already lost most of their leaves, a mere scattering of brownish-gold survivors visible here and there. Although Marjorie said the weather was good for September, I was already chilly, my face longing for a suggestion that the sun behind the ominous grey clouds would eventually show itself.

A metal sign that read *84 Wokingham Road* dangled under the mailbox outside a redbrick house trimmed in eggshell white. After examining every detail of the evidence that I was indeed a student with a stipend to cover accommodation, the landlady with the pale, pleated face laid out the arrangements curtly, her inquisitive eyes moving carefully from my sister's face to mine. She was visibly relieved that our Jamaican accent and our brown skin were offset by the fact that I had listed under "Contact Persons" not only the university's accommodations officer, but a sister who'd lived in London for more than fifteen years and named Guy's Hospital as her full-time employer for almost as long. The woman's satisfaction was obvious as she briskly counted the crisp pound notes I handed her, and she shoved them in the pocket of her apron. She promptly fished a key from the other pocket and pointed us up rickety stairs.

"Welcome to life in your first attic," Marjorie said with a mischievous smile as soon as we were out of the landlady's earshot. Drawing me in for a hug as clumsy as the one at Heathrow, she whispered a more comforting message. "But it's near to the campus and it's small enough, so the little one-burner heater will keep you warm. Those are the two most important things. Oh, and once November comes, you have to make sure you always have coins to feed the meter, or you will definitely freeze." I focused on the wall, inspecting the unfamiliar coin-consuming contraption that would become central to my survival in the months ahead.

With that, my sister left me to settle in. I was smothered by my growing apprehension and the unbroken blueness of the four walls that would be home for the next nine months. I walked from one corner to the other, peering through the thick double-glazed windows Marjorie had said were "good for keeping the heat in the room". The furniture was as old as it was scant—double bed with headboard affixed to the wall by some invisible contraption, well-worn dressing table with a detached mirror hanging from a rusty hook, narrow clothes closet with four wire hangers, two chairs, and a tiny eating table that would double as my desk.

Everything smelled and felt like someone had pressed down on the nozzle of a spray can of enamel and just looked away. *How did I come to be alone in this musty old place, my life upended, my marriage adjourned, my thinking scrambled, and no boys to teach or coach? How can this be me, standing in this off-blue dankness, with nowhere to get a shower except a shared bathroom two flights down?*

Not ready to face the unknown condition of a bath shared by three tenants I hadn't yet met, I drew on my experience of months of water lock-offs every year at home and made the best of a metal pail and sink in a little enclosure off to the side. Rid of my travelling clothes and relatively clean, I stuck the cup-size immersion heater into a cracked mug, sipped the comfort of warm milk, and soon succumbed to my first dose of jet lag, telling myself I would sleep for a couple of hours and then investigate the bath.

I woke to the sound of rain pelting the windows, startled that for the first time in months, I'd slept through the night, wrapped in a stranger's scratchy blue blanket, my head on a pillow that was familiar only because it smelled of the camphor balls my sister had sprinkled in the closet with her pillowcases.

The disarray I'd left at home cast lengthy shadows over my early days and nights in the blue room. But there was no time to dwell on all that had misplaced me within these walls. A thousand more forms sat waiting for me to fill them out—to prove once again that I was really me and I had really been selected for the programme. There were drugstores, post offices, and grocery shops to look for in the Wokingham Road area, classes to register for, campus locations to discover, strangers to become acquainted with—dozens of battles to wage. *Now that I've used up all my will and energy to get here, how will I get through all this?*

Separation and Discovery

We were coming to the end of the orientation meeting. The eyes of our lead lecturer/facilitator roamed over the room and settled, unwelcomed, on my face, seeming to pin his words on me.

"We rely heavily on group sessions that emphasise self-disclosure. Just as you will expect your students to share, we expect you to share while you are here."

Of course, I can just see it—me baring my soul to twenty-two strangers!

Half an hour later, I stood before the chief form-checker in the student records office, waiting to be released so I could grab a yogurt-and-muesli lunch before my first individual session across from the threatening laser eyes of the man who'd led us through orientation.

"You are missing one form here, ma'am."

"What is it?" I asked, unsure he was speaking to me.

"Results of your English test for foreign students."

I looked around at the other persons waiting, sure now that he couldn't be speaking to me. *So why are his eyes fixed on my face?* "Excuse me?"

"Here, this one," he said, showing me a blank copy of the form that he was demanding.

Scanning the contents with little to no interest, I braced my shoulders and found my most patient tone. "You don't understand. I am a native speaker of English."

"Are you a foreign student?" His tone made it clear there was only one answer and that would take care of everything else.

"Yes, but I am from Jamaica. We are a Commonwealth country. English is our official language. I don't want to take up your time, but maybe you should look at the other papers you have for me."

"I've looked; this one is missing." This was not a customer service representative who was trained to veer from his prepared script.

Losing confidence in his ability to grasp what I was trying to explain, I quickly asked, "Can you show me to someone else who checks credentials?"

He disappeared through a door into a hole where I could see nothing, and I began to fear no one would show up to speak to me. In a few minutes I would be late for my session, but I had to sort this out. I knew one thing for sure: I would not be taking an English test.

"What seems to be the problem, miss?" An older woman had emerged from the hole, but the more she spoke, the more it seemed she would be incapable of believing I knew what I was talking about. She was pretty much going over the same ground her predecessor had covered.

"Didn't your colleague brief you?" My irritation was growing, but I knew it wouldn't help, so I called upon my "whisper technique" from my first year with my boys in 4A. "Look, someone has made a mistake. He is insisting that I should have results from some English test I know I cannot be required to take. English is my first language, and not to put too fine a point on it, I teach English, including A-level literature. You know—your own Cambridge University syllabus and exams? And, by the way, I have a bachelor's degree in English."

"We will have to look into it. Can you wait?"

"I have a class in twenty minutes and it's way across the campus. I have to go, but I will be back to sort this out."

I landed at my lecturer/facilitator's door, hoping he would not detect my annoyance or my hunger. Instead of my session turning into a dreaded investigation into my emotional state and readiness for group therapy, we focused on solving the immediate problem—me tapping my loafers on the floor, him on the phone with Student Admissions.

"We will catch up on the pre-group session tomorrow," he finally said to me. "Do some more reading until then. And try not to make these small hurdles interfere with what you are really here for."

Small hurdle? Man, do you know what it is like to have people question an essential part of who you are? Tolerance, Frances, tolerance.

It was the beginning of a stormy relationship with this man who, in addition to all his roles, was supposed to be my personal tutor but fancied himself as my therapist. *Good luck with this aspect of the year ahead.*

The days contracted into a few hours of curtailed daylight, and the nights stretched from four o'clock one day to eight o'clock the next. I suffered from never seeing the kind of real sunshine to which I was accustomed. This sunshine was a liar, promising warmth and bringing only the same wearying dampness to the grass and the mailbox and the people. My shoulders ached under the weight of my brown ankle-length coat as I walked the frigid miles from the campus to the blue room.

Every evening, I peeled off the weight of the coat and the day, wondering how I would get through eight more months of being "open" about who I was and what had brought me here. All the lecturers had succeeded in convincing us that we could not counsel if we were unable to freely engage in the counselling encounter ourselves. Every day, they preached the same gospel: "Group process is integral to the learning experience and there can be no meaningful group process without each student's openness and willingness to self-disclose."

The talkative Americans were a godsend. They seemed born to self-disclose, ever ready to grab time from the rest of us who hadn't been brought up on talking about ourselves. Maria from Malaysia was not far behind them, her dark eyes and white teeth flashing as she narrated stories of her turbulent childhood.

That left Anand from Ahmedabad and Kamau from Arusha, who shared information about themselves just a fraction more than I shared about me. Over morning coffee and lunch, we three hung out together, comparing notes and planning survival strategies as we learned to imitate the menu of students who feasted most days on mounds of cheap potato "crisps" drenched in the cafeteria's free ketchup. It was the best way to stretch the British Council stipend that seemed so generous on paper. But I was always transporting bags of leftovers from my visits to my sister. I stocked up on muesli and yogurt in the blue room, and on the way there, a Chinese restaurant and a fish-and-chips shop guaranteed that from time to time I could make up for the drab lunchtime fare.

As the weeks turned into months, the classroom interactions became easier and my network spread beyond Anand and Kamau. I soaked up the theories and practices of guidance and counselling. I read everything I could get my hands on, furiously underlining words and inserting notes among the sentences that captured my experiences at home. When the assignments provided options, I doggedly neglected the reading matter from the Tavistock Institute, refusing to pay too much attention to the reams of information about the self, the group, and the therapeutic process. I was not looking for therapy; I wanted help for the students I had left at home. I wanted skills and techniques to help me work with them. I was in no hurry to talk about the turmoil safely buried inside me—especially not with people who I feared would judge everything about me, based on where I came from and how different I was from them.

And there was never any question that I was different. Why else did random acquaintances keep marvelling at my "impeccable English"? And why did my classmates and lecturers keep asking question after ridiculous question: What kinds of buildings do you have there? How do they withstand hurricanes? What are some of the jobs people do? Where had I studied to be a teacher? They could never get enough of my persistent attempts to increase their limited information and broaden their views about what Jamaica was like. Yes, some had heard of Negril, Harry Belafonte, and Bob Marley, along with a smattering of political leaders, but their curiosity knew no bounds when it came to everyday characteristics of Jamaican life. I could see how hard it was for them to grapple with the notion that my country was not just sand, sea, and music, that it had a city like Kingston and had produced outstanding individuals across the worlds of sports, industry, politics, and academics. How lucky I was that the SCQ training had filled my head with facts and figures that rolled off my tongue without effort. My patience wore thin at their incredulous faces and their unconvinced eyes.

And yes, I cringed as I groped for sociological and historical explanations that could smother my embarrassment when they probed for answers about crime, violence, and political discord.

Once a month I hopped on the train from Reading to Clapham Junction, where I caught the bus to Crystal Palace and then walked the mile to my sister's house to spend the weekend. This kind of walking was new to me, but in Reading, I had already discovered the bliss of long walks when the temperature allowed. As I walked, I ruminated about everything under the sun, even mentally dismantling the unfinished business I had abandoned at home.

Schoolboys prancing along the streets of Reading and London in their cricket caps, grey trousers, and blue blazers stirred my longing for the laughter of my own boys along the sixth-form corridor. I longed for the light of discovery in the eyes of the boys behind the columns, those leaning in distraction against the window and suddenly drawn back into the lesson by a word or incident that struck a chord. My days were bland without the pranks and jokes of my fourth- and fifth-formers, without the outbursts of excitement when one team or another hoisted a trophy at assembly, without the light echo of the trebles in the choir, leading us at worship in the chapel.

And what of the drawn, frightened faces of boys who were in trouble at home or at school? Even those would have brought life to the damp mornings at the stop where I trembled for the bus that would take me to my field assignment at a school near Windsor Castle.

The long train rides between Reading and London brought me the satisfaction of a rescued fish thrown back into the ocean. I swallowed up the sights and the sounds and the volumes of psychology each lecturer prescribed, piecing together the insights they offered into my own woes and the troubles of my boys back in Kingston. Against the backdrop of the shrilling whistle, the repetitive rattle, the unbroken clackety-clack, and the occasional whoosh of this new way of traveling that fit me like a well-tailored suit, thoughts of the past and the future meandered through my mind. For long hours without any chance of escaping from myself, I watched the cities and towns between Reading Station and London Paddington whizz by.

In the beginning, I searched inside every train for something to connect with. I scanned the maps outlining stations and environs I knew I would never see. I studied the faces of strangers for clues about what movie characters they could be and what lives they lived when they left the train. They stared back, unseeing, their eyes addressing nothing inside me that mattered. I feasted on scraps of poems dangling between the window frames, silently reciting the familiar lines, committing the unfamiliar to memory, and jotting down random couplets that were on the way to becoming my growing collection of *Blue Room Poems*. Sometimes I shut my eyes tight, relishing the black space in which the scenes of my life replayed themselves from the safety of this distance that skewed memory and dulled edgy emotions.

I soon varied my journeys, making my way straight to the heart of London and riding the Tube all over the entertainment district. Thankfully, the Underground was clean and well-lit—a far cry from the New York subway, whose dark stations and ominous faces always brought me visions of bloody knives and the chilling eyes of serial killers. In London, I hurried from one movie to another or from one play to another, filling entire days with the excitement and stimulation of old and new stories brought to life on stage and on screen.

Images of the places we had studied for SCQ came flooding back as I stepped into the entranceways of the Old Vic and the Globe, hopped in and out of the Tube, and followed narrow criss-crossed streets from Piccadilly Circus to Soho. *How thrilled the boys would be to see this world that they know so well in their minds' eyes!* At least once per outing, the absolute allure of a new dream hit me. *I could lose myself in this place. I could be entirely anonymous, rid of all the chaos left at home. I could throw away the packet of thin blue airletters waiting in the blue room for me to scrawl hopeful words and drop them in the mailbox at the corner of Wokingham Road.*

The seminar room spawned new insights, exciting me with the prospect of going home to make a huge difference at school. We would no longer be amateurs at career guidance, and I would no longer feel totally ill-equipped when faced with the daunting realities with which so many students grappled.

The transition to a state of mind from which I could speak out in group sessions about my own confusion took more out of me than any of the classes in evaluation, measurement, psychological testing, or theories of guidance. But it did come, and I began to surprise myself with snippets of disclosure about the circumstances that had led to my presence at Reading. It was not a steady journey. Every now and again, I stepped on one of the many minefields that lurked on the path to "getting in touch with our experiences and our feelings". Every now and again, I reminded myself why I was not given to sharing my innermost thoughts or feelings with people I didn't know.

My instinct had always been to withdraw to quiet places to reflect on what was going on inside me. *But has anyone ever encouraged me to do it? Haven't some people always eyed my quietness with suspicion or walked away from what they called my "moodiness"?* I had never known of an acceptable or structured way to engage in such reflection.

Only one type of experience from my youth came to mind, one that had actually encouraged some kind of introspection. Every year since entering fourth form at Alpha, we had spent three or four days "on retreat". We sometimes complained bitterly about those days of mandated silence as we walked in twos or threes from stirring sermons at Mass to spaces earmarked for quiet time. Of course, we longed for our normal teenage chats, and we sometimes stole a minute or two for hushed exchanges before hustling back to our classrooms for inspirational talks as we huddled around tables littered with books and pamphlets about the "Catholic way".

By the time we had reached to sixth form, we would sometimes whisper that retreat days were not all bad. In fact, as I'd cleared my apartment and packed to come to Reading, several holy pictures and retreat schedules had fallen from an old box of mementoes. A few faded notes my closest friends had pressed into my hand in exchange for mine had brought it all back. Time and life had robbed me of a way to replicate my high school retreats, but they had not stolen my gifts of quietness and a propensity to reflect on what was going on inside me.

Group process at Reading was no retreat, but I was good at the silence that sometimes prevailed. The introspection it encouraged was very different from just withdrawing or feeding my natural tendency to isolate myself from too much "noise". I was now getting the tools and the feedback (resolutely rejected in the beginning) to experience it in the right way. Self-disclosure and feedback often brought hidden and overt storms whose winds resonated into the chilly darkness of the blue room, bringing heavy silences or rage as often as they brought tears. Then, in the dim light of the winter morning, a layer of baggage would shift ever so slightly from my shoulders. The eyes that stared back as I brushed my teeth more furiously than ever would lose some of their glaze. A few months of this type of experience was admittedly too short, but it was a start.

And it was enough to set me thinking about how I would ensure that my boys did not have to wait as long as I had waited to experience it.

I had watched many of my more mature students grow emotionally and psychologically during class discussions that encouraged them to share their experiences and express how they felt about characters and stories we explored. The friendships developed in SCQ and the emotional roller coaster of challenging competitions provided many opportunities for helping students claim and manage their emotions. But these were limited contexts. *How will the boys react to counselling experiences designed to help them get in touch with their feelings about themselves, their lives, and their relationships? How will I help them to walk the path of self-awareness that they need to help them understand who they are and how they can be better, not just as students but as young men?* The books on counselling theory tumbled from my bedside, making way for those that focused on promoting self-awareness and emotional maturity among adolescent boys.

Meanwhile, back in our seminar room, our evolution as a group had begun to demolish some of the barriers evident in our early sessions. We talked more freely of "next steps" that were soon close at hand. But the price of openness was conflict; even discussions about the future could stir the remnants of misunderstanding and suspicion.

"I imagine you won't be at that school for too long after going back home, Frances." It was our indomitable lead lecturer/facilitator, predicting my future once again without any basis that I knew of.

As I swallowed hard to contain my impatience with him, a tall, hairy-faced teacher/guidance counsellor from a military school in Arkansas piped in. "I bet she won't even be back on the island."

"Yes, Mr Guidance Counsellor from Arkansas. You know all about me, right? So where exactly will I be?"

"You tell me," he replied, with an inescapable taunt in his voice.

"I guess you think because our countries aren't wealthy, we all want to be somewhere else. I wonder where."

The fly on the wall waited to see who would break the loud silence. It was a recurring theme of our sessions, and the Arkansas man's suggestion always infuriated me because of what I saw as his glib, self-satisfied belief that everybody wanted to go to America. Still, I had to agree with my lecturer/facilitator that I owed it to myself to consider whether "my usual strong response—bordering on overreaction" was an indication that the Arkansas man's unwelcome prediction had pushed my button.

It didn't help me to put the exchange behind me when my tutor himself started repeating the same announcement at least once a week. Very often, he explained, the university collaborated with the British Council to offer additional stipends each year to allow promising graduates of our programme to remain at

Reading for another year and complete their master's degrees.

I was seriously tempted to hang on to all the wonder and appeal of an extended stay between Reading and London. But neither one was home, and although I was intrigued by my new universe of academics, theatre, cinema, museums, historic sites, and ruminations during long train rides, I was daunted by this world with its vast open spaces. The damp and the sunlessness of this world numbed me. I longed for the light and the restricting borders of my own tiny world. It was a limited and limiting island from which one could easily step backwards and fall into the sea. But it was mine, and I thrived within its invisible fences that made me certain I was home.

Away from the immediate impact of the clatter and rage of political and social factions constantly poised to attack each other at home, I grabbed the chance to reflect in peace. At that distance, the wars at home seemed out of proportion. I was living in a completely different environment, one in which people did not seem to make politics so central to their everyday lives. Certainly, the people I met didn't seem to identify with their political parties to the same extent as so many in Jamaica did. From my vantage point as a casual observer, no one seemed to be a die-hard anything, and they didn't allow differences to wedge boulders between themselves and others of a different political stripe.

Faced with more and more questions about life in Jamaica, I moved from blind loyalty to defensiveness and being protective, pulling explanations from the stories lodged in my head and my heart about where we came from and who we were trying to become. I proffered answers from our history—not least the role of the "mother country" in shaping that history. I drew on achievements that were noteworthy in light of our fleeting foray into political independence, encouraged by a Britain anxious to dispose of territories that no longer brought her fortunes from King Sugar. I called out the miseducation that left generations of us unprepared for either effective political leadership or responsible citizenship.

But I could produce no defence for the recent actions of our politicians or their role in leading the country's apparent descent into lawlessness and violence. I was no economist or sociologist, but I wondered why it wasn't obvious to everyone at home that we had a right and a duty to change the course of a history that had never brought as much benefit to ordinary Jamaicans as it had brought to outsiders. Groping for my own insights into what I now saw as a much more complex maze of issues, I asked myself more questions than anyone else asked me. Why didn't more of us see both the logic and the urgency of policies and laws designed to redress history and help the country make its way in a changing world? Why shouldn't a country with our history, size, and resource limitations seek new alliances in a world whose superpowers didn't see our survival as their business? Most of all, I wondered why both parties couldn't seek common ground and forge a path to the future that would make life better for everyone. Surely both sides could see that we needed drastic change?

The government I'd left behind had made promises about change and progress. The opposition stoutly opposed all that the government said. Everyone else scrambled to line up for or against the policies articulated on one side or the other. While some policies looked outward to the country's international relations, many were designed to address issues that had long torn holes below the surface of a society that holiday brochures marketed as "happy, fun-loving, out-of-many-one people", offering the world our island in the sun. Some of the problems could only be solved if we changed how we viewed ourselves and how we related to each other.

And it was to this type of change that the government had directed some of its efforts. Mr Manley's rallying cry for self-reliance went to the heart of the national dependency syndrome, no doubt spawned by a history of slavery and reinforced by the system of patronage that characterised our modern politics. *Why doesn't everyone see this? Why do so many of us believe that our problems are insurmountable, that our solutions are in England or America? Why am I tempted to stay?*

My routines in Reading and London exposed me to only a few people from Jamaica, but I used my few opportunities to seek answers to some of my questions. Through her work and social activities, my sister had many Jamaican connections, but my visits on the weekend were too brief for me to interact with them to any significant degree. On the bus and on the train, I did have glimpses of my own people playing their little parts in the general landscape. Once we opened our mouths, we could not be mistaken for anyone else, no matter how many years some of us had spent in England or how hard some tried to ape the accents of the British. From the back of a bus or a few seats down the aisle of the Tube or a train, a sweet Jamaican sentence would arrest my attention, sometimes embellished by a proverb or two and even the colourful seasoning of a uniquely Jamaican "bad word". I could never resist turning sharply to put a face to the words, sometimes laughing to myself and attracting questioning stares from others around me.

Often, if we were close enough, this would lead to "You come from Jamaica, right?" Sometimes a conversation would follow, always laced with questions that I could not answer about "what going on at home" in exchange for their cagey answers to my probes about what it was really like living in London. Brixton felt like Kingston, and when my sister and I went there to perk up our taste buds with curry goat, jerk chicken, patties, or the closest thing we could find to real mangoes, the pervasive aura of Jamaica awakened my yearning for home. These glimpses into the lives of some Jamaicans who had made the move to England many years before, or during the more recent migration surges caused by crime and politics at home, did not equip me to make any judgements about their decisions to make lives outside of our country.

Brief conversations and observations did suggest that, although life in England provided Jamaicans with opportunities for work and overall improvement of their lives, it did not always lead to the feeling of being truly at home. Like me, many enjoyed the facilities and the opportunities that the mother country offered. But for most of them, the feeling of being at home was never there. For some of us, the loss of home created the need to paint bright pictures of what we had left behind. Together, we romanticised our recollections to overcome the fear that the Jamaica we knew and loved would be lost forever. For others, it was easier to forget the warmth of the sun on their faces, the rippling blue of the ocean, the rhythm of the music, and the laughter that could break out for no reason in Jamaica—anywhere, anytime.

Some lined their explanations of their decision to stay away from home with images of sacrifice and resignation. "What to do, my dear? Jamaica don't have anything to offer my children. I can't stand the cold and the distance in the eyes of the people who make me know with one look that I don't belong here. But the children will have a better life."

Others were convincing in their assertions about their lives. "This is a good place, man. You can get work and nobody not going shoot you or take away you things."

"I couldn't manage as a nurse in Jamaica. Up here, I am somebody and I get good benefits."

"Is a nice nice place; you should stay right here and make a better life."

"I work two jobs and my missis and the children have what they need. I miss Jamaica, yes, but things down there too hard."

Sometimes, barely masking that ever-present "but" that lurked behind the words, their assurances stirred conflicting feelings inside me. I understood what they said, and yet I couldn't bring myself to that place of resignation that would make me accept that they were right. I saw this conflict most in the poems I wrote in the blue room. My longing for home sometimes dragged me down into a dark space, where I was incapable of doing anything except filling page after page with images of the captivating land for which my very bones yearned.

I kept my longing to myself, the coward in me opting to partake in conversations in which transplanted Jamaicans painted the bleakest possible images of what was going on back home to justify their departure—and in my case, to yield to the temptation of lengthening my stay in Reading or London as much as possible. At such times, I could not put out of my mind the words of a woman on the bus who had asked me, "Why a nice lady like you going back down there to them wicked people with them crime and badness? You know how much Jamaican families up here would love a teacher like you to help out our children in school?" *You know how many people waiting down there for me to go home with some solutions to help out our children at KC?*

With all the longing, displacement, and confusion that confronted me in the blue room and in my journeys around London, the lengthy walks, the getaways offered by long train rides, and the grey hours gradually became the ideal prescription for escaping from myself and my troubles. They gave me the time and space to crystallise my maze of thoughts and feelings about what I had left behind at home and what I was discovering about Jamaicans living in England. Dreamy images sketched by Jamaican Londoners "hoping their way" through British living conspired with the fulfilment of my academic pursuits and my relative immersion in a different culture to fill up my senses.

Anonymity brought the freedom to experiment with new ways of being, and some of what I saw in my experimenting self was appealing. I relished the respite from the crassness and violence and confusion that pervaded the Jamaica I had stepped away from. A part of me wanted to stay in this bubble of being a foreigner who could walk blithely past the less attractive realities of London life without taking on its burden. It was not mine to carry. In Jamaica, I had no protection: everything that was wrong was a part of me and I a part of it. As a foreigner in England, I could leave whatever was wrong to those whose country it was and to Jamaicans who'd adopted it as theirs.

The noise of my arguments with myself played on for months, like a soundtrack to everything I did. But, in the end, I had to confront what was before me. This was not my world or my real life. I did not want to be an outsider in a country that might accept my qualifications for a job, but would always keep the rest of me on its fringes. My real life was on pause, waiting for me to press the "play" button. My school needed me there to add new dimensions to my role and justify the study leave I'd been granted.

The facilitator dangled his final invitation for three of us to extend our stays. The luxury of becoming an anonymous academic feeding on an unending diet of train rides, museums, libraries, movies, and plays was almost irresistible. But I could not afford it.

Once the decision was behind me, the pull to remain gave way to a new excitement about the prospect of going home, equipped to make a difference.

Something Bright and New

Not even the sight of my oversized suitcase lying next to the carousel with its zipper broken, my books and clothes disgorged all over the floor, could slow my heart rate. Braving the scowls of the customs officers, I negotiated my way through the narrow spaces, comforting my luggage and hugging its contents together. All the way along Norman Manley Highway, I smiled as if staring at an old photograph and reliving a time long gone: the coconut man with his ear-to-ear grin, the billboards with their peeling paint, and the nonchalant ocean lapping the shores along which fishermen lingered in the afternoon sun.

Just past the roundabout, I leaned to peer through the overgrowth into the famous circular supermarket of Harbour View, the stomping ground of my youth.

Windward Road was unchanged, its hungry urchins still stooping beside their sidewalk-vendor mothers, ever peddling five oranges, six dried-out heads of skellion, and six bunches of callaloo perishing in the dust and the sun. Mountain Terrace drew my eyes to its grey walls and white aluminium louvre windows. On the left, the stadium stood silent, longing for the shrieks and howls of boys' championships.

We swept past the building where I'd shared my brief home with cockroaches and my fleeting consolation. In my absence, he had moved on to possibilities that stood a chance. It was hard to believe that before escaping to Reading, I'd spent my last few weeks in that scruff, relieved only by the fleeting light he had shone.

In ten minutes, I stepped across a new threshold into the cave where my erstwhile husband had waited next to his music, writing his anxious entreaties and poring through the reams of confusion I'd penned in the blue room. This was the space he had prepared for us to work on mending what we had broken. The distance between Kingston and Reading had already prepared us for the slog that was ahead. Our perspectives on family and marriage had begun to grow up, and we had a better understanding of the work they required. His characteristic lightness and the roar of his laugh tempered my apprehension, and we smiled at small things again, setting aside those that had driven the wedges between us. Things we had never spoken about floated in and out of the room, surviving the transition from airmail paper to the real world in which we now stood.

In a few days, I could not escape the signs of an unfamiliar gravitas that had crept into his laughter and his words, and it gave me pause. I saw it too in the eyes of a close friend and my brother-in-law. I wondered what was not being said.

It wasn't long before it slipped out. Each of them had been pushed to the ground and made to stare into the muzzle of a crude gun waved across his face by a stripling or two, demanding wallet, chain, and wedding ring. Unknown to me, these encounters had become commonplace, often turning into the last straw to break the spirit of numerous Jamaicans who soon joined the trek to the US. My sister too had made up her mind. In a few weeks, the core of my support system was gone. Home was not quite the same.

The changes at KC were more numerous than I expected. Principal McNab had moved on after his outstanding restoration efforts following the fire, and ever-faithful Carlton Bruce had come over from Melbourne Park to take up the position of acting principal. The post-fire rebuilding process had been turned into an opportunity for improving the entire Clovelly Park campus. Refurbished classrooms and a spanking new staffroom greeted me on my first day back. A space had been identified for the new guidance counsellor. It took me a few breaths to realise this was me, but I quickly set about transforming the old, unused office area. The room was soon decked out with the relevant paraphernalia of posters, pictures, books, and inspirational sayings that would send the right messages about what would happen in the guidance and counselling (G & C) room.

Excitement and optimism fuelled me for the mammoth task of implementing all the setting-up procedures I had learned. From the first day I visited the tiny guidance unit at the Ministry of Education, I knew I would need to call on my natural tendency to squeeze and shove theories so they would fit into the realities of my environment. Policy guidelines and educational material were in short supply, and despite the enthusiasm of the limited staff—whose primary task was to conduct workshops—tangible support was limited for schools establishing the new initiatives. G & C orientation sessions replaced language and literature on my timetable for the September term.

I sped from one building to another, spreading the new vocabulary of student support, social skills, study skills, individual and group interventions, career education, and preparation for life and work. This was the groundwork that was supposed to bring students, teachers, and parents to my door, but I knew I would only succeed if everyone understood what the services would be and how they should work. If parents or students believed I was there to deal with boys in trouble or those getting bad grades, they would sidestep the pathway to my new little room, and I would be no more than another disciplinarian. This would be fatal to my plans. Painstakingly spelling out the details of what was ahead was the only way to manage expectations and pre-empt misunderstanding.

Some of the principles I espoused brought rigorous questioning and pockets of resistance. It was difficult to gain acceptance for the idea that students should not be "sent to me" in the way that teachers dispatched them to the office of the grade supervisor, vice principal, or principal—because they were in trouble. Some doubted the validity of my explanation that with only a few exceptions, I could not disclose certain types of information that students shared in counselling encounters. We had all been brought up on warnings against "washing dirty linen in public", and some parents saw people at school as the public.

It was plain to see that, apart from justifiable questions and behind the doubts and objections voiced by some administrators and teachers, there hovered a great fear that I would be harbouring complaints against them, taking the side of students, or mollycoddling boys instead of toughening them up to be men who could handle the realities outside of school. My reputation among students and my previous roles as teacher, grade supervisor, and SCQ coach presented both opportunities and challenges. I had learned long ago how to navigate the waters between these responsibilities. Now, I had to call upon all the theories I had absorbed about the dangers of role conflict, unclear expectations, and mixed messages about how the new services would fit into the structure of the school. We had been warned enough at Reading that guidance and counselling should work with students to help them understand why they were in trouble, but it could not replace disciplinary measures prescribed by school rules and policies.

Most of my colleagues were as animated as I was about the new services, but I had to contend with the arguments of the inevitable cynics who doubted their relevance. Others felt counselling had nothing to do with their role as teachers. I understood well that we were all in the difficult position of having to structure a new image of who I should be as I set about playing a role with which we were all just becoming familiar. My natural inclinations, bolstered by the theories I'd studied, made me emphasise a collaborative approach to my new tasks. I stressed the importance of getting buy-in from all quarters, selling the idea that the programme had to operate as a network to which students must be channelled for help by vigilant teachers with a first-hand view of them in the classrooms.

By the end of the term, the basic routines and procedures for guidance and counselling were up and running. We were part of a network of guidance counsellors and Ministry of Education officials who were increasing their involvement in the infant movement to standardise operations and practices in the field.

Enter a new principal, Mr Woodburn Miller, who ushered in a period of relative stability and rebuilding— not of structures, but of commitment and resilience in the face of well-known challenges. Confident that we had a working system, he drummed up support from the PTA and the old boys to expand the old welfare programme into a more comprehensive system of support to students needing special help. To this, I turned my attention, reluctantly facing the fact that my small UWI study of the impact of deprivation on school performance now had more than ample support from the circumstances around us. It was the kind of vindication that no one appreciated, but at least I now knew ways of alleviating their impact.

The work of the committee put me eye to eye with a human hurricane from the Melbourne Campus. Miss Helen Douglas had joined KC in the same year as I had, but until now, we'd been on separate campuses, so we'd had little day-to-day contact. By the time her new roles increased her presence at North Street, her name had already been etched in the annals of the school as an exceptional French teacher, student advocate, administrator, fundraiser, and supporter of all things "Fortis". For sheer energy, devotion, and commitment to the school, few could match Miss Douglas. She was closest to being Missa Johnno's equal in the fast-walking department, but the fact that she did it in high heels was a source of constant amazement. Just as the decades of the fifties, sixties, and seventies had been marked by boys scampering from the approach of Mr Forrest and whispering "Dougs a come!" so the eighties and nineties would be marked by similarly energised boys calling out, "Dougie a come!"

No matter how strict she was (and she could equal any of our best disciplinarians), the boys knew she was one of their chief advocates and one of the best and most enduring friends of KC. Miss Douglas and Missa Johnno were stalwart supporters of everything to do with establishing the guidance and counselling programme. Both had their ears to the ground, and they knew the importance of getting students the help they needed.

Despite the challenges, most teachers gradually threw their support behind the initiatives, and the links between counselling, career guidance, and health services provided by the energetic and committed school nurse, Mrs Samuels, were up and running. Understanding and support inched along, and soon I began to feel that my new role was a reality.

I often dropped in on the SCQ programme, in the capable hands of a young and animated teacher and KC old boy, Gervaise McLeod, who had taken up the reins while I was away. Under his guidance, the momentum had continued. The 1979 team of Adolph Barclay, Lincoln Wilson, Ricardo McPherson, and Paul Thomas had performed well, succumbing to Munro College in the semi-finals. A year later, Barclay, Thomas, and McPherson were joined by Trevor Pickersgill, and they'd prevailed until they came up against Wolmer's Boys, who took the trophy home. Mr McLeod, along with several SCQ alumni, were continuing the strong tradition of successful KC old boys helping their young brothers. SCQ was no longer my baby; it was the growing child of a crew of new fathers to whom I'd given custody and continued to give support. Still, like a midwife and the babies she delivers, we remained inextricably connected.

Sometimes, Behind
Their Eyes

My work as guidance counsellor was quite different from that of the teacher and grade supervisor that I had worked so hard to master. In my old roles, my timetable was structured and planned, with regular classes, testing periods, setting exams, meetings, and days of grading papers. There was no such structure in the guidance and counselling programme. A schedule of visits to classes took care of a few hours each day, but the remaining hours were set aside for counselling sessions with individual students, with or without their parents, or small groups needing interventions recommended for various reasons. On some days, these slots were filled by prior arrangement; on others, students, parents or teachers walked in without appointments to deal with unplanned incidents and spontaneous discussions. There was no telling what these sessions would bring, and the unpredictability of my days became both an irritation and an attraction.

My routine allowed blocks of time for planning, meetings with teachers, preparation of class material, design of group counselling activities, and follow-up contacts with parents, teachers, the school nurse, and external agencies. On other days, it left me scrambling from one unscheduled drop-in visit to another, sometimes without enough time to do my follow-up notes, which were essential to maintaining up-to-date files on students. This was an art that required a delicate balance between, on one hand, observing rules about confidentiality, and on the other, meeting the need for records and student profiles that allowed me to chart their presenting problems, their personal situations, decisions taken, and the progress of our discussions. They included records of whether students walked in by choice or had been referred by teachers and others in authority.

My interactions with students focused on a variety of needs and concerns. Career guidance activities involved expanding the work we had started before my job change. They targeted average, trouble-free, high-performing students who were busy planning their next educational steps. They needed information about training opportunities, tertiary-level institutions, entry requirements, contacts, effective study skills, and pep talks that would motivate and encourage them to keep their eyes on their goals. For these purposes, I met with individuals and small groups with common interests.

Everyday behavioural problems brought others in because their teachers had used up the progressive levels of disciplinary measures available to them, and detected factors that were contributing to recurrent problems. My work with these students was designed to help them explore those factors and identify underlying psychological needs and conditions outside of school that were contributing to inappropriate behaviour. Once we knew the causes, we could pursue corrective measures. Some needed more attention and supervision at home; others were testing boundaries or mismanaging the confusion of adolescence. They "hated" math or history or writing. They couldn't sit still. They played more than the "normal" boyish pranks on classmates. They complained that "the teacher hate me and pick on me all the time". Others were waiting for the day to end so they could explode on the football or basketball field or burn up the track.

Of course, we encountered a few "bad boys" who got into recurrent and violent fights, missed school once a week, were disrespectful to their teachers, or smoked ganja every chance they got. At meetings and seminars for school counsellors, it became clear that these were the problems of the day, and at KC, we faced them in numbers that reflected the growing size of the school.

Predictably, many issues necessitated interactions with parents. The more I saw of parents, the more I understood the complexity of the typical student's world. At school, we treated each boy as an individual, and we tried to shape his experiences and behaviour to facilitate the best academic outcomes. After all, every student's academic success was our first priority. In my new role, I discovered each boy was part of a network of situations and relationships of which we, and very often he, had little understanding and even less control. What we saw at school was often only a ripple in the ocean of their lives; sometimes it was a furious storm surge. But as I questioned, probed, nudged, and waded through rage, confusion, and protracted silences, we plumbed the depths, dissecting domestic issues and personal or family crises that reinforced the concerns that had originally driven me to explore the counselling role for myself.

Time brought even greater astonishment at some of the realities that students contended with every day. They reinforced my belief that many of our students showed astounding resilience and determination in the face of odds that approached the insurmountable. The realities strengthened my conviction about the need for more of what we were trying to do. They also confronted me with the many barriers that stood between where we were and where we needed to be. In an all-boys' school like KC, this gap was particularly wide in one area that had given me cause for concern ever since Mr Forrest told me why he wanted capable young women to join his team of teachers. In my own ongoing journey to self-understanding, I had come to terms with the fact that mine was a society that excelled in bringing up a resilient, determined, ambitious generation. But it was also one in which many child-rearing and socialisation processes paid too little attention to the emotional and psychological aspects of child development.

This was not always about economic conditions. Most parents kept their eyes relentlessly on the physical well-being and educational needs of their children. Some spent copious sums of money. Others summoned up their last few dollars on supplies for home and for school, sometimes stretching what they had to cover a few inessentials. Most exerted all their energy to live up to the biblical exhortation to "train up a child in the way he should go, and when he is old, he will not depart from it".

Conversely, paying attention to the psychological growth and emotional development of children was beyond the experience or skills of many parents, regardless of socio-economic status. Our culture simply did not emphasise that we should pay attention to what went on behind the eyes of children. It did not encourage the expression of feelings, fears, or aspirations beyond "So, what you want to be when you grow up?"

And our men suffered most from it. I knew this not just from books. The men in and around my life were often capable and successful, but many were woefully incompetent when it came to managing the complexities of their feelings and the feelings of others. The causes were numerous, and sociologists had already documented many, tracing some to our history of enslavement and colonial domination, along with the near decimation of the male spirit that not all had been able to escape.

The answers were not only available to historians and sociologists, though. Growing up in Jamaica, we knew, without ever framing it in words, that what was going on inside of us was far less significant to our elders than whether we were behaving ourselves, working hard enough at school, or eating enough. The cure for every look of anxiety, fear, or disturbance was "Go outside and play" or "Go and find something to do" or "Go and study your book". I never met a teenager, who, when asked by an adult, "What's wrong with you, child?" could answer "I don't understand what's going on inside me" or, even less likely, "I don't feel good about myself, Mama".

For boys, the likelihood of such exchanges was much less. Many of them didn't even have the advantage that most girls had of growing up nestled under the arms of their mothers and grandmothers. Typically, mothers saved their hugs and caresses for their daughters, keeping us close at hand as much for our safety as for bonding and for assistance with "women's business" in the house. At the same time, they sent their sons outside for the rough and tumble they considered normal, even necessary, for boys.

Many traditional fathers stayed away from physical contact with their sons except for rough play and, unfortunately, physical punishment. In some homes, there were only female adults, and at many primary schools, boys were surrounded by female teachers.

Taken all together, these factors nurtured a strong resistance to being under the thumbs of women. Much worse, they bred a lurking fear in the national psyche of absorbing too much "woman" behaviour—in other words, being perceived as effeminate. Resistance and fear concerning any inclinations towards expressing their "feminine side" were as visible among grown men as they were among schoolboys.

One way such fear manifested itself was in the excessive emphasis that many men placed on being tough and unfeeling because "that's how men are supposed to be". It was not uncommon for the socialisation process to reinforce these beliefs. At home, at school, and even on the streets, men (and women too) fed young boys the idea that they must spurn everything about themselves that had to do with emotions and sensitivity.

I had often seen this in my classes when characters and situations in literature forced the expression of deeper feelings. Some boys heckled one another for expressing or identifying with those emotions. Though their words were usually spoken in jest, I could tell they were covering deeper messages. Some withdrew into stillness, and others wore discomfort just behind their eyes.

Then I had understood the words of Mr Forrest, as strong and as gentle a man as anyone could want to find. He wanted young women as teachers because his boys needed to be exposed to the softer side and to discover it in themselves. This may not have found favour with the many men who feared over-exposure to female influence or who associated the distaff side with smelling salts, sewing machines, and weakness or nagging.

The dread of being viewed as a "sissy" or "mama-man" was deadly. It drove some boys to wear heavy cloaks of aggression and roughness, even to parade complete lack of feeling. For some, it was a short step from these tendencies toward bad behaviour and negative attitudes to school; they believed this was what "real boys" did. Getting into trouble for being disruptive and boisterous was a far better option than facing the possibility of the persistent and hurtful shaming that was inflicted on boys who were not "man enough". Unexpressed confusion about themselves, along with anger and aggression, could build up into rages that gave teachers no option but to send the trouble-maker out of class, and, increasingly, to my door. It took hard work to penetrate the tough exterior and help them express their needs and their feelings without shame. Confronting these situations, I made it my goal to strip off the protective layers and find the real concerns and emotions they'd worked so hard to mask. Whenever it happened, the breakthrough for them—and for me—was always worth the effort.

Some breakthroughs only came when parents were willing to participate in the process and own the part they may have played in situations that involved their sons. The more I interacted with parents, the more I saw evidence of how overwhelming everyday life was for many ordinary Jamaicans. Despite their best efforts, some were ill-prepared for the challenges of managing adolescents and for the processes I was asking them to take part in. Sharing my observations at staff meetings and PTA meetings brought both denial and recognition. *Some parents need help before they can do what we are asking of them. Interventions here at high school level are late! When we discover that "something more is going on" behind what is obvious at school, it may be too late to repair the damage.*

Though discussions were often controversial and even heated, they helped me frame questions that were critical and thus far, mostly unanswerable: How could we help teenage boys whose parents also needed help to understand themselves as a first step to learning how to cope with the demands of being parents? Where were concerned or disturbed adults supposed to get help in a society that encouraged us to keep our troubles to ourselves and "not tell strangers your business"? Mental health facilities were not widely distributed in our society; both their orientation and their priority were the treating of mental illness. This only perpetuated the notion that anyone who admitted to having emotional and psychological problems also had something "wrong in the head" and was a few steps from the madhouse.

Of course, the parents I saw were not emotionally disturbed or anywhere near mad. They were just stretched by the everyday challenges in their personal, domestic, and work lives, and this caused many of them unnecessary shame and embarrassment. Most would have done much better if they had access to trained practitioners and processes that could help them sift through what was going on in and around them. But even when they wanted to seek help, the average person could not get it except from family, community, and church elders who might be too close to the situation or too judgemental.

School counsellors were limited in number, and we were seeing growing evidence that most parents were committed to their children's well-being, but many were overburdened and did not have the wherewithal to do all they wanted for them. These questions and insights were planting seeds somewhere inside me, but for the time being, I kept my focus on doing all I could to find at least some answers through our interactions at school.

One new development brought a small part of the answer. A second guidance counsellor was soon in place at the Melbourne campus, ensuring that the younger students were not left out, and those who might be on the wrong path could benefit from earlier interventions. It was just in time. In addition to everything else, we were all sounding alarms about the realities facing our country and the effects these realities were having on the well-being of our students as well as their ability and commitment to remain on track.

Some of the causes of the breakdown were associated with socio-political forces beyond our control. The governing party was holding on by a thread as members of the middle class, now shrunken by migration, withdrew their support in the face of devaluation, unemployment, shortages of basic supplies, and increasing crime. Mr Manley's return to the rhetoric of socialism as a basis for creating a more equitable economic system continued to worsen relations with the US and the IMF. The resulting struggles within and outside the party brought more disagreement and division everywhere. The austerity policies tied to loan agreements with the IMF led to loss of jobs, even in the public sector, and it was clear that the "new international economic order" was a dream whose time had not come. Disaffection and opposition soared. Supporters of the government dug their heels in and defended its actions fiercely. Debates turned strident, sometimes erupting in physical altercations. In the middle, the grumbles of ordinary people grew into a mighty roar.

As the prospect of new elections loomed, a new vocabulary held sway in the local and international news, painting a picture of a country at war, characterised by images of massacres, guerrilla training, brigadistas, garrisons, assassinations, arson, roadblocks, assault rifles, and gangs dressed in military fatigues. Newspaper headlines screamed "114 Murders in 14 Days" and almost a thousand murders in the year leading to the 1980 election.

Demonstrators took to the streets, protesting gas-price hikes and politically motivated evictions from government housing schemes. A few of our students who lived in poorer areas were left homeless. It was not unheard of for boys to miss a day or two from school because they had been detained by police randomly rounding up groups of young men on the street. Others came to school exhausted after spending nights on their roofs, looking out for signs of invasions by rival political gangs.

My determination to return home had been fuelled by the desire to provide a new type of support that would go to the heart of conditions threatening to derail our students. Despite the significant headway we were making, we sometimes felt besieged by the forces against us—a social and economic framework that seemed unmanageable, a political culture intertwined with violence, a criminal class newly independent of politics and bolstered by drug money, a generation of men in danger of losing their way. Schoolboys witnessed it all, and in their hearts, the seeds of discontent began to change who some wanted to be. We fixed our sights on keeping as many as possible focused on the belief that education would still provide the path to the lives they wanted. The vast majority complied, responding to our pleas to stay out of trouble and keep their minds on their work and on the safe harbour they enjoyed at Clovelly Park.

I Felt a Parting

It started as a whisper in my head, a repetitive hum of uneasiness—about what, I wasn't quite sure. I shrugged it off for as long as I could, choosing instead to focus on what I had come home to do. It was not that the problems became less daunting or the circumstances around the school improved; quite the contrary. If anything, both sets of factors were feeding into my discomfort. But it was also emanating from something inside me that, at first, I could not pinpoint.

Was I disappointed that my new initiatives had begun to settle into a predictable routine of interventions that seemed inadequate in the face of mounting challenges? Was I missing the intellectual engagement that only a full teaching load of language and literature had brought me in the past? My friend who was a social worker had already warned me of the dangers of "taking home the days with me" and becoming too immersed in problems I could not always fix.

My general paper classes continued to be a beacon on difficult days. Our discussions of topical events at home and abroad were stimulating for all of us. Counselling interventions increased my exposure to the circumstances of some students and enriched my insights into the way they saw the world. My weaning from the SCQ programme had left a void too, but I could still participate in their activities as much as I wanted.

I had not shaken the loss of my sister and her children. I had come home filled with anticipation about renewed adventures with my 7- and 9-year-old nieces, as well as the one little boy in the family, who had grown into an irrepressible 5-year-old fan of the Incredible Hulk. Instead, they had left within weeks of my return, and I had not filled the void. Friends had migrated, colleagues had moved on, the circles in which we moved had shrunk, and I feared that my work was not enough to replace them.

My unease was the child of all the above, and it was something else. The staffroom buzzed with complaints about the lack of resources in the school, despite the ambitious revamped plan for free education and the introduction of social programmes to provide additional support to schoolchildren. Most of these did not touch students in the high school system, and many parents did not qualify for help. It was a catch-22: they earned too little to manage, and they earned too much to meet the qualifying threshold for assistance.

Some youngsters were increasingly aware that their counterparts were finding options to education. They saw entertainers, school dropouts, and hustlers flaunting the symbols of material wealth. They were familiar with the workings of the underground economy. The arduous route of education looked like a hard choice, and we who continued to uphold it felt our messages would wear thin. Teachers were giving their all to their jobs, and yet some worried that their income remained too measly for them to move out of rented houses or replace sputtering vehicles or pay for their own children's higher education.

A boy who had left school a few years before, with no more than three O-level subject passes, drove his flashy car into the school and parked amid the dented and dilapidated vehicles in which his former teachers had chugged along for years. Little boys huddled around his fancy wheels and rims, excited at the prospect of being able to drive "a fast car just like that one". Another graduate stepped from his new vehicle, dressed in a spanking suit, and sat down to talk with his former teachers about buying his company's life insurance policies—only to find that their monthly income was less than his commission.

It was not all about lack of material rewards. No one could deny the evidence of a growing disrespect for teachers. It was not always spoken or even directed to us as individuals, but to the jobs and the environments we chose to stay in despite the lack of support and regard for what we were doing. Increasingly, friends greeted us with the question, "So, you *still* in teaching?" In their eyes, we could see the unspoken suggestion that the answer ought not to be yes.

And if it was, a thinly-veiled accusation stared back at us—we lacked ambition and self-esteem, or worse, the wherewithal to be "somewhere better". When the question came from a graduate to his former teacher and mentor, it took on even more significance. "But wait, sir. You still down here so, man?" This type of question was taking root just as it raised a bigger one: Was education losing its position as a priority in the government's budget and in the social conscience? In my own mind, this gave way to another question that was much more personal: Was I losing my own conviction about my place in the world of teaching and counselling?

I faced half the truth in a particularly difficult staff meeting. The principal reacted to a newspaper column lambasting "the failing teachers of this country". Chafing under the onslaught that followed, the ministry had despatched a flurry of directives. In turn, principals weighed in one more time against "teachers who continually fail" to do something or the other.

I had always hated that practice, perfected by so many leaders. Unwilling to tackle individual transgressors, they harangued the entire staff complement with generalised accusations. I hated how they painted the faultless with the very same brush as the guilty. It always smacked of cowardice. *Who are these people attacking us while maintaining a safe distance from the world we have to navigate day after day?*

The impact of the meeting stayed too long. It was not like me to be unable to shrug off something like that and remain immersed in my own work. I continued to be immersed, but my anger simmered for weeks, and I needed to know why.

My confinement in the blue room and my awakenings in the seminar room at Reading had changed me too. The faded paint, the permanent chill, the long train rides, and my unbroken gaze at my life had brought new ways of looking at my world and the part I should play in it. Even in those dank days, an unknown voice had been whispering to me about stepping into unfamiliar worlds, but I had not been ready to hear it. I had pushed the options to coming home from my mind, uncertain of myself and fearful that if I pursued any of them, my lecturer-tutor and maybe even the hairy-faced Arkansas man, would have been right to predict I would not be at my school (or in Jamaica) for long. Inclinations I had buried in order to return home surfaced again, spreading my unease, growing it into the admission that, in the main, the "something was not quite right" was taking hold inside of me.

Once again, I stood at a crossing. It was time to apply to myself the assessment and analysis in which I engaged boys at school who were confused about the career options they should contemplate. I subjected myself to the same questioning and probing that I inflicted on my students. Just as it did for them, the process brought me to new levels of self-understanding, along with the second half of the truth about what was going on inside me: I did not want to leave Jamaica. I had not wavered in my commitment to teaching and counselling. The meeting was only the last straw. Increasingly, I'd felt I was chasing the wind, trying to help students who had too little control over the circumstances in which they lived. I was ready to water the seeds that had been sprouting in my mind and shaping the question as to whether I could be more effective if I worked with the adults in their lives. The adults were the ones struggling to do right by their children. Many were buffeted by forces that they could not manage. I could not yet identify the means through which I could bring these ideas to reality, but the call was unrelenting.

Some of my classmates at Reading had become engaged in mental health services just a notch below psychiatric, psychological, and social work practices. Some had gone on to further studies towards advanced qualifications in counselling psychology. I did not have the interest or the opportunity to pursue such paths, but I became convinced that in time, if I found the right setting and focused on working with adults, the benefits would accrue to their children, thereby reaching students like those at KC.

I was incapable of surviving as either a preoccupied teacher or a half-committed guidance counsellor. Neither did the boys deserve either of the two. I could not be half-hearted anywhere, least of all at Clovelly

Park, for I had learned over the years that KC merited all or nothing. It was time for me to go. It took me several months to find certainty, and it would take a few more to brace myself and quiet the voices both within and outside of myself that urged me to stay.

The separation brought a profound sense of loss, but I felt no remorse. I'd stumbled through my earlier tempests and made it to a clear field in which I could see the crucial questions. Though I didn't know all the answers, the struggle inside me was settled. This time, I left with the certainty that I had taken in all that the ten years were supposed to give me. And I had given it my all. I had taught every boy to the best of my ability. I had established a foundation for the school's involvement in SCQ. KC was one of the few schools that had a counselling programme. It was well established, it was viable, and there were strong hands in which to leave it. Unlike my premature departure after just one year, this going was the natural end of the journey that had taken me into the lives of hundreds of boys I never would have known without stepping into that Number 22 bus that took me to Clovelly Park.

Epilogue: 2014

I heard it as a sudden tap-tap breaking into my thoughts every now and then between the rapid clunkety-clunk of keys on my computer keyboard. At first, I paid no attention. But it persisted, like a child saying "again, Mama" even after the fifth telling of a favourite story. I tiptoed into the family room, from which the sound seemed to originate; nothing to see there. Satisfied that "it" was over, or at least not worth my attention, I returned to the humdrum world of typing comments on the assignments that my online students had dutifully uploaded in the drop box. A half-committed resident, relocated in Florida to take care of family issues, I longed for the crucial parts of myself I'd abandoned in Jamaica. I was working as a "virtual" writing tutor, my days littered with disorganised paragraphs, plucky plagiarism, verbs that disagreed with their subjects, research papers, and persuasive essays hastily pulled together without a cause.

Two error-riddled papers later, the sound was back, rising from a tap-tap to an insistent clamour. As I neared the side window facing the street, a flash of movement riveted my eyes to the spot between the leaves, where the maker of the disturbance had landed. Its colour was somewhere between burnt orange and rust, almost indistinguishable from the colours of the shrub I had nursed for months into a thick, protective guard against curious eyes moving along just beyond my yard. It darted among the leaves and landed on my window, captivating me with its stunningly gorgeous, feathery coat. Relentless, and oblivious to the clear danger in its action, it barged into the hurricane-proof glass, thrusting its beak against it over and over. The bird seemed on a mission to break through to some undefined destination or destroy itself in the effort.

Google had no images to match the richness of its colour. Unable to locate a name for my visitor, I dubbed her Rustbird. I had decided on the flimsy evidence of her penchant for self-destruction that Rustbird must be female. For the next seven days, she crashed into my window every day, in the same way and almost at the same time. She seemed tireless, unstinting in her commitment to a purpose I couldn't decipher.

On Day 9, I forgot to leave the blinds closed. In fact, except for a vague echo in my head, Rustbird was not on my mind. I struggled to focus on the words swimming on my computer screen, but I couldn't shake the need to creep out to the living room. The feeling of impending doom fell over me out of nowhere; this kind of recurrent apprehension was one of the consequences of my loss of home.

In all my years living in Florida, I hadn't once felt truly at home, despite the solace of my immediate surroundings. Every sound, every mishap, every day of longing for a peep at the Blue Mountains I could see from any spot in Jamaica had taught me to fear the unknown.

A trace of blood smeared the window. Two or three small feathers were stuck to the sill. Rustbird lay in the thicket below, her coat blemished with a stream of red leaking from her mouth. I wiped her with warm water, drying her feathers and comforting her, laying her on a bed of leaves warmed by the sun. In an instant, she was gone. I groped for an explanation of what it all meant. *Nonsense; it was a bird and it meant nothing. Get back to your work.*

I struggled to get my thoughts together and finish my comment on Marcelline's literary analysis paper, which badly needed a thesis statement. As I hit "send" and sat back in my chair, "You have mail" jumped up from the right-hand corner of the screen. The subject field shouted, "Fwd: 'Fortis' Prevails!" And there it was: a mile-long message thread with dozens of comments celebrating KC's victory in the SCQ competition in the fortieth year since our first victory.

My mouth fell open as the thread stretched out, preceded by a lengthy list of email addresses of old boys scattered around the globe. In message after message, SCQ alumni and other KC old boys scrawled their reminiscences across my screen. They were baring their souls about their days and nights on the inside of the KC quiz enterprise. Up and down the screen I scrolled, captivated by their words—rescued from the colourless world into which I had been plunged by my Rustbird and the deep yearning for home that my interaction with her had brought.

A story began to write itself.

I first became involved in Schools' Challenge with the hope of improving my students' attitude to learning and enhancing my effectiveness as a teacher. In all the years of the competition, KC marched into battle at the JBC studio almost every year. They reached the quarter- and semi-finals numerous times, qualified for a spot in twenty-two finals, and took home the trophy eleven times—almost twice as many as the next most successful school. KC has prevailed against Wolmer's Boys, St Jago High, Jamaica College, St George's College, and Munro College, schools that existed long before KC emerged on the scene—

My fingers froze! This was not the real story at all. Quiz participation at KC was never just about turning up at JBC to compete. It was not even always about winning the competition. It was a movement that opened the eyes of scores of boys to a new possibility— one of the many possibilities that Bishop Gibson and

Mr Forrest had glimpsed in the stars, all those years before any of us had come along. A few teachers and the hundreds of boys who had felt the pull of something new and ventured across the threshold into quiz practice discovered a world of new possibilities, mostly within us. And our discoveries had inflamed all of us with the desire to follow wherever the adventure would take us.

It took sixth-formers across the campus to the lower forms to conduct quiz competitions, whipping up interest and discovering boys with the potential to become "quiz men". They were also enriching their roles as student leaders expected to bring something special to their young counterparts who now had a new reason to look up to their role models. It took me on a path where I could experiment with my theories about increasing academic effort and building relationships, finding a way to enrich what went on in the formal classroom.

Its true purpose was not just to create winning teams. It was, rather, to help reshape the attitudes of students towards the pursuit of knowledge, to channel their incomparable "Fortis" spirit in a new direction, and to provide an experience of team work in an arena outside of sports. To be sure, these goals were not crystal-clear to me at the outset, so I never articulated them to the boys. Neither did we ever state that our sole aspiration was to win. All we knew for sure was that our involvement became its own reward. Whether it was in Big Yard, Cassava Piece, the physics lab, or under the ackee tree at my sister's house when teachers were on strike and we were unable to enter the school premises, it was always the same—a search for knowledge in an atmosphere of stimulation and discovery.

The school's motto was known by every boy, and we often dissected its meaning, making it our mantra. But we needed something of our own and after researching numerous options, we came to embrace the words of Queen Victoria: "We are not interested in the possibilities of defeat."[11] I withheld the queen's follow-up words: "They do not exist", which for my taste, took her over the edge into bombast. I wanted to instil confidence without breeding arrogance. I explained that for us, this motto meant that although we knew defeat could occur, it was not an outcome on which we should waste our minds or our time.

Our quiz culture spawned a passion for seeking out new information, sharing knowledge and ideas, exchanging facts, coming alive in spirited debates about everything under the sun. We read widely and avidly, enabling everyone to answer questions posed by curious participants about issues that went way beyond the desire for quiz mastery. Practice sessions surpassed the tasks of gathering and checking facts, developing strategies, honing skills, and increasing speed. They became all-purpose "reasonings" in which boys from ages 14 to 18 engaged in discussions of music, art, science, literature, religion, sports, entertainment, world affairs, politics, race, and class. In an environment of safety and respectful openness, we dissected the problems

---

[11] A statement Queen Victoria made regarding the Boer War.

of the world and problems of our own: the narrowness of the school curriculum, the threats to safety along Kingston streets, the imbalances of the world order, the awkwardness of adolescence, misunderstandings with parents and teachers, confusion about girls, and … more confusion about girls.

Sometimes it was nothing short of stunning to watch the transformation that occurred when competing hopefuls assumed their positions in the eight practice chairs we set up in front of a roomful of enthusiasts, wherever we prepared for our matches. Their faces became solemn, their eyes focused, and their shoulders hunched over, ready to display the results of their hours of private study. Slow, nervous, or stuttering boys, known for saying no more than ten words all afternoon while they waited for a turn to take a chair, grew tall before our eyes. Once seated in a quiz man's chair, they displayed new levels of self-assurance, assertiveness, and agility, their fingers quickly finding the buzzer when they were certain of the answer even to the most obscure question. As the others looked on hopefully, they would fill the nervous silence without hesitation, eyes shining with satisfaction.

The names of the winds in India and Africa fell from their lips as easily as those of the gods of Greek and Norse mythology. They identified the theories of scientists who changed the world and composers of classics from Bach to Bob Marley. They inspired each other with quotations from Shakespeare and the Bible, from the stirring words of Jamaican heroes and

Caribbean authors missing from the school syllabus. They murmured lyrics of mento folk songs, ska, and reggae. They cited Latin and Greek origins of obscure English words and admonished one another with proverbs passed down through Jamaican folklore. They borrowed my warnings and brandished them before one another until the walls echoed my own mother's sobering admonitions, "Chicken merry, hawk deh near" and "Crab walk too much, lose dem claw".

But it was never just about knowing. It was a glorious expedition in which we came to understand much more about ourselves and one another, about what we could achieve and how we could rebound when we fell short. And for me, still growing into the teacher I wanted to be, it was a way of learning new approaches to enhance my work in the classroom.

Within the walls of "quiz", we reinforced the role that KC had always played in the lives of those who found themselves there—building lasting and unlikely relationships among boys whose circumstances outside often differed widely. In any one training squad, you could find boys from well-barricaded, well-appointed homes in St Andrew, whose professional parents would drive them to school and who rushed off to music lessons at private piano studios. Right next to them, there were boys boarding or just staying indefinitely in Rollington Town or Allman Town with struggling relatives or friends of their parents who were fighting life in small rural villages. Huddling with them were some who came to practice having not eaten more than a patty all day. At the end of practice, they would make their way to lower Kingston addresses behind zinc fences and walls defaced with graffiti and rusty bullet holes.

Cramped in one classroom, sons and brothers of prominent professionals broke bun-and-cheese, sipping from orange juice boxes passed around to colleagues who were sons of struggling mothers and to friends without fathers, dismantling social divisions that prevailed a few streets away. It was a place to forget, even for a few hours each day, whatever crisis might be brewing uptown or downtown. In the cocoon of quiz practice, a boy could displace the struggles he faced within himself or with someone else. Another could forget the images of conflict at home, of gunshots ricocheting all through the night, of landlords raging for overdue rent. And whenever the time came for me to escape from my own challenges, the room and the boys became my refuge too.

Under the blinding lights, the suffocating heat, and the tension that hung in the air at the JBC studios, those who wore the prized purple blazers sweated and pulled through because they had become one force— irrespective of everything else. Whether they bounced out victorious or limped out defeated into the night, every one of them could be equally certain that the crew of supporters outside in the semi-darkness knew what they'd been through, wanted what they'd wanted, and felt what they'd felt. After our post-match hamburger haunts, we often made our way from Trafalgar Road to

North Street, across to Windward Road and Mountain View, and up to Cross Roads and Meadowbrook, criss-crossing the dividing lines of the society. None of the diverse addresses had any bearing on us or on the boys whom we deposited and watched until they disappeared into the same night, carrying in their hearts the same joy of accomplishment or the same wounds of loss.

A casual observer may be forgiven for questioning the significance of a school activity that, from all appearances, involved fewer than three hundred students in forty-five years. Unconvinced onlookers have asked, "So what?" Detractors have protested that students should not be pulled from their preparation for important school-leaving exams to seek short-lived glory by winning a TV competition. They wonder about the benefit of having students accumulate "trivial information" that has nothing to do with their exams or with developing skills for the job market. No one should deny the relevance of these observations, but they should not obscure the real story.

Those who have been on the inside of the SCQ walls understand that the deeper meanings stretched far beyond accumulating information, basking in the glitter of the trophy, or experiencing the sting of defeat. They know that the call to quiz practice opened the door to a new space in which many more than four students per year experienced something that supported their academic endeavours and their efforts at navigating life.

For me, the real prize was sharing in a special way in their lives, getting to know them not as willing or unwilling students sitting before me in rows of desks and chairs, not just as prospective statistics when exam results were published, not just as good boys or wayward boys, but as real people pursuing real dreams, battling real issues. If I rescued them, they rescued me right back. And the experience gave us all a glimpse of something more important than ourselves.

That was the real story behind the messages that took over my inbox for days, reinforcing my own assessment of the true meaning of our shared experiences. The words of the men, now mostly in their fifties and sixties, echoed each other, sharing new perspectives and offering up gems from their memory banks.

"Our involvement in the competition succeeded indeed in elevating knowledge to the same level as our school's legendary sporting prowess."

"From recent discussions among the boys of '74 … we all agree that the experience was pivotal to our growth."

"Getting a chance to represent a great school we all love and culminating in our first win is a legendary achievement."

"[SCQ was] on par with all the school's great sporting titles."

"I remember my first days at UWI when a former head boy of a prominent Kingston school confided how intimidated some of his fellow students were [by KC's reputation in SCQ]."

"We all know that SCQ changed our lives forever."

"We are all eternally grateful for how SCQ shaped the men we became."

"[One member] developed an interest in music because of the competition. I certainly developed an appreciation of art which made me ensure that I visited Le Louvre ... On that day, a whole lot of memories of SCQ came flooding back."

"I remember the great practices ... I remember Mountain View. I remember the treats and the challenge trophy. I remember Trinidad."

"[The fact that] we have all achieved our academic and professional skills was due in no small part to the invaluable contribution that [SCQ] made to our lives."

"We were merely the tools of KC's first School's Challenge success."

"In the 15 seasons from 2000 to this year we have been in the final four all but three times, been in the finals seven times and we have won four times."

"I suppose to those looking in from outside these last 15 seasons have been nothing short of excellent, but such is the standard of our quiz programme at KC that we are always looking to do better."

"The foundation and formula have only got stronger due to the cadre of old boy coaches."

"SCQ had [such] a great and profound influence on me that I eventually married an English Language and Literature teacher!! I remember the word 'serendipity' and its meaning. ... Oftentimes when talking to my wife she would marvel at my knowledge of literature and I would always attribute that to being on the SCQ team."

"The single most influential event during my seven years at THE College occurred in 1974 … I knew my life was changing when I was taught/given the tools to decide who should represent KC in SCQ! In every other school endeavour, the decision was solely that of adults! I am eternally grateful for the quiz which broadened my interests."

The SCQ alumni had spoken, and for weeks their messages continued to bring light into the shadows of this home that I'd unwillingly adopted but had never considered truly mine. Now as their grown-up words leaped across my screen, stirring warm memories of the times we shared, I could recall their hairless faces, their copious afro hairstyles without a trace of grey. I could hear the boyish laughter that, evening after evening, had turned a drab classroom into an unforgettable adventure. And now the evidence was right before me: What we shared had left them with cherished memories too—memories that, just like mine, had outlasted the years. Their words brought me certainty that, although circumstances had misplaced me in this flat expanse of land where Rustbird's last visit had left me feeling so empty, I had at least once done something that outlasted the passage of time. The evidence lay littered across my screen.

SCQ was not the entire focus of my journey at KC, but it played no small part in opening my eyes to the unique delights of an occupation that was never easy or materially rewarding but was always a source of profound fulfilment. Unsure of my place in the world, I had entered that unknown universe of desks, chairs, chalk, and tracks of dust I feared would suffocate me. It was only fitting that I had been terrified on that first day. The responsibility that life was thrusting upon my unready shoulders couldn't have been more daunting or more important.

Though unprepared and uninformed, from the moment I'd stepped into my first terrifying class, I had known one thing for sure: the boys sitting before me were promises the world was waiting for. I could be their poison, causing them to droop and wither, robbing the world of what they could become. Or I could be their nurturer, feeding their hunger for knowledge and growth. My own school experience had exposed me to teachers who stunted and teachers who nurtured, but I had not known how to make sure I would end up in the right category. That ignorance had fuelled my fear, leading me to walk away too soon. But Mr Forrest and his boys had planted a seed that survived beyond my attempt to escape. It had brought me right back to Clovelly Park, where it grew into a mighty tree. That tree blossomed and bore fruit in the shining eyes of boys who came alive when they discovered what they could achieve, boys once lost and then found. Interacting with them was like nothing I experienced in my work before Clovelly Park or since. Effortlessly, they had insinuated themselves into my consciousness, filling up my thoughts and dreams, shaping the person I would become.

A day with any one of my classes could drag me into the quicksand of despondency, convinced that I couldn't make the slightest difference in their scheme of things. One minute or one day later, they could raise me up to the top of the highest mountain, where I breathed in fresh air and savoured all the meanings of what was truly important. A warming radiance had always spread out inside of me in those moments when previously indifferent boys caught the magic of a word, the delight of storytelling, the intrigue of critical thinking and argument, or the accomplishment of moving a grade from D to B, a journey much more arduous than standing still with the cherished A.

Mrs Riley had confessed soon after I started at KC that the most significant reason why she agreed to my employment was the excitement I'd displayed about reading and literature. In my first year of uncertain wobbling, I'd flinched in the face of the barrage of questions and objections from the boys about the school's insistence that they all must study literature. In time, I could give them the real answer without doubt or hesitation: this was the subject that had allowed us to explore stories about life and living. It opened their eyes to the wonderful adventure of escaping from everything real, for an hour or a day, by roaming through the pages of a book. There, they had become aware of the human condition, awakening to their own humanity and bridging the space between our classrooms and the streets where we lived.

Today, I take comfort in the strategies I called upon to deal with the challenges of leading my students to proficiency in English. The issue concerning English as a first or second language and how it should be approached in Jamaican schools has become the basis of raging debates over many years. Some argue that insistence on mastering English stands in the way of children's learning because it steals their natural expressiveness, assails their confidence in the worth of the Jamaican language, and diminishes their self-esteem. Others contend that allowing students to use Jamaican speech in class causes interference with their use of English. They hold that students do not need to use Jamaican in the classroom because they already know it and need only to master English.

The challenge is not unique to Jamaica. Over recent decades, experts in ways of teaching and learning language have weighed in and the arguments have multiplied. Today, theories and practices related to teaching English as a second language (ESL) occupy numerous texts. All over the world, students wear multiple labels describing their status as English language learners. Teachers have access to a wide variety of strategies that do not necessitate a choice between a learner's first language and the target language being taught.

Essential to our understanding of "what to do" about teaching English in our Jamaican classrooms is the fact that tried and tested approaches share a common feature. They shun philosophies and methods that deprive learners of their "first" language, whether it be a mainstream foreign language, an emergent dialect, or a developed Creole language like Jamaican.

Despite the numerous arguments about the features that characterise each of these, one thing is certain: for most Jamaican children, the first language they master is Jamaican. To deny this based on the assumption that English is the first language of the typical Jamaican household is to bury one's head in the sand. Modern language teaching methods are based on the recognition that, when appropriately used in the learning process, every student's native language is a powerful tool in the acquisition of other languages. There is no need for our children to face the well-documented disadvantage of losing their first language. By banning it from the classroom, we deprive them of part of who they are, and we take away their competence while stifling their spontaneity.

At the same time, we should not deprive them of the opportunity to master English, which is a necessary tool for participating in the numerous types of discourse demanded by everyday living in a world that is more complicated today than it was when I first tried to teach. We do not have to make this choice; we must use proven approaches that recognise the value of the first language in acquiring the second.

Making the switch to a role in guidance and counselling opened my eyes to both the strengths and the limiting consequences of some of our child-rearing and educational approaches. It took me deeper into the hearts and minds of students and their parents, uncovering their hopes and fears and the struggles they encountered. We didn't always have the remedies, and the process was sometimes painful. But in the stillness that came with each turning point, I could see the light coming through the uncertainty that had inhabited the eyes of a troubled boy for far too long. That light, if only momentary, made it worth every effort I put into preparing myself to facilitate those moments.

There is no longer any question about the absolute necessity of these services in all educational settings, as well as in other environments where normal, responsible adults are sometimes held back by our own anxieties, inadequacies, and dysfunctions. Our errors in socialisation, education, and parenting may only be the tip of the iceberg that looms between Jamaica's potential as a country and the level of underachievement in many spheres of our national life. It is not a stretch to question whether there is a relationship between stunted emotional or psychological growth and our record of persistent aggression, our propensity for violence, and our intractable crime statistics. We may have become inured to these realities. We may even have arrived at the self-defeating conclusion that this is just how we are. Thankfully, many dynamic leaders and other experts in various sectors are making a difference by helping others to realise we do not have to fall short of our potential. We must rid our children and our adults alike of the tyranny of low expectations.

It is now recognised that it is not just children and teenagers who need guidance and counselling. Needing help and support does not equate to weakness, incompetence, or mental instability. New opportunities are available to adults through churches, communities, and organisations that recognise the importance of counselling services as part of corporate strategy and human resource management.

I didn't make a life-long career of teaching or guidance counselling at KC. I stumbled often along the way, sometimes grazing my knees and bruising my heart. I fell short of the expectations of others as much as I fell short of my own. I started and stopped and started again, taking more than one detour in the hope of seeing more clearly where I was going. Often, I started to walk away defeated from boys who fought off learning, only to hold my breath as they turned around momentarily for a second thought, and then embraced the process with everything they had. Many started out being badly behaved, uncaring, and as insolent as I had been in my own time. Some stayed off track and came to less than they should have. But it was not always their own doing. As adults in their lives, we often let them down, and sometimes the forces at home and in the wider society were too powerful for them to win the battle.

It is not for me to know what I would have become had I not returned to the classroom after my first false start. This I do know: I never looked back with regret that I did not stay longer, only with gratitude that I stayed long enough. The journey took me out of myself, along a meandering path back to myself, but I was not the same person. I'd stepped into the classroom as a woman in the making. I left as a teacher for life. The impact of Clovelly Park travelled with me no matter where I turned. Since leaving there, I have not occupied one job in which one workday passed when I did not guide or counsel or teach. Being at KC taught me that nothing less would ever bring the same kind of fulfilment.

Whether it was in telecommunications, where I established the first employee counselling programme, or at a corporate training institution or at a university, all my jobs found me sooner or later in a role that involved me in the development of others. I valued all my jobs and gave each one everything I had, but in the end, none can compare with teaching at KC. None made me realise that what I did every moment could determine the next move in the life of a young and vulnerable person. None gave me the feeling that one word or action of mine could help to shape a 14-year-old's feeling about who he was or who he could become. It was a feeling that nourished and terrified me in equal measure.

Once in a while, an experience comes that is never repeated. We may not know it at the time, but in a moment of stillness and clarity, we come to realise that something matchless has happened. It may have lasted as long as a mere flicker on the eyelid of time, or it may have lingered just long enough. Such was my time at KC. It brought trepidation, agony, unrestrained joy, and unequalled clarity about what was important.

That clarity had come to me twice in the presence of Mr Forrest. The first time was when he told me why his boys needed me to say yes to his offer of the job. It came again later as he explained that I should not apologise for leaving the classroom and returning only when I was certain I truly wanted to be there. It was fourteen years after I'd left the school that it came again. This time, Mr Forrest was not sitting or standing before me at Clovelly Park. This time, Half-Way-Tree rumbled as "hundreds of deep-throated male voices of varied vintage resounded through the St Andrew Parish Church with 'Now thank we all our God with hearts and hands and voices'".[12] They were proclaiming their gratitude for the life of that man who had moulded generations of them, someone who made the world better by being in it and by shaping and moulding hundreds of boys who turned into men doing the same.

I sang the words too, but all I could think of was my gratitude for the day Mr Forrest convinced me that I belonged at his school, teaching his boys. I knew then, as I know now, that a part of me would always remain at Clovelly Park. And thanks to the bonds that endure even now, I know I am still a part of something of immeasurable importance. In a few brief years, KC

---

[12] I am grateful to the late Wally Johnson, who wrote of this event in his "36 Years of Random Recollections", a compilation of his memories of special moments in KC's history (unpublished).

will celebrate its hundredth year of existence. In such a history, a decade is no more than an instant. But for me, it was the instant that changed everything—the instant in which scores of boys making their way to manhood walked with me on my most important journey. Because of them, every page of our shared narrative overflows with the knowing and the meaning we uncovered in the classrooms and the corridors of Clovelly Park.

They are my finest stories.

The end